Other books by Gordon Baxter:

13/13 Vietnam: Search and Destroy
Bax Seat: Log of a Pasture Pilot

Gordon Baxter

Village Creek

The First and Only Eyewitness Account of the Second Life of Gordon Baxter by Himself

 Summit Books / New York

Copyright © 1979 by Gordon Baxter
All rights reserved
including the right of reproduction
in whole or in part in any form
Published by *Summit Books*
A Simon & Schuster Division of Gulf & Western Corporation
Simon & Schuster Building
1230 Avenue of the Americas
New York, New York 10020

Designed by Irving Perkins
Manufactured in the United States of America
1 2 3 4 5 6 7 8 9 10

Library of Congress Cataloging in Publication Data
Baxter, Gordon, date.
Village Creek.

1. Baxter, Gordon, date.   2. Journalists—
United States—Biography.   I. Title.
PN4874.B336A38   070′.9′24 [B]   79-18758

ISBN 0-671-40088-6

To

Molly
Gordon III
Roney
Bonnie
Marjie
Margie
Jim K
Laurie
Martha
Jenny

Contents

Acknowledgments

To this little string of newspapers that printed me first:
The Beaumont Enterprise
The East Texas News, of Buna
Hardin County News, of Lumberton
The Highlander, of Marble Falls
Huntington-Zavalla Herald
Kountze News
Midcounty Chronicle, of Port Neches
Opportunity Valley News, of Orange
The Vidor Vidorian
    —all in Texas, and the *Vinton News*, of Vinton, Louisana.
And KLVI radio, Beaumont
and *Flying* magazine, New York.

Chapter 1

The War

Village Creek

Clear morning light is bouncing off Village Creek and lighting the cabin from within. Leaving shadows on the ceiling of wavery water patterns. The new leaves, lighted from underneath, are a screen of pale-green dotted swiss all around. Tree trunks stand in water, the boat swings peacefully, tied to the front step railing. It's the March flood, chuckling in the forest, running free and clear across the county road. The old nesters here say this is the time when the catfish sneak through the bushes and catch baby rabbits.

Sister Creek has played with me for a week. A few years of no floods, then once each month this year. Bringing my nose down to smell her fragrance, kneeling to read the yardstick, stuck in the ground by the steps. An inch-an-hour rise. It's been raining in deep East Texas; now three days later in the sun it's all on its way down to Beaumont, through Village Creek and the Neches River. Inch-an-hour rise. Six hours more and she'll be running in the front door and out the back. I don't live on Village Creek, I·live in it. It's ok, the real house sits upstairs on the pilings. Those isolated creatures of us that are drawn to her know this; if you nest on Village Creek, nest high. In the summertimes, out there in midstream where the willow tops are swaying now, you can cool in the heat waist-deep, sitting in the dappled shade and watching the shadows of little fishes darting over clear white sands.

In the next day's early stillness Village Creek was running sweet and clear across my cabin floor. I stood where the stairway ends strangely in water, watching the swift schooling minnows curving away from my shadow. A bubble of laughter started to rise up in me. Upstairs I heard Jenny wake up and call her mommy. Then her little pony footsteps thudding, running across the floor. Next she'll be looking for me, arms out wide. Eager Jenny with hair the color of new copper in the sun. Her oldest sister is thirty-four. And Jenny lives in a house that little fishes sometimes swim through. I started up the stairway, the bubble of laughter breaking through at this and other strange and wondrous stories of what all went on in this cabin on Village Creek. Here deep in the flowered rain forest of the Holy Ghost Thicket.

We Saw Santa

What I am is a teller of tales. "A rainmaker," said my brother Tommy; "he can march around beating on all those drums and telling you lies . . . but sometimes he makes it rain."

My little brother Tommy was a soft and brown-eyed five years old at the Christmas of 1933, and I was ten, red hair, freckles and rangy and mean as hell to him sometimes. Tell him he could go with us big guys on the exploring down the railroad track, and then run off and leave him crying alone out on the trestle.

But the big kids were getting to Tommy, telling him there ain't no Santa Claus. I had read to him " 'Twas the Night Before Christmas," and I promised him he'd see Santa this very Christmas Eve night. It gave me goose bumps too.

I climbed the cottonwood tree that grew up beside our bedroom window and stepped silently off onto the roof. I carried a loose bundle of dry sticks and placed them high up on the rooftop, near the center ridge, and came down, leading a ball of twine, and punched a tiny secret hole in the window screen, bringing the end of the string inside to where I could reach it from our bed.

This was to be Tommy's first bike Christmas; I knew, I'd already seen it. And I had walked nine rails along the track without once stepping off and made my wish for a BB gun, a long, sleek Daisy 25. A wish made with that much magic always comes true. Ask any kid.

Christmas Eve night was almost more than we could stand. They got us to bed, we were faking sleep. It sounded like squirrels in there. Daddy's voice came right through the walls.

"Aw'right you kids!"

"We're asleep, Daddy, honest."

At last Tommy's breathing changed, deep and regular. I woke him up. "Tommy! Listen. I just saw Santa and his sleigh and all those tiny reindeer out there against the moon. . . . I think he's about to land on our roof . . . sh-hh-hh, listen. . . ."

And I gave my secret string a tug and that bundle of dry sticks came halfway down the sloping roof, clattering over dry wood shingles. I could see Tommy's eyes shining in the dark.

"I hear him!" he cried.

"Sh-hh . . . listen." And we listened, straining, as Santa with his pack of toys now crept faintly jingling and tinkling into the living room. We could see the shadow of his boots moving in the crack of light under the door. I swear I could smell new bicycle.

Then it got real quiet in there, and the light went out. I gave the string a real hard jerk and the bundle of dry sticks clattered on down the rooftop, struck the metal gutter with a clang, then lay hidden in it. Perfect.

Tommy and I were at the window, swaying slightly, holding onto each other. He glimpsed Santa and the sleigh and the tiny reindeer, curving away against the face of the full moon. We went back to bed, chilled, trembling. It was beautiful. I had seen Santa too.

Christmas afternoon the kinfolks started coming over. Tommy was out happily spilling in the driveway, learning to ride his first bike. That's when our Cousin Hughie got ahold of him. Tommy told Hughie the wonders of what all had happened last night. Hughie was only a year older than Tommy, but Hughie was never young enough to believe.

He got to poking around the the bedroom window, found the string, made Tommy climb the cottonwood tree with him and look down on that bundle of sticks lying in the gutter.

You know Tommy never did learn to ride that bike. Forty years later, over the wine and telling it again, we would always come to this part of the story and agree we should have killed Cousin Hughie. "Should have pinched his nappy little head off." Then me and my brother Tommy would get up and stagger around the room some. "It ain't too late . . . let's go do it now . . . he still needs it!"

But me and Tommy let Cousin Hughie live.

Getting Ready for War

Jim was my best friend. Still is. We only see each other once a year now, and we talk in the code of when we were boys. Our wives, who hardly know each other, sit and smile, but not laughing at our friendship, arrested and held in time for forty years. We retell of how we got ready for the war.

In 1939 war was seeping out from under the doors of Europe. Nobody came to school and told us that we were going to be fed to the cannons, but we knew. Hollywood was the only one to give us our roles. The little girls would see us off, only a kiss, from tippy-toes, then remain forever faithful by the white cottage door where the red rose vines twined round.

We would go out in the biplanes with Jimmy Cagney and Wallace Beery and a kid from Texas and a kid from Brooklyn. We would grimace at each other from behind our goggles, Beery would jab a finger down at the battleship below, Cagney with his white scarf streaming, would give us a jaunty thumbs up, and we would peel off one by one, flashing our stars and bars in the shell riddled sky and pitch over into the death dive. Enemy fighter planes would swarm us, the rear gunner cowboy returning a deadly fire. Then as some of us went straight in, wrapped in flames, a tiny dot of a bomb would detach from one of the Helldivers and go straight down the smokestack of that evil battleship, the *Itchy Maru*. A boiling caldron of fire, a pillar of smoke, and one of us would try to make it back to the carrier deck.

Colin Kelly really did this. Any of us would have.

Hollywood had made us American Kamikazi. We had never met a Japanese person.

Now the gunner lay wounded, a trickle of chocolate syrup streaming from the corner of his mouth. The top wing of the Helldiver was beating up and down against a machine-gun riddled strut, about to come off any instant. We brought our riddled plane back to the edge of the carrier deck, Old Glory was snapping in the wind there, the biplane crashed and skittered along the landing deck. They got to the wounded gunner before the flames burst out.

Later, when the carrier got back stateside, the whole squadron flew low over your girl's house, rumbling brave engines, spelling out in the sky the letters U.S.A., with one plane missing from the formation in your honor. Your girl, ever true, stood looking up by the vine-covered door, her bosom heaving 'neath white lace.

It was all a kid could hope for.

Jim and I built a full, boy-scale model of a Helldiver fuselage. We hung it by clothesline wire wrapped around it, swinging free from a scaffold in the backyard. She was made of wood crates with old window shade material fabric covering. We fought her bravely, then Jim reached down and set the fabric on fire and I took pliers and cut one side of the wire sling.

Our Helldiver spun, crashed and burned. Jim and I pulled each other out of the wreck, rolled over and over in the grass, putting out real fire.

"I can't keep sending kids up in crates like this . . ." gasped Jim, mocking the major, and we rolled over and over in choking gales of laughter, kicking up our heels.

Mamma looked at me, standing there in the house, smelling of real char. Shook her head over her book.

"Suppose they gave a war and nobody came?"

"Aw-w, Mom . . ."

Jim and I had to find out if we had any guts. We shot at each other with the .22 rifle. One of us would crawl into a steel culvert and the other would crouch down in the ditch and take careful aim at the curved steel just over the other's head, and squeeze the trigger. We had to find out what real bullets sounded like.

"Boy! This is keen!"

"Kee-een!" the flattened bullets would go, off the steel by our heads.

I would come home with my boy scout uniform tucked into real leggings laced up and a leather chin strip on my campaign hat with the brim turned up, go-to-hell style, and tell her about war.

Mom would look at her warrior and softly close her book. "What if they took away all the uniforms and made the generals wear pajamas with sleeper foots in them?"

Mom was way ahead of her time. And she was sick a lot. She would stay in her room for days, in the dark, with all the shades down. But when she was well, and in days when she stood singing in her beautiful voice in the light coming in the kitchen window is how I remember Mamma most. She took me and Tommy with her to the library every time. She didn't say anything about it, but we knew books were something precious. Tommy ate the library paste. And grew up to become an Episcopal priest.

Times were hard until just before the war. We lived in rent houses and we moved a lot. Mom called us "The Joads," after that family in *Grapes of Wrath*. But she could take some flowered-edge, shelf-paper trim, a can of ivory paint, and some pin-on lamps and make any bare new house look like "us" by the time Daddy got home from work.

Once, we had just moved into a new neighborhood and the lady from across the lot came over to make friends. "You sure have a couple of fine sons . . . and the daughter seems quite active too."

Mom looked at her puzzled, head to one side; we never had a sister. The neighbor lady went on: "You know, the girl in the blue gym shorts who was sliding off the garage roof on a washboard with the boys yesterday."

That was our Mom.

Jim and I had to know if we had any guts, enough to go to the war. There was the radio tower. It stood 404 feet tall. The flashing red beacon on top was a ridged glass lens, framed in brass, standing about two feet high. The metal plate it was bolted to capped the tower framework and the rim of it was about one tennis shoe wider than the beacon itself.

The test was, would you climb the tower and stand on the rim, one foot each side of the beacon, clutching it only with your knees and holding your arms out wide, feeling the tensions tremble in the tower and ride its slight sway in the Gulf Coast winds.

Then could you unbutton your fly and reach in? Could you find that terrified little thing and coax it to come out? If you could get it out you were a brave. If you could make it pee, sending your golden mists off on the winds into two counties, then you were a hero.

Jim and I were heroes.

Skeet

There was one major difference between Jim and me. At school he played by the rules. I always figured the rules were designed to protect the slow-witted from each other.

His mom saw to it that he did his homework. Our mom was off in the hospital a lot, or in her dark, shade-drawn room, sick. I had more important things to do after school than to help them with homework anyway. When we were eleven, Jim and I finished reading the life of the Wright brothers and built our own glider, *Fishflakes*. I had six months' production of them sold at school if the prototype had not crashed so badly with us in it on the first two flights. Jim, with his fine mathematical mind, later figured our wing loading of *Fishflakes*. It would have been the same as a brick with a ten inch wingspan.

Then we had a sailboat to design and build. *Kanvas Kitty* was workable. Wet, but workable. We sailed summers off the Port Arthur waterfront in her, and later down Village Creek. God! To someday live in such beauty as this.

Of course, Jim did all this and his homework too. But Jim accepted the system. I resented the school not being able to educate me in their allotted all day of time. Why should I bring stuff home and contribute to the failure of the system?

"Do you have your homework assignment, Gordon?"

"No, ma'am."

"And you didn't wear shoes to school today like I told you to."

"No, ma'am."

I was not going to put my feet into little boxes either.

"Then you go stand out in the hall."

For this teacher who insisted that a barefoot boy could not be educated I kept an old pair of red Keds in a locker by her classroom door. Made a great show of getting shod, hopping around the edge of her forbidden threshold.

In social studies class the teacher asked, "What was the first material thing man ever worked with?"

I yelled, "Eve."

She made me go stand out in the hall.

I became one of those hall ghosts. You've seen them. There are some at every school. I would not deny their authority. The "hell, no, we won't go" wasn't to be invented within our culture until the generation of my children. All I knew was that somehow, for some reason, I was falling through the whole grid of twelve years of a fairly good educational system and not hardly touching any of the bars. This did not delight me.

At the end of the hall a window opened out onto the second floor and there was easy climbable offset brickwork up to the third floor and over a cornice and onto the roof. I sat on the high-school roof, feeling the rough slate of its steep gable tingle the soles of my feet. Down in the courtyard the kids played, their bright-colored sweaters forming and breaking in ever-changing patterns, then somewhere inside the building a bell rang and the bright dots down on the campus grass formed and funneled into the building like the sands of time. I began to suspect that I didn't really belong anywhere. But I enjoyed the mysticism of the aerie, feeling the school pulse with all the lives and emotions crisscrossing inside. And when

some girl would point up and I could thinly hear her voice, "Oh-h
. . . there's a boy-ee on the roof. . . . !" No. An Eagle.

By his senior year Jim was a standby teacher in chemistry and
physics. He made the dean's list at Texas A & M too. What I like
about ole Jim was he did that and his folks never knew it until they
got the letter. Jim went on with Patton then, and crossed the Rhine.

If you were to ask for a picture of my university it would be a
long line of hot stoves. Some of them touched twice. Or a picture of
Skeet.

Skeet was a box bodied, 1927 Model T Ford coupé, my first car. I
got her for a summer's wages, $20 to a thickset man name of Worley
whose face never moved when he spoke.

Skeet was not her name at first; it was an ad, painted nicely on her
black door in carnival-red glitter paint. It was to advertise Worley's
skeet range, which subsequently failed. She became *Skeet* to me
because that was sort of the sound of the spirit of her when she ran.
A sort of a tinny roar: skee-eet!

Skeet was born out of time and out of place. She was the last
Model T. Next year, 1928, the Ford would be the wonderful Model
A, Ford's first step in nearly twenty years toward civilizing the Ford
car. The '27 T was so ugly that they quit looking at her when they
built her.

Over bodied, underpowered, she showed the lines of the coming
Model A. She had grown fat around the cowling, lost her little cat
face. Lost all the virtues and the Remington bronze hard lines of the
real Model T, the car that won the West. She was the last ox, dying
on the trail.

The worst improvement in the '27 Model T was that it had a
self-starter and needed a battery. The real Model T Fords had to be
hand-cranked to start, and you could take the battery with you or
not.

Only a man could start a Ford car then, and thus it had always
been. A man would arise early, eat a big breakfast of steak and eggs,
then go out and get ahold of that crank. He would heave on that
crank with all his muscle and might. If he could turn it hard enough,
fast enough, there was a thing inside called a magneto which would

create a spark, and the spark begat life, and the cold iron of the engine would commence to run.

Praise the Lord.

And in its running, the magneto produced more and stronger sparks, which kept it running. The Model T was fundamental. Right out of the New Testament. The only way a man could start the thing was with his vital energy, right out of the proteins of the earth, the way God and Henry Ford intended things to be.

It was General Motors who invented the self-starter, and put it on the Chevrolet and first freed the women and set them upon us evermore.

I got *Skeet* in the summer of 1940, when I was sixteen years old and only knew two things: that I'd never be sixteen again. And that I would probably live forever. *Skeet* taught me the rest.

She taught me that if I ran the car fast enough at night to keep the lights burning bright, this excess of speed and power, sometimes approaching nearly thirty miles an hour, would beat out the connecting rod bearings in the bottom of the engine. The Model T Ford engine had skinny and tender connecting rod ends, much like the fetlocks of a fine-bred horse. It was possible to lash her onward until she would do harm to herself.

And so I learned that for each night of bright lights and blond-haired women there would come a day in the pits. A time later of being under there in the dark and oily droppings, a time to tighten up the connecting rod bearings and to repent.

A battery salesman told me that a good battery, although expensive, would provide an easy answer to all this. That it would start the car, and burn bright the lights too. What he did not tell me was that a battery is only a box of promises that begin to wane from the first day you possess it. So beware of men in soft clothing, and the buying of things that promise too much.

Skeet led me to lust and crime. With only Wilma in there we were suddenly free from the soft footsteps of her mom. Both of us were uncertain, but the old car and the warm nights fairly tingled with the idea that the possibilities were unlimited. And when Jim double-dated with his girl Sippy, all four of us crammed into that tin box, there was no way we could avoid getting shoved up against warm yieldy stuff we had only dreamed about in wildest imaginings.

Tiny had even let me kiss her in *Skeet*. She wore thick purple lipstick that was slippery and tasted like grapes. If she let me do that once, she'd let me do it again. I had a date with Tiny that night, and I had a dead battery too.

By stealth I did go out and swipe my neighbor's battery. I left him my own dead battery, of course, installed this false witness into his car, and hurried back to *Skeet*, still tasting wild purple grapes.

That stolen battery was even deader than my own. In his innocence, my victim had made a victim of me.

Almost late for the date, panic rising in me, but spoiled now to worldly ways, I hated cranking that Ford.

Part of the Model T folklore was that cranking could be made easier by jacking up one rear wheel and letting it kick free like a rabbit's leg.

The reasoning behind this strange-looking procedure was caused by what Mr. Ford called "the planetary transmission." It was a forerunner of today's automatic transmission, only it had no *P* or *N*. The Model T was never really in neutral. On a cold day the whole car would creep up on you as you cranked it. Jacking up one back wheel was one sure way of putting it in neutral, although you still had to waste all that cranking against the draggy transmission, down the drive shaft and axle and out to the mockery of that idle rear wheel kicking free in the air. I hated it. And *Skeet* knew I was cranking in hate and refused to start.

Skeet knew. Round and round went the crank, breast to breast; the two of us groaned to the strain. The only sound was my gasping breath, and the raw gas dripped and stank. I picked up the brick that was chocking the front tire and slung it through her windshield with all my might. Glass flew everywhere. It was wonderful.

This, also, did not start the car.

Next, I found out how cheaply I would sell my soul. There in the driveway sat Dad's brand-new '40 model Ford V-8. And there I was before him, promising all the things I would do if only he would let me have his car for this night. That I would wash it every day, that I would keep the grass mowed, that I would never again sass Mom, nor bully my little brother Tommy anymore.

I drove off in that shiny black Tudor humpback, playing the radio, grinning, the devil himself sitting cross-legged in my lap.

Usually, if she would start, I drove *Skeet* to school. Not many kids had a school car then. But she could humble me there too. Her radiator leaked. It was a basket of water, weaving and wickering as we drove along. There was no way I could set enough cans under it to catch all that water as it leaked dry during a school day.

So I parked her on the shoulder of the road; the water trickling out of here and there would collect on the greasy front axle and all drain down and gather and run off at the low point. That's where I put my five-quart Havoline oil can each morning. At day's end I had collected five quarts of greasy, rusty water, enough to pour it back in, with all the kids laughing, and make my way back out to the house before it ran dry and burned up the engine.

One guy tried to sell me a heat gauge so I would know before she got red hot. Same guy that sold batteries. I drilled a hole in her brass radiator cap and put a loose-fitting bolt in it. When the bolt just perked up and down, it meant find water soon. When it stood straight up against its nut on a whistling column of steam, it meant stop now and do nothing until things cool down. If I had put one in the top of my head like that, I would have still had a windshield.

Skeet taught me about free advice. In those days no American boy grew beyond puberty without having heard of some sure home remedy that would stop radiator leaks in a Model T Ford.

One theory was to crack a few raw eggs and pour them into the radiator. The eggs would mix with the water, you drove the car until it got boiling hot, the boiled eggs would congeal in the leaky places. Another remedy along the same theory was to pour in a cup of oatmeal. The flakes would be drawn down to the leaks, swelling and plugging them forever.

As a result of all this, *Skeet*'s radiator leaked as bad as ever, but when she got red hot, she smelled like a good English breakfast.

Uncle Johnny gave me the best advice. He was what they called a "Ford man." He said, "Son, if it's running, don't fool with it."

In *Skeet* I learned about critics. They stood row on row on Walgreen's corner, wearing peg tops and pleats and wisecracking and jiggling the change in their pockets. They scored us on the Saturday-night drag, graded us out according to what kind of a car we drove and what kind of a girl we could get to ride in it, and whether or not she was shifting the gears for you at the stoplight or was she a door pusher.

Reviewed and passed, it finally occurred to me, by these judges who had neither car nor girl of their own, and stood only a few feet from the gutter.

I didn't need outside help to confirm how bad my act was. Even the kids who drove Nashes sneered at the tall, ever trembling *Skeet*. I learned to kill with comedy, same way little Jewish boys in Queens, New York, were learning at the same time. And for the same reasons.

Doug was as good a man as Jim when we were out in the salt cane marshes in a homemade boat and a blue norther storm was whipping Sabine Lake to a frenzy of whitecaps. But Doug was from Griffin Park. He had the clothes, the manners, and on Saturday nights he had Lovie Marie tucked down in his dad's long, gray, torpedo Buick. When Lovie walked down the hall at school, guys just fell up against the lockers and groaned. When Doug looked at me out of that Buick, he sneered. He couldn't help it. In those days there were still the haves and have-nots.

Not knowing exactly why, I reinvented vaudeville down there in Port Arthur, Texas. I took the floorboards out of *Skeet*. From the driver's seat I could look down and see the pavement. I took my five-quart water can and filled it half full of black sludge oil and the rest with all the bright, shiny engine junk parts I could get into it. A bent connecting rod, a broken piston, burned-out bearing shells and jumpy valve springs.

With this tall can of syrupy black oil and junk carefully balanced on the frame over the hole in the bottom of the car, I eased up to the stoplight and challenged Doug's straight eight Buick and a blazing little '33 Ford coupé to a drag race.

Gunned my engine, rattled my pistons at them. They turned, astonished. I gave them the stare. The line of jelly beans standing in front of Walgreen's began to shift their sharp shoes and make low clucking sounds. This would be murder.

Then just before the light changed to green, I jumped *Skeet*'s clutch. She reared, pawed the air, died. The oil can dumped all that stuff and it spread and rolled out from under the car. It looked like *Skeet* had emptied her engine.

The jelly beans doubled up guffawing, shoes striking fire off the sidewalk. Lovie Marie was grabbing Doug and pointing, her cute little nose all crinkled up laughing.

During all the cheers and jeering the light went back to red. I climbed down, went around to the front and grabbed *Skeet*'s crank with a prayer. Gave it a pop turn and the hot engine started. I mounted her running board as she went by, climbing in through the window and waving bye-bye to Lovie. Shoe and Other Shoe.

That came nearly forty years later. I took a black magic marker and printed a big "Shoe" on one, and "Other Shoe" on the other of the new tan pair of soft shoes. Going up the elevator of the publisher's building, everybody staring at the floor, someone would giggle, "Like your shoes." In New York they don't even talk to each other; now a little warmth could spread down to my cold fingers clutching that manuscript.

"Why didn't you mark them 'right' and 'left'?"

"Well, sir," not ashamed of the cottonmouthed accent in this play of my own setting, "when I was just a little bitty boy my Mamma said, 'Son, this is your foot. The shoe goes on your foot.' " And the elevator stopping, them always rushing, would delay it a delicious moment. New Yorkers love a good act. "And the other shoe?" "Well, the other shoe goes on my other foot. Been like that since I was born. Y'all are quick for New Yorkers . . . bye-bye." And I could go in and face that publisher in the echo of a good laugh instead of my hair all standing on end.

Skeet died while I still owned her. She just sort of collapsed and died. I opened her up and her spirit flew out. I dismantled her and sold most of her parts. I tried to sell her body shell to Big Boy James who ran the junkyard across the tracks but he wouldn't even let me give it to him free. We sneaked back that night and threw it over the fence.

I got $5 for *Skeet*'s old cast iron engine block which never did get busted. I last saw it lying on its side on the floor of the garage where I sold it. I paused a moment in leaving and looked back at it. There was its crankshaft, gripped now in red rust. I stood there thinking, Once it had been new and made its first single turn. Now it had made its last.

And there at the age of sixteen I first realized that all things have a beginning and an end.

Soon enough I would go off to the war. And at midwar return home and marry one of those girls who had sat up beside me in *Skeet*. I would leave her safely with my seed to tend as so many young couples did then when the future looked so uncertain.

After the war, and in the long years to come, there would be life to be lived, and careers to be won and more babies to come. Then I would leave her again, leave her safely with all that I had owned, as so many old couples did when the future looked too certain.

There is a technical term for all this. A medical phrase that I learned from some of the professionals while going through the agonies. It's called "the middle-aged crazies," or, "Is that all there is?"

I returned to the sunlight and sandbars of Village Creek, for we had raised a cabin there. Back to the joys of my youth, but the cabin was dark and silent now. This was before Diane came, to bring light and laughter back to this place, and Jenny. Now in the silences I rummaged through the meager junk that a man grabs out of a marriage and I found *Skeet*'s bell.

Skeet didn't have a horn, for more reasons than you'd want to hear. She couldn't go "Ahh-OO-gah!" like real Model Ts did. She had a bell. A real cowbell, hung under her frame. Not a tourist bell; this was a real dong-a-longer that used to belong to our cow, Ida. I had punched a hole in it with a nail and tied a string which ran up through a crack in the floor so I could reach down and ring it from the steering wheel.

It also swung free and *Skeet* could ring it herself when she hit bad holes in the road, adding to the general sounds of merriment and loose metal having a party.

The bell was for strangers at the stoplight, staring at that old box-bodied coupé. I would stare back a moment, then carefully point a finger at them, and as the light changed, *Skeet* would go "donga-longa-longa," and they would pull away laughing. Here was a different spirit. Or here was something so bad it may be better than anything you'll ever have.

All those years later, in the junk carried out of the past, I found *Skeet*'s bell, brought along from the first camp to this last one. The unleavened bread.

I hung the bell from the capital of a low beam in the underframe of the cabin, a place where I was always cracking my head going by. Now I hit the bell. And *Skeet*'s voice comes clearly over Village Creek. "Donga-longa-long." I stoop, laughing, holding the place. "Still learning things by cracking your head against them, aren't you?"

Nobody, not even Henry, got so much mileage out of the Model T Ford. But first, the war . . .

On the Banks of the Ole Pontchartrain

In the summer of '42 the American merchant marine was being sunk at the rate of one a day, sunk right on our own doorstep; the U-boat commanders called it "The great American turkey shoot." America desperately built new ships and needed warm bodies to sail them.

The new Merchant Marine Academy at Kings Point cut its four-year course to eighteen months. They taught us all they could in ninety days, of seamanship, engineering, gunnery, and then shipped us out to learn the rest at sea. Teacher was waiting, submerged right at the mouth of the river; teacher was a German submarine.

The only distinction of the Class of '43 was its 25 percent casualty rate. Line us up in our dress whites by the old cannon on the quadrangle at Bayou St. John, have us count off by fours, let every fourth man take one pace forward; that's how many of us died.

I came to the basic school at New Orleans with a group of six. One sleeps forever in the engine room of a destroyer blasted off

Okinawa. One was barbecued alive on a tanker off Norfolk; I got mine, but survived it, on a tanker in the South Pacific.

It was a casual, wonderful way to go off to The Great War. The first night they put us in the YMCA, for they had no other place. We talked in the dark while the streetcars rumbled by outside on Jackson Square. We talked of our homes, of high school just yesterday, we spoke back and forth in the dark, and when it grew silent I buried my face in the pillow and wept with homesickness. I cried in the dark, and lay there thinking of my opposite number in Germany. Some other cadet at the submarine school. Would I be as good as him? Could I hate him?

The next day they took us down to The Marine Exchange, a little shop on Canal Street, and there they bought us our uniforms. Dress whites, khakis, and winter blues with six white dress shirts and a little box of six stiff detachable collars. Such a lovely Victorian touch against sonic guided torpedoes. The collar boxes burned up in bright red flames in our rooms, the blues went unworn. They were winter clothing, and so many did not live until winter.

They took us out to the barracks on the banks of the old Pontchartrain in taxicabs. And the same yellow cabs took the first six to graduate down to the wharf. At sunset the cabs brought back what was left, eyes staring hollow, new uniforms sagging in seawater and bunker oil. The U-boat had met them at the mouth of the Mississippi, blew them out of the water, drowned them in the engine room. For them the war lasted one day.

Those nights then, after innocence, knowing we had just a few more weeks to live, we went into New Orleans to meet the girls. It was knowing we had only a few weeks to live that made the living all so sweet.

We found the girls where they had come to meet us, 'neath the bright lights of Canal Street. We took them out to Bayou St. John on the West End Street Car. It was a long ride. Time to look at each other, to know a little, to let her see you as you were, the pure warrior, so handsome, so far from home, so lonely.

And there at the end of the line, on the banks of Lake Pontchartrain, was the Old Spanish Fort. Soft, moldering brick from some other war, some other fine youths who died before us, let them look after themselves. It was we who needed the old fort this night, for its low walls, its thick carpet of grass, its sheltering mossy oaks. There amongst the crunchy acorn shells, a man could look deep into the dark, starry eyes of a beautiful girl whose name he had not yet learned, and never would, and he could utter those great unsung words of war: "Them U-boats is waitin' for me out there. . . . Yours may be the last lips I will ever taste. . . . Your arms may be the last to ever hold me and warm me before my body sleeps forever in the bosom of the cold sea. . . . How can you send me away like this?" It worked. Nearly ever time. The Maids of New Orleans sent us off to war as best they knew how.

And we were not unfeeling, unknowing. We would unclasp the gold metal insignia worn over our hearts and bestow it upon the girl. Pin it to her blouse, so she would have something to remember us by after we were dead, since she would not remember our names either.

I had the usual bad luck. I met a girl. She was dark and beautiful. She was from a large family of daughters who lived on Ursulines Avenue. And always being greedy and curious, after I met the girl, I met her sister. And from her sister, I met her other sister, and finally I got to knowing so many of them that they started bringing me home. And then I met Mamma.

Mamma was big and fat and beautiful like all New Orleans mammas, and she put her head to one side and looked at me and she said, "Ah! he's so young, so pretty, but so skinny! He needs some of Mamma's home cooking!" And that was the beginning of the end of it. Each night I sat there listening to them all talk, and I had to eat all that okra and stewed tomatoes, and eggplant, and dirty rice and sweet potatoes, and all that kind of gish. That lady like to have killed me. She was feeding me to death.

I was glad when in September it was my turn and I went down to the sea where there were only submarines.

There really were "wolf packs." Our convoy was a ten-knot moving platter of fat ships. Each night the wolf packs of U-boats trimmed down the edges of it like a butcher trims a steak. There were six cadets on the ship; me and Dood shared the four-to-eight watch. Him on the bridge, me in the engine room. She was diesel, big, slow-beating, direct-drive Nordbergs. In port I could open a crankcase door and walk up and down on the crankshaft, shining my flashlight up the oil gleaming connecting rods to the piston skirts above, trying to imagine that the hand of man could make forgings that big. The clean honesty of the machining was beautiful. I walked through the engine like a poem. Under way I would lean my whole body against the metal warmth, singing to the thudding of her power. She boogied.

Me and Dood would meet in the galley at 3:30 A.M. before going to relieve the watch. The gleaming, four-foot-tall coffee maker in there was the heart of the ship, but we were too young to drink coffee yet so we made peanut butter and jelly sandwiches.

"You hear all that crashing and thudding last night?"

"Yeah, the Canadian corvette was trying to save that little Dutch freighter after her smokestack caught fire."

"Naw, man, torpedoes are too expensive for a rust pot like that. What you heard was them U-boats clashing all over each other, a wad of them, getting lined up for a daybreak shot at us. Now why don't you just hand over that little black book of all that nookie you got lined up in Port Arthur? No sense wasting it in the engine room. I'll go back and comfort every one of them. Tell 'em your last gurgle was their name on your lips. C'mon, give me the book," holding out his nonjellied hand. Dood was about to go on watch up on the nice safe bridge, right by the lifeboats.

"Listen to me, you half-caste, misbegotten, Tangipahoa Parish quadroon. While you're up there mooning at the stars, this ship wandering all over the convoy scaring Liberty ships to death, I have committed to my mind the total plan of the construction of this vessel. I know holes and tunnels out of that engine room that not even the builders know are there. When this tub gets it, I'm going to open a hatch in the top of the smokestack and step out of it onto your fancy white cap just as it floats off your head." Hitching a dungaree handful of crotch at him. "There are whole generations, yet unborn, squirming around in there. I promised them I would bring them through this war. . . . Mrs. Baxter's li'l boy ain't never gon' be found floating belly up in no engine room." We guffawed loudly, but didn't look at each other's eyes. I went below, carefully dogging down all the watertight doors behind me. Man, this is keen.

A few months later, back in Baltimore, the most odd shot of the dice you could ever dream up bounced off the wall and put us into the Navy.

The Navy took over the ship, and along with this deed went a set of rules which said, "—any Naval Reserve personnel on board who are on inactive status will be activated into the Navy." That swallowed all six of us cadets. They gave us the Navy equivalent rank of midshipman, but we did not fit into any Navy midshipman program. And we didn't belong to Kings Point Academy anymore either. So they scattered us and sent us out to sea where at least we would be useful. As permanent midshipmen, I guess. My service serial number was 6.

I was shipped off to a new construction tanker on the West Coast because it was supposed to have Nordberg diesel engines and I was an experienced Nordberg engineer.

Whoever was matching up this set of cards was missing the one that said there were no more Nordberg engines to be had from Nazi-occupied Norway and the builders of this tanker had made the cheapest, quickest substitution they could find. They filled up the engine room with four General Motors locomotive diesels. And I had never seen one in my life.

I went aboard and reported to the captain, who up until the urgencies of war had never captained anything more serious than a harbor tug. His gold braid was as new and uncomfortable looking as mine. He gazed upon me with sorrow.

"Do you know anything about a diesel-electric engine room?"

"Nossir."

"What is the extent of your experience with the Navy 3"/50 cannon?"

"I've seen them before. From a distance."

"How old are you, son?"

"Nineteen, sir."

The captain seemed to be gazing far away and speaking to himself. "A schoolboy. Three weeks and we set sail out into the South Pacific Ocean which at this time is being owned and operated by the Imperial Japanese Navy. I need an engineer and gunnery officer, and they have sent me a schoolboy. . . . Son, you better go hit the books because as soon as they load this tub full of hundred-octane aviation gas we are going to haul it out to the Solomon Islands and you are now the third watch engineer and the second gunnery officer."

Once again the feeling of being the hall ghost, like when I was in high school. I tried to fit in.

The gunnery was easy. I can talk to guns. But those high-speed V-16 "screaming jimmy" engines were impersonal. They came from the factory as "units." They ran as units. Hot and screaming.

I really don't know, or much want to know, what happened off Canton Island. I had the 3"/50 cannons elevated to their maximum 85 degrees, firing. I woke up in the Navy hospital at Pearl Harbor. Birds were singing outside the window and some crazy Asiatic survivors of the 1st Marines from Guadalcanal were wheelchair racing down the corridors.

There is always a backwash eddy of a big war. The flotsam that chugs back and forth in the shaded tides up under the wharves, then casts up on the beach to rot away. I was part of that now.

The Navy had "surveyed me from sea duty," as they phrase it. I also did not fit into any Navy shore duty. They gave me back to Kings Point, which just sent me home until someone could decide something.

Manners and morals have changed so fast in America in my lifetime that I need to tell you how we were in the class of '42 or the things that happened next won't make any sense. The word patriotism is a kook word now, best used to illustrate the dated and daffy character of Archie Bunker in TV comedy. It was real to us then.

I was home at midwar, ashamed to be seen on the streets with all my arms and legs and both eyes. I wore my uniforms and all my ribbons and swaggered with my hat cocked at a go-to-hell angle

. . . lest they say, "What's *he* doing home?" Behind the windows of every house along the street there was someone whose man had gone to war.

Daddy told me Mary was a widow. Mary was one of the nice girls who sat up beside me in ole *Skeet*. She was tall and pretty with a thick mane of chestnut hair. She moved good when she walked, a tall girl with a tall girl's face. While I was in the Pacific she had sent me notice of her wedding to Otto and I was glad for both of them. They had been married only a few months when he was killed in a B-17 bomber. Mary was a widow at seventeen.

I was picking up the phone to call her when Daddy said of widows, "Never miss a slice off a cut loaf." Lecherous old man.

I dated Mary in the excitement of midwar.

Then the Navy solved itself of me with a stroke of the pen. I got a letter from Secretary of Navy Frank Knox himself, suggesting I resign. I still got the letter, and his signature, along with the wonder of having resigned from World War II.

I couldn't let it go at that, of course. My song had not been sung yet. I volunteered into the Army Air Corps. The flying cadets. Gone be an Ace.

They washed me right out. Sent me down to a crash boat squadron in Florida. I was the captain and only crew of a derrick barge that sat out in one of those big shallow lakes right at the end of the runway. My command drew five feet of water in a lake that was about three feet deep. It was moored in a special hole dug for it. If you expected me to use my big hook to get the wreck off your back, you better crash close to my barge. It sure wasn't going anywhere.

There I was, a buck private in the Army, wearing Navy dungarees and a white sailor hat, moored in a circle of coffee grounds and thinking how funny things can turn out.

I'd been an officer and I'd been an enlisted man. Officer is better. I'd been in the Navy, now I was in the Army. Soon I'd go to the river and be baptized. I had been gone from home about three months when Mary called. She was from a good Catholic family. I started studying my catechism; always wanted to be a Catholic someday anyhow.

I received the sacraments of confession, penance, baptism, first communion and matrimony all in the same day. The Army shipped me out that night, which is about all that the Holy Roman Catholic Church and the U.S. Army can do for a man, short of last rites.

Mary had a cheeseburger in the same PX where I bought her wedding ring and followed me to my new post down the coast next day. We got a one-room kitchenette in a long, brown, row government project, and I guess you could say we started our lives.

I was too swamped with having a woman, right there, in the house, all the time, within reach, to be thinking of much of anything else. "Wife" took some time to soak in. And "husband." And soon "Daddy." My God, Daddy is "Daddy": I'm not twenty-one yet.

This was serious. I tried to think it through and realized I hadn't thought anything through past the war and being a hero. Maybe it wasn't so serious. Maybe this is just how it turns out for folks. How could it be serious with everything going along so good? Come home to a clean house, green ivy in the window. My window. Supper on the table and the bed smoothly turned down and Mary giving me little sheep's-eye looks across the table.

Yet I went alone back to the crucifix and knelt in the stillness. "Well, I've really gone and done it this time . . . no . . . excuse me, God." And I remembered some of the stuff I had just been reading and looked up again with a better face on. "Dear God . . . please . . . let me love her as Christ loved His own Church. . . ." —that's pretty good. The strongest thing I could think of. Christ died for His church. "—let me love her. . . ." My balls crawled at the satiated thinking that drifted off from that. There was some distant unformed thinking that maybe all I knew about love was in my balls. "Well, don't knock it. That'd been pretty good for openers . . . sure got this show on the road . . . heh heh heh. . . . Naw, God, I'm sorry. This is serious. Or at least it seems like it ought to be."

It helped, but I came out of the church feeling like I really didn't belong in there either. Not like the little old lady with the black shawl over her head, grown to the pew in the back. But just being outside and walking felt good, and I struck out down the railroad

track that cuts across to the field our project was in. I'd tell Mary I'd
been to church, praying. Surely God understood sinners like me.
He made king snakes too, didn't He? They're snakes, but good-
looking ones, and they don't hurt anybody.

Molly was born that winter.

It was a mean time. My war was over, I was working at getting
out of the service. They didn't need me anymore, I didn't need
them. In the summer to come a solitary bomb would drop from the
belly of a B-29 high over Japan. It was the last war any of us ever
went off to singing.

Mary and I were one. A spent ball in the pinball machine, rolling
free of all the flashing lights now, headed for the home slot. Germany and Japan seemed far away, my real enemy was right down at
the end of the street, pecking out shipping orders on his typewriter.
They randomly shipped me back and forth across the country, looking for a place I would fit. Mary kept one foot locker ready. It held
everything we owned.

And she always kept bus fare home from wherever we were. That
was the last dime, but we never got down to it and we were toughly
proud of that. At one place I took a night-time civvy job unloading
boxcars.

Let me tell you something. Never work at anything that has to do
with boxcars.

We lived in rented rooms. Once to get half a garage, which was
the only place open in a uniform-jammed town, she worked as a
maid. The infant Molly slept in dresser drawers; at one place we
hung her bassinet in the shower. It was the roomiest, quietest place
we had.

Molly reddened and screamed a lot and she filled up Mary's arms.
I seriously suggested we give her away. To Mary's mother. All the
women seemed to enjoy a wet, dirty kid about the same. Mary just
listened to the idea and nodded.

By April, I had become what they call a "guardhouse lawyer." I
studied all the books of rules and regulations and after two or three
stalled attempts, sprung myself out of the service. I took our little

caravan home to Port Arthur and we moved in with Mary's folks. Quiet, decent people. We had absolutely nothing to talk to each other about. Molly banged away at her crib bars. Now there was screaming in my house too. Well, actually, Mary's house.

I slung my seabag on my shoulder and went down to the docks looking for a job. Diesels were all I knew.

In the rows of tugs and barges there was a towboat nosed up to the wharf, the skipper looking down from his pilothouse, arms folded on the curved, varnished windowsill.

"Hi, Red, you on the beach?"

I nodded.

"What do you do, deck or engine room?"

"All of it."

"Well, c'mon aboard. My engineer just quit."

There was a crap game going on the deck of the crew quarters forward. I stood in the door, seabag still slung, blocking the light. They looked up, one of them jerked his head toward the three-wall stack of bunks, indicating the one the former engineer had just vacated. With great manners I stepped over the game and crumpled stacked money, pitched my bag on the bunk and sat down beside it, puffing up a reek of diesel fuel. The sheets were brown with the pattern of the former throttle bender. Not yet glazed, but brown.

"You want in the game, Red?"

"Not just yet."

The circle of heads closed and the dice went clickety in the shooter's hand. He looked like he was hot and trying to get the spell back on them again.

Towboats

I towboated awhile on the Mississippi. That great lady, lolling in her bed between halves of a continent. In the evenings by the twilight we would sit in front of the wheelhouse and talk in low voices, watching the lead barge brush the overhanging trees. We could smell the willows and the rich loam.

The *Lee La Ferney* was too underpowered to breast the river current, so we ran the eddies near the bank. It took three days from New Orleans to Baton Rouge and nine hours for the wild ride sweeping back downstream with the empties "on the hip."

Our sister ship, the *John McCullough*, swept round a bend like that one night and right under the bows of a tanker. She had a one-eyed mate at the wheel and he never stopped to call the watch below. He just flew out of that wheelhouse like a big bird and the tanker carved exploding steel and the watch below drowned fighting their own mattresses as the river foamed in the door.

One night that same one-eyed mate was sailing relief mate in the *Lee La Ferney* and I was on watch down in the engine room. I heard him ring three bells and a "double hookup." I lifted the throttle stop and shoved her up into the overload notch and left her raving wide open and went topside to see what he was trying to miss. It was the same situation. We were being swept down on the lights of a ship coming up in midchannel. I called all hands, we put on life jackets and stepped out onto the barge alongside. A little cluster of men waiting to see if he was going to make it. Ready for a night swim. The mate divided his time between missing that ship and glaring down at us.

I think I decided to quit the river one day in that string-straight section of the intercoastal canal. Where the canal runs through the flat marshes between Lake Charles and Orange, it notches the horizon at both ends. We stood watches of six on, six off. I went off watch, there was an old red cow, ambling along the canal bank in our direction. When they called me for the watch she was still out there, keeping pace with us. I folded my arms on the Dutch doors into the engine room that evening and watched the sun go red down into the canes and decided that I wasn't sure yet of what I was going to be, but it was going to have to be more than this.

Chapter 2

Radio

I came ashore looking for easy money. Walking along Procter Street in Port Arthur, hands jammed down in my pockets, thinking, "—Someday I'll be mayor of this town, but right now I'm out of work."

I met Roney Petersen on the sidewalk behind KPAC, we stopped and talked about it.

"Why don't you go over to the radio station and try. They've got bigger fools than you."

They were still getting rid of the wartime women announcers. Dusty Rhodes grinned and ripped off about a yard of press wire news copy.

"Go sit in that little announcer's booth and read this into the microphone."

He hired me on that July 22, 1945, and I've been talking into the microphone for over thirty years.

The new postwar manager was John Lofton. He was the first high roller I ever met. He wore fine pinchback suits that fitted him like a black beetle. He was quick moving, graying hair slicked back; he sent for me in his office.

"Damn programming. The name of this game is money."

His pale eyes crescented up from the bottom when he smiled. His sharpened face had a baked ruddy cast to it that reminded me of how the steady exhaust flame of an engine will bake the exhaust manifold red and brittle. When he was in a temper I expected to see a jagged crack break out in this casting and orange flames shoot out of it. I wouldn't have given you a nickel for his heart.

"Never mind the scruples, get the rubles."

His laughter clacked like an iron ratchet wheel turning. Al Legget laughed when Mr. Lofton laughed. Me and Al had gone to high school together, Mr. Lofton said Al was his boy, going to make a real crackerjack salesman out of him.

"Remember, son, they can slam the door on your fingers, pee in your shoe, but they can't ever hurt your feelings."

Al stood there blushing, with Mr. Lofton's arm around his shoulders. Mr. Lofton even favored the kid by coming out to his house for dinner sometimes. Curvy Carolyn Legget was also one helluva good cook too.

Lofton's brilliant stay as manager was short. He bounced right off our dry boards of directors. KPAC–Port Arthur College was an endowed institution; all the board members belonged to the First Methodist Church right there on the campus. Ole man Carter, who signed the checks, wrote carefully with a dipped pen in a fine Spencerian hand. They all voted no when Lofton proposed that he could double the station's revenue, and his too, if they would lift their blue law on beer advertising.

Lofton left town in a brand-new black Lincoln coupé with luckless Legget's little blond wife sitting up there right beside him. The last thing Lofton ever said to me was, "You get out too. That self-perpetuating group of horses' asses will someday put this place in the ground."

Carter's son was running it years later when they sold the station to a chain outfit out of San Antonio.

But I stayed on a few years. I was making $125 a month and Mary was round with child again. Molly wasn't going to be the baby anymore. "I never was," she said many years later; "I look at those old photographs and every other year there was a new baby in Mother's arms and I was pushed farther down the line."

We bought a little house and I started working night gigs in the honky-tonks across the river in Louisiana. "Got to take care of Mary and the kids." And that's all true. But I had also quickly learned that just being the voice on the radio attracted chicks. The teenyboppers would call me at the station, their voices dropped low. They would dance by the bandstand, shaking their fannies then looking back to see.

I'd get in about one or two o'clock in the mornings and sleep until showtime on the air. "Sh-hh, you kids be quiet. Your daddy's sleeping."

Never true to them. Never knew them. One Christmas when Molly was thirty she gave me a long, slender, wrapped gift. It was a barbed and feathered arrow, the shaft broken, the two halves tied together with ribbon.

Molly was watching me steadily as I turned this over in my hands. Then I knew.

"This mean the war is over?"

"Yep." She was smiling. Was it defiance or pity in her eyes?

Jesus! All that time and I hadn't even known she was trying to work something out between us. Bax, you never really belonged anywhere, not even to them.

I called my show *Jambalaya;* that's a Cajun French word for a stew, made mostly of ham. That's the first time Hank Williams ever heard the word too. We had booked in Hank and the Louisiana Hayride for the Beaumont City Auditorium that night, and he was getting drunk already.

Hank propped his boots up on my desk and told me that if a song took over thirty minutes to write it was no good. "Jambalaya," he said softly to himself a time or two, looking far away.

We looked all over town for Hank that night while the second-stringers kept the show going. Found him in Walgreen's across the street with his head in a cup of coffee. We shoved him out into the spotlight, weaving and buckling, but he came on. His long shadow slanting back across the stage.

If you were to put all the Hank Williams records in a row according to serial numbers, you could hear him singing the story of his life.

After he and Audrey gave it up and tore the blanket, he married Billie. He died not long afterward, died alone in the back seat of a big blue Cadillac speeding through the West Virginia hills on his way to a show. We put on a benefit show for him back at the City Auditorium and his band came down to play it. I was emcee, and introduced the new Mrs. Hank Williams. I moved back and stood behind the steel guitar man as she came on. She jutted out onstage in a white cable-knit sweater. Biggest, finest-looking set of jugs you ever saw. Without looking up, the steel man said, "Ole Hank . . . he lived right up until the day he died."

I kept getting hired and fired. Back and forth between the radio stations of Beaumont–Port Arthur. Once when I was really down and busted, Al Legget gave me a job at his station in Orange just because he knew I needed it while lining up something bigger. They always hired or fired me for the same reasons, five times at KTRM. Jack Neil, who owned KTRM, said it best one time. He was standing in the door, shaking his fist at me and shouted, "You are incompatible, unpredictable and incorrigible!" The newspapers printed that. Blake Locke, who ran the oldest station here and never hired me at all, said, "Baxter invented nearly all of what is radio today . . . and I would have fired him for all of it."

One of the times that Neil fired me was typical. The Top 40 craze was just sweeping in from the left coast, and KTRM had switched over to play this playpen-mentality format. I announced each one of the Top 40 records as formatted, but actually played the Kingston Trio's "Coplas" forty times. I told one outraged listener who called in that I really was playing all those famous pop tunes, that her radio must be stuck. "Hang your radio out the window and I will blow the soot out of it for you." Then I let out a bloodcurdling rebel yell, since known as my sig: the whispering voice of the piney woods.

I knew Neil was going to fire me, but planned first to jump flat-footed to the top of his desk and pee "I Quit" in his blotter. But the old man threw a whiskey glass at my head as soon as I peeked in his door and I didn't remember to do all the good stuff I was planning for him until I was down the road again. You can't go back and recapture a moment like that.

The years wore on swiftly. Now my teenyboppers were grandmas, smiling back at me through dentures. "We'd follow you up sewer pipes . . ." one of them wrote. The sponsors were loyal too; they dragged back and forth across towns with me. The ones that were going to quit, quit the first day or so. Like the really big fat account I lost, a Chevy dealer. He was switch-bait advertising a striped Impala. Only "nineteen ninety-five . . ." back in those days. And I added to this for my listener's sake, "—and for only nineteen hundred and ninety-five dollars more you can buy just about all it needs." The Chevy dealer wanted to cancel retroactive. I mean he was mad. Wanted money back.

Sometimes the listeners got really mad too. Port Arthur is a union town and back in the early fifties when they were voting closed shop they enforced their choice by cracking skulls on Procter Street at high noon. The police, the sheriff, they didn't see nothin'. It's democrat-union town; you don't get reelected by jailing union goon squads. I spent a lot of time commenting on this on the air and saying that terrorism was a poor way to gain the support of a man who chose to be nonunion. Un-American too.

I know that labor violence is one of the few socially acceptable forms of terror in America, took my ch'ice and paid my price. They boycotted thirty of my thirty-two accounts into canceling and would call up, the heavy voice on the air saying, "—boy, we gone git you tomorrow."

"You better send seven men. The first six ain't getting close to me."

Just like a John Wayne movie. I carried the six-shooter in my hand during most of the 101 strike days. Or in the basket of my bicycle. I had lost the car when the money ran out. One of the old union chiefs, with scars on his own head put there by the refinery-hired Burns gunmen, said later, "No hard feelings, Bax; at least we knew where you stood." When his kid grew up and ran for the

Senate, I made his TV commercials and helped win his seat in the state capital. A union town needs union representation, and the kid is smart too. No hard feelings.

I guess more than anything else I spent all those radio years mixed up in the marrying and the burying of these Eastex piney woods. When a home burned, someone would call me and give me all the sizes the family wore and before noon we'd have their yard piled up with clothes again. Sometimes furniture and appliances too. When a little girl was lost and wandering in the cold wet woods, that radio show could right now pull together enough men to walk a square mile of woods hand to hand. Found the kids too. One little girl we found facedown, her hair fanned out around her, floating on a river sandbar. When the flood was about to knock out Deweyville, I had a hundred men there in the rain and the levee was built by sundown. I always went too. So they could say, "—and ole Bax was right there too . . . he's really one of us. . . ." At the weddings, the beauty contests, the rodeos, a part of the marrying and the burying. The kind of stuff that lasts.

"How come you guys named a buckin' horse after me?"

"You'll find out soon's he comes out of the chute."

Ole "Bax" came out of the chute high diving, and every time he hit the hard-packed ground you could hear him farting a mile away.

And I always shared with them about Mary and the latest kid. It was just like living inside of a real soap opera . . . only I could tell it better than I lived it.

"Ole Bax tells it like it is."

Yeah. Nearly all of it. And the music. That awful music. The music never lied.

The Music

First with the music there was my ole Indian grandma and that tall, cabinet-model Atwater Kent with the batteries underneath it. Setting four hours at the end of the dark living room every Saturday night, hearing the dying-in and dying-out sounds of the *Grand Ole*

Opry coming from Nashville, WSM, Tennessee. I would just stare up at that little yellow celluloid dial light with my mouth open, like trying to get it in all my body openings at once. Uncle Dave Macon and the Fruit Jar Drinkers, the Gully Jumpers, the ancient, atavistic, crackbow fiddlings crawling and scraping out of there stirred gray ghosts of bagpipes in my blood. It was beyond the Appalachians, it was all the way back to the misty moors, and skirlings and tartans, and sharp-edged long knives and rushing feet. It was years later, hearing Her Majesty's Massed Pipers and Drummers that I linked it up, recognized it, thrilled to the red bloody lust of it. My ancient mountain fiddlings were the war-crawling man sounds of bagpipes going into cannon smoke.

Listen to it, if you can, it's the same everything, the same long-heads and socketed eyes, pale blue and mad, the mating and fighting music of the Anglos. At that time and place and I would have come up off the firing step at Ypres, long bayonet slanting off my Enfield, and strode grinning through the shell holes and wire behind the pipers and drummers, a crawling mass, earth covering, relentless, driven to that skirling in the blood and drumbeat in my balls, and gone in among the German tuba players and laid them to waste and died and gone up in smoke of glory to darken the rafters of the mead halls where they come to live it over and over afterward.

And in the living room dark I was up jigging my pale little skeleton about, shaking the beaded shades on the lamps, while my old Indian grandma threw back her head in a gap-toothed, cackling laugh because she knew too. And all the others were asleep.

And then there was the other part, the aching crooning coming up from the soft white throat of a woman. Corinne, sitting cross-legged on the edge of her bed, head bent over the big, yellow, flattop guitar, the light of a bare bulb shining in her black hair tumbling down. Her hands moving, fascinating, shutting out all else but her voice telling me of the kind of love that never dies. Of lonesome cabins and mountain valleys low, in the slow motion of the chords of music there was Ole 97, "coming down the hill makin' ninety miles an hour when his whistle broke into a scream, and they found him in the wreck, with his hand on the throttle, scalded to death by the steam" . . . and in the slow silence I saw the locomotive falling through the trestle, turning, falling, and I could see his wife as she had kissed him good-bye at the humble cabin door, and she would be waiting evermore.

In the dark of Corinne's room with only me and her son, both nine years old, to listen while she played her guitar of love and faith and garlands of ballads while her husband, Catfish, was out in the dangerous night making his bootlegging rounds. All she had was the little .38 under her pillow, and king snakes that she liked and we brought to her, peeping silently about. Waiting for her beloved Catfish to come safely home and poke his leathery face around the corner and give us that grin they named him for. She played the ballads of a beautiful woman in love, and sang them into my heart. "They buried him in the old churchyard, they buried her in the choir, and from his breast there grew a red rose, from hers, a green briar. They grew up to the old church top, till they could grow no higher. And there they tied a lovers' knot, a rose, and a green briar." From Corinne I learned that true love was deathless. How many, or how often, I cannot now recall, but this I know, I never loved but true.

And full of my love and music I came into the first music class-room in the seventh grade. A room made just for music, and I was ready to embrace it all. And the teacher, one with high chest and short black hair and a way of coming up on tippy-toes, asked each of us to stand and sing some of our favorite music. And when I sang to her "Jack o' Diamonds," imitating Corinne's husky voice, hearing it in my head, she stopped me. Told me to sit down, that such songs were trash and not music and that I would now learn of Bach and Beethoven and Chopin. And she put some horrible mishmash on the record player, and I sat there, head down on my fists, trembling, red with shame and rage, and vowed that if she would not hear my music then I would not hear hers.

I'm sorry now that I missed all that, for the hatred and hurt are still there. The snob thing. I was learning that what I had learned was different, it was not enough, and that others would look down on me. And damn me to hell before I would ever change and try to be like them.

And the decades rolled by and I was playing this music on the radio. First Burl Ives. He knew Corinne's songs. Then The Weavers on the old 78s. And then it got to be "Folk," and I began to dare to dream that America's classic music had been found at last. Like the stories of the opera with their plush and gilt that I was shut out from, our own classic music was surfacing from the earth. From shacks and shanties and undying love across the broken trestles in the valley's low. And I have lived to hear it played at Carnegie Hall and by the Boston Pops, who made it even sound like orchestration, perfected from the raw ore dug out by Chet Atkins. It's in the pot now, mixing, stirring, bubbling with blues, rock, and zonk and gospel and all that crap, but what will come from it will be American classic, dear teacher, and the hell with you. Sincerely, Jack o' Diamonds.

I saw Corinne twenty years later, playing the organ in church. Black-haired, still beautiful; true love. She picked up her guitar and played the songs back to me, into each other's eyes, and the crowd never knew what passed between us on that stage, but we did. Thank you, Corinne, for the songs of softness and true love.

My music. I am a feather before the winds of it. I cannot write it, I cannot play it, I cannot even describe it to my fellows because I am ignorant of the language, the terms of the art. But when I am open and it comes pouring up out of me, they know out there in the crowd, and they are with me. And I see my music make their hearts remember out there, and I hear them open up like some great sigh, remembering a lost love they never knew. Or I can whiplash them with it, the pipers and drummers coming out of the mists of fiddle dust, and I see their ranks stirring, moving in unison, coming through the wire and the shellfire and cannon smoke with me, grinning, splitting the air with high screams and rebel yells. And that's rich stuff. When you have done this, everything else is second best. When you have held people's hearts wet, in tender hands of song, then that's as good as it gets.

A newspaperman whose bowels had long since turned to ashes once asked me if I got my rocks off to my own music. I told him yes. The poor, miserable creeper of the cement, it's something he'll never know.

In the fifties, when steam was dying to the diesel centipedes, I used to have a regular show, "Railroading Monday, songs about them train-wrecked engineers." I ran it all together in a montage, a rush of sound and motion, "The Wabash Cannon Ball," "Orange Blossom Special," "The Mystery of Number Five," "The Engineer's Child," "Hobo Bill's Last Ride," "The Wreck of the 1256," "The Wreck of the Old 97," the "Wreck Between New Hope and Gesthemane," "Freight Train Boogie." By God, I was firing those turntables red hot with a nigger squattin' on the safety valve and the whole studio pounding the rails and the paint flaking and blowing off the towers. I felt the power of it so much I felt like I could pull her back one more notch and blow the whole radio station into one hot, steaming hole in the ground, with driving wheels found as far as ten miles away. And they would find me in the wreck, with my hand upon the throttle and my eye upon the grade, true to the end.

I always thought of myself as fair and good and true, no matter what I was doing. Fair-haired and honest, I was standing on the bandstand at the Top Hat Club on that ten-mile strip of sin between Sulphur, Louisiana, and Lake Charles. The fiddles were crying, I had my hand cupped in my ear, singing "Warm Red Wine," and making a little brown-eyed, Cajun girl with my eyes over her man's shoulder.

And later in the sleazy tourist cabin in that swaybacked, spring-raunching bed, getting marked up by that faded, tufted chenille bedspread because I didn't dare look at the sheet, I heard the Sunset Limited coming. The Southern Pacific mainline ran ten feet behind that shack. Glory, God amighty, how many women ever got it from an S.P. decapod? She was short-coupled and still hard-assed, and I knew there was a second section on the midnight train. And I held it, singing in the tension of the rails until I heard that second section coming, and then it was all hot steam and roaring and driving rods, and the blast of the locomotive rushing by and the scream of that little Cajun curled up around me. The ground thundered and shook, and the cabin fell out like a deck of cards and we rode it all the way back over the boxcars, and down in the gondola cars, and across the splintery flatcars, and sliding down and around the tank cars, until at last the caboose came flapping by with all the trainmen cheering and throwing their hats away, and the red lights faded into the distance toward the Pacific Ocean, leaving their ruby gleam dancing on the cooling, popping rails.

And on other nights alone I would race the Sunset Limited on the narrow, two-lane blacktop Highway 90. Keeping my blood-red, souped-up '50 Ford hub to hub, looking at the firebox glare when I dared, and screeching around the dark narrow turns, listening to the rap of the locomotive exhaust, and hearing the sounds of my smitty's running up my back and into my ear, and life hung by a delicious thread.

Now how could I go confess all that as a sin? Pulling back the curtain which felt like the chenille bedspread, and kneeling down on the Lysol-smelling floor amidst the candle wax drippings and whisper, "Father, I have sinned. Me and the fiddles have been raunching the locomotive of the Sunset Limited again, and howling through the night, smelling the Evangeline oaks and the honeysuckle in the dew of the little towns and listening to the whistle blow and those casings squall." I'm sorry, but I wasn't sorry. It was as good as it could get. But I wanted tame Sunday mornings at the communion rail with my wife and kids too. There ought to be a separate set of rules for the riders of the night song, the throttle benders, for those who want to drink deep of all of it.

A separate set of rules for the fair and golden ones, lest they look up someday and see themselves blackened in what corruption?

Elvis

I never played much Elvis; I never even liked him. Not even after he went into the Army and took that standing up like a man. Not even when they came out with all that about how much he loved his mother. The Army part, I always wondered how much was ole Colonel Tom Parker. Parker never let Elvis make a wrong turn, so I don't think Elvis did anything for love, and I'm sure the colonel didn't.

Elvis just put me off for some reason. He was what we would have called a jelly bean. I was fourteen years old and going into my first season of rut before I would even hang around with a kid that carried a pocket comb. The Elvises were down at the pool hall wearing fire-striking shoes, and I knew none of them would last long on a life raft. That's just not the kind of stuff they thought about.

The night we booked Elvis into Port Arthur was the first time I ever saw him. Back stage Colonel Parker told us he had just signed Elvis with RCA. I knew it was star-making time and asked him to sign one of his pictures they were hawking at intermission. He did. Wonder what that's worth now?

Then I asked Elvis if he wanted me to put him on cold, or run out during the opening theme and introduce then. When any of the Opry stars came through, they always had the local DJ do that. Then the guy could say, years later, as I am doing now, "—that night I worked with ole Elvis . . ." It was good for all of us. They still do it.

So when I asked Elvis how he wanted me to bring him on, he just turned his hooded eyes on me and his pouty mouth said, "Man, who needs you?"

Then instead of pulling the curtain over the music, and all the band jumping up and down, the curtain opened on a bare stage. Dead silence. Blue borders only.

One by one the musicians slouched out, not looking up, and set up their equipment. More silence. The packed house holding its breath was a long tide pulling out. Then Elvis came on from left. Peg tops and shirt open; nobody was wearing cowboy stuff. And he was dragging a Martin flattop by its sling. Dragging it. A big, or-chestra-model Martin. Enough right there to send him to hell for me.

He put an arm out to the standing mike and I swear every woman in the house felt it slide round the small of her back. Then he hit "Blue Suede Shoes," or "Hound Dog," I'm not sure. It was one of those jiggety ones. And Elvis could have had every woman in Port Arthur. The waves of sound broke over the walls, every seat was wired to his voltage. I never saw anything like it. I looked at those women and thought of all the stuff I had missed in Port Arthur that it would have never occurred to me to try for. Their mothers too. And a few uncles.

The pounding sounds and screams never died down. They blew the curtain away, swept in toward the dressing rooms. Elvis stood a minute on a chair, "Y'all go on home, we got more women at the motel now than we can take care of. . . ."

The auditorium was a walk from our house so I had not brought the car to get it into the traffic jam. Some Bax fan would usually stop and scoop me up anyhow.

Tonight I walked down the shoulder of the road, unbothered. I had a ways to go in the quiet of the night and a lot of stuff to think about. Life changing, important things. One was the shock of finding out that women would lower their horns and go snorting and pawing after it too. I guess I had always thought that although it was always on my mind, women had to be sort of surprised gently into it, like it was the first time they had ever felt like that. And afterward a man could go in the bathroom and secretly admire the fingernail rakings she had left down his back, but it was not the sort of thing you would mention over the coffee.

And the second thing to think about was not just the sour grapes of being left dead by the roadside right in my own hometown, but that after Elvis, music was not ever going to be the same again.

Some of the old folks in porch rockers might still want to hear about Mother and God and that Little Old Cabin in the Lane, but hillbilly music had gone to the mattress. Except for a few Eastern college professors, who collected the Carter sisters like butterflies, me and Bill Monroe and that good ole blue grass music were gone. And so were all the humor and real stories. The name got changed too; "Country and Western" became a product. I call it the "Purple motel room drapes, dying calf in a snowstorm blues." All the songs are about whiskey and women and them rhinestone cowboys can't hold either one.

So I never did like Elvis. I did enjoy aggravating the public by cracking at him. "Save your money, Elvis," would light up all the phone lines.

I never could understand Elvis's immunity from the press either. They kept up the illusion, Elvis died in the nick of time, and I think he may be the first genuine saint to sprout up from among us.

Bopper

Buddy Holly and The Big Bopper are sainted now too. Not sanctified like Elvis, out of the crotch and dreams of a million women, but lesser saints out of a movie, *The Buddy Holly Story*. They come on scrubbed clean in their white shoes and flattop haircuts from back when rock 'n' roll was just fun.

I couldn't see the Big Bopper, or hear him, but I could feel the thud thud thud of his heavy leg through the radio station floor. He was in the darkened news booth on the other side of two panels of soundproof glass. I could see his cigar glow in the dark. He was just J. P. Richardson then, night announcer, KTRM, trying to write a song in his off-duty time. Said he was going to make good.

"Chantilly Lace . . . with a pretty face . . . aw-w, baby,
you KNOW-W what ah like . . ."

Then he would come out and prop one foot up on my control room chair, "Now listen to this one, Bax . . ."

I would listen and watch his transfiguration. A chunky-faced kid, sweat beading his crew cut, he would start to play his guitar and sing and his face would glow, eyes glistening. "Eeee-yow! White lightning! . . ."

"What do you think of that one?"

I always told him the same thing, "Jape, it'll never sell."

"Aw-w, c'mon. What if I write one just for you?"

And in a little while he was back with this story song about an Indian brave name of Running Bear who lost his life in the raging river for just one stolen kiss from Little White Dove.

I felt the hair rise up on the back of my neck.

"That's too close to the house."

He laughed, and parodied himself, "Aw, baby, I know-w what you like . . ." Jape was straight; I had been best man at the wedding when he married Teensie, but he knew I was running the roads.

He always said he was going to be famous. He tried to build a name for himself by setting the world record for continuous broadcasting. He did too, but the Jape-a-thon only got one line on the AP state wire.

We took turns staying up with him down at the lobby of the old Jefferson Theater. After he began to hallucinate, I was walking him around the deserted streets one night, him mumbling and stumbling up against me. He called the hallucinations "going to the cinema."

"Bax, I've died. Honest to God. I've died, been across and back. They talked to me. It's ok, Bax, don't be afraid to die. It was light over there, and warm. I didn't want to come back. . . ." He sagged against me, asleep, still walking and talking. The break time was over, I slapped him gently across the cheeks, shoved him back into his chair between the turntables in the lobby.

After that he took up with another kid who was then broke and unknown, Bill Hall. Jape would write the million-seller gold records, Hall would go out and find him a big-time contract. Bill Hall is still a big producer in Nashville. Back then he was the only one of us even knew that J.P. could sing.

A lot of great art has come out of this Bible-thumping, red neck corner of Eastexas. Harry James, Ivory Joe Hunter, Janis Jo Joplin, Milt Roschenberg, Babe Zaharias. Only the Babe ever got a shrine built for her trophies, but then Babe was an athlete.

We ain't much here, so I guess we figure that anybody who comes out of here can't be much either. We couldn't really believe it when The Big Bopper and Bill Hall came home riding on a solid-gold record. At least we didn't cut him dead like Port Arthur did Janis Jo, but then J.P. never told the audience to bug off, or swigged Southern Comfort onstage. The Bopper was good, but Janis Jo was grand. So our hometown broke her heart, but we just sort of ignored J.P. when he came home from the stars. This was not the sort of thing to ever eat on Jape, he rode easy.

Once, between tours, he knew I was getting excited about flying and asked me if I would take him up. We bobbed along in sunlight in the little Cessna and Jape loved it. "I don't see how people can get killed in one of these little things. How come we always read about them falling out of the sky in bad weather; does rain kill the engine?"

Being a fresh forty-hour expert I explained about vertigo. That when the weather is bad and the pilot can no longer see the horizon line, he can no longer tell which way is up unless he has had instrument training. And that's harder to do than just learning to fly.

"Aw, I don't see how you couldn't tell it if you were falling."

"Close your eyes and tell me what it feels like we are doing."

I started a turn and let it get steeper. The airplane began to lose altitude. I applied full power and hauled back on the controls to make it climb. This only steepened the turn and we were headed for the ground in a "graveyard spiral," but in the seat of our pants it felt like we were pulling up sharply in a climb.

With his eyes closed J.P. said it felt like we were climbing. I told him that if a noninstrument pilot flew into weather where he could not see the horizon, he would have about ninety seconds to live before he lost it.

We had just rehearsed the Big Bopper's death.

The little plane that he and Buddy Holly and Richie Valens chartered that night climbed into the dark and light snow; the pilot was not instrument rated.

From where they winked out of sight into the night to where the plane augered into the corn rows at full throttle was about ninety seconds of flight.

Wondering if J.P. knew has haunted me ever since. I tried to write it out of me in a song. Benny Barnes sang it, and there were only five hundred copies ever pressed of "Gold Records in the Snow."

> "On a lonely farm in Iowa,
> Beside an old fence row,
> They searched the wreckage, just to find
> Gold records in the snow. . . ."

We were all in Jack Neil's office when they called to tell us. He listened, paling, "Are you sure? . . . Jesus." He turned to us. "J.P. is dead."

The next horrible thing we did was to stampede into the control room and bust it on the air. Teensie was pregnant, driving the car, listening to the radio. That's how she found out her husband was killed. She heard it first over KTRM.

I sat up with his coffin the night before the funeral. It's an old custom. In the stillness I laid my head against the cool, rounded bronze. "Jape," I promised him, "I'll make you a going-away promise. I'll promise on your body that I'll never mess around again. You never did, I won't anymore. That's me trying to get something good out of the power of death, I guess."

So little Miss Sweetbuns came to find out where I was, why I wouldn't see her or talk on the phone anymore. It was a few months later, during the "Quiet Hour," when the station was quiet and empty and I played my favorite old come-to-Jesus music into the dawn. Satan had sent me my first temptation. "No."

She slipped off her skirt.

"No. I promised."

She stood there moving slightly; the cross of her garter belt was the cross of Christ.

Bax, you're hopeless, I thought, as I swung her up onto the control board between the turntables.

Back on the day they had buried Jape I was the only one who didn't go. "I'll keep the station on the air." What I did was talk to Jape and we did the show together. The place was full of him. We gave him a real Dixieland jazz funeral sendoff. All his favorite songs. He went with "The Saints," with "Tailgate Ramble," with Pete Fountain and Trudy Richards' "Big Butter and Egg Man," and his own "Chantilly Lace." They said that every big black car in the procession had the radio up and the windows down, that people came out and stood on their lawns to watch him ride by. At the gate I said, "You ought to be just about turning into the big gate now. . . ." It was eerie.

When Jape and I used to work together, he would listen to some of my downer shows. I would sit withdrawn and hang the air with curtains of blues. Afterward we would go over to Pete's greasy spoon and sit an hour in the booth over coffee.

"Bax," he said, "you got to make a happy sound. . . ."

Shang

Old man Pete Mathews used to raise fighting chickens. One morning he went out to the pens and they had all gotten in amongst each other. There was nothing but blood and feathers and dead roosters. All but one. Shanghai Red, the rooster, was alive and strutting around on top of the pile. Pete said, "He is either the best, and he whipped them all, or he is a coward and hid out until the fight was over. Either way you can have him."

"What would I do with a fighting chicken at a radio station?"

"Why, man, we'll build you a little pen out back and you can open the control room window and you and Shang can bring in daylight together. There's a lot of folks moved to this city that would love to hear a rooster crowing in the mornings again."

Folks loved to hear old Shang. For a while they would call up and ask if that was a recording, or, "Do you know we can hear chickens on your radio station?" Shang even got Christmas cards. One rural listener even brought him a couple of wives. That liked to have been his undoing as a performer on the air. Folks would call up: "Where's your old rooster? Wake him up, we can't hear him. Is Shang still there?" He was there all right; you just can't hear a grinning rooster.

He had a little brown banty that was a settin' hen wife. She wanted to stay home and raise a family. And he had a shiny black banty that was his sportin' wife. She liked to run the roads with him.

I used to let them have the run of the place until one morning ole man Neil stepped in some on the front porch of the radio station. "Bax-i-ter," he called me, "pen up those goddam chickens. If there is going to be any more chickenshit at this radio station, it will continue to come from my office." He threatened to cook Shang. You could have cooked Shang a week and still bend a fork in him.

Shang was pure mean to the very core. His home wife kept hatching broods and Shang would perch on the top of the henhouse, waiting, as the chicks came out one by one, blinking at the first sight of day. Whammo, Shang hit them like lightning from above. He was taking care of the competition when it's easiest to do.

I saved one of the chicks, outgrabbed ole Shang, and got him before his daddy did. Gave him to a listener who called back in a few months. "What kind of a chicken did you give me? I went out this morning and he'd killed off my whole flock." Son of Shang, we named him.

Shang got me too. I made the mistake of getting friendly with him at feed time after he got used to me. Had him eating right out of my hand. One day he came up off the ground in a blur of feathers; one spur opened up the feed sack I was carrying, from top to bottom. The other spur went into my hand at the web of my thumb. Felt like I had been shot with a .22 short.

By the end of the show at 10:00 A.M. the place was swollen up, sore, turned bright green and yellow. I checked in with Baptist Hospital emergency room.

"What is the nature of your injury, Mr. Baxter?"

"I got spurred by a chicken."

"Mr. Baxter, we listen to your show, and we appreciate your comedy, but this is a serious institution, now, please . . ."

I showed her my hand, like a Mexican fiesta mitten. She liked to have let me stood there and die for laughing.

Next time I went out to feed Shang I went through the coffee room at the radio station, carrying the feed sack in one hand and Slim Watt's Colt Bisley Model .45 pistol in the other.

"My God, Bax, where you going with all that?"

"Out to feed my pet chicken. If he so much as lifts one foot off the ground, I'm going to fill him so full of lead you could dice him and use him for trotline sinkers."

Nobody said anything about the loaded .45 being there because Slimbeaux always wore them. He had a matched pair, pearl grips, wore them in a buscaderro while he was on the air. He did that right up until the day he was practicing a quick draw outside in the parking lot and his thumb slipped off the hammer of the right one and he shot himself through the calf of his right leg and the toe of his left foot.

"I'm shot," said Slim, in his quiet voice, as he fell like a telephone pole. "Ruined my jeans. Boots too."

Anyway, from then on at feeding time me and Shang would circle each other, me with the pistol cocked and aimed at him, him with his ruff raised up, all green and gold, bobbing and circling me in his gunfighter crouch.

After they ran me off from the radio station, years later, my engineer J. C. Dorrell took Shang out to his place in the country. Got him some big Rhode Island Red hens. Said Shang lived to be an old, old rooster, found him dead one morning, hanging upside down, those spurs still clenched around the roost, a smile on his face.

—And Now the News . . .

Ole man Jack Neil had been a newspaperman long before he pirated radio KTRM. He built the station, he was strong as snuff. He was the majority stockholder, but one night all his partners pooled their shares and voted him out. Nobody really had the nerve to go in next morning alone and tell him, so they all went. He already knew, of course. If there was a mouse poot in that building he knew it. The story goes that after they were all in and seated, Jack opened up his middle drawer, laid his .357 S & W magnum down on his desk blotter and asked who was the spokesman of the group.

That may be just another Jack Neil story, but this one is true. We didn't have a "news department" in early radio. If you were a broadcaster you were a broadcaster, and if the refinery blew up while you were home with your wife and kids, and you felt the thud, and didn't call in from out there with the earliest story, then just don't come back. We didn't call "sources" from a news office, we rode into the fire hidden in the ambulance and interviewed the survivors while they were still gagging, and rode out with the curled-up corpses.

In later years the old man hired a "news director," and found that morning's *Beaumont Enterprise* laid out on his desk with stories razored off the front page. "Son," Jack said, as he wrote out the fellow's check, "I did not hire you to broadcast at the speed of light that which has arrived here at the speed of truck."

When I walked into that station on the day of November 22, 1963, Neil was pacing the hall, looking for the first man. "Kennedy's been shot. Get to Dallas. Now."

It was still Trans Texas Airways then, flying DC-3s. I busted the gate getting on it. It seemed to take forever, and then they put us in a holding pattern at Love Field. Later I found out that Air Force One, taking off with President Johnson, and bloody Jackie and Kennedy's remains, was the only traffic in the air over Dallas. Not knowing where to go, I headed out to Parkland Hospital.

The two officers were still astride their police Harleys outside the hospital in the clear twilight and chill.

Me: "Been one helluva day, hadn't it?"

Cop: "Gahdam, you can say that again."

"How close were y'all?"

"How close? Man, looke heah at this stuff on my jacket, that's how close I was. I was riding by the fender."

Kennedy's brains. Pea-sized clots of them clung to his jacket front, gray on gray. The brains that saw the Treaty of Rome as the greatest document of Western man since the Magna Carta. The man whose sense of history and his place in it, the long line of what had come before and what was yet to come, had seen this as his distant golden shore, of nations doing international business instead of nations doing international war.

The brains that topped Khrushchev and ended forever the ploy of nuclear blackmail. I had been in the State Department auditorium the day Kennedy got the hard intelligence that there were Soviet missiles cocked and aimed at us from Cuba. We asked him about it, but he had not yet decided to risk surrounding them on three sides and telling them to get out or else. He said it was still in the oven. We did not accept that, pushed him further, belittled him some. And Kennedy put his hand in his coat pocket, tipped his head and paused, then said he would like to quote the Spanish poet, Ortega: "—the critics sit, row on row, but only one can really know, and he must face the bull. . . ."

Later at the cocktail party I asked Dean Rusk how close we came. Rusk sighted me over his Scotch and gave me one of his great one-liners. "We were within reach of a nuclear exchange."

Now outside Parkland Hospital the memory of the Kennedy head tipped to one side, his timing, his humor, his mastery, it all came back to me. Those brains, right there on that jacket. The cop said, "It went ker-plock, like shooting a pumpkin. They had it on the news for a few hours that he maybe wasn't dead. Man, he was dead. Right then."

I shuffled on off toward the hospital, went by a pay phone station, thought, I got the first and only eyewitness account; I ought to call the wire service, or the network. Then I thought of what I had to say. Somehow it seemed wrong. Poor taste or something. I never told it until just now.

I followed the thick trail of TV cables into the hospital. I didn't know where to go, where I ought to be. There was shooting and killing in Big D, Oswald was still unknown and on the loose. Maybe I am at the wrong place, even if I can find the right place in the hospital. I envied the big-time guys who spread out as a team and cover it all. What can one man do on a story scattered out like this?

I followed the cables into a makeshift pressroom. The reporters were sprawled, lolling at desks. Looked like a classroom. What we were waiting for was the returns on Governor John Connally. All we knew about Silver John was that he was hit. He might be dead. Good a place as any to wait.

I stood up at the front desk, looking over the room for a familiar face to sit by. There was a phone on the desk and I picked it up and placed a collect call to our local radio station newsroom. Might as well keep the story alive, tell them where I am at.

Just as the guy in Beaumont answered, and put me on 'live, a doctor came busting through one of the side doors like a boiler full of steam. He had a paper in his hand and I could tell from the look of him that we were about to get the Connally report. I handed him the phone as he stepped up to the desk and he absentmindedly held it in the normal speaking position, but he was looking at and talking to the nation's press. Our people got it live and direct. And first. This is called blind luck.

Later after they caught Oswald, I was upstairs in the Dallas police station when they came through the mob with him, clearing a path through the press with poked sticks. Just before I got mine in the solar plexus I leaned into Oswald's ear and shouted, "Did you do it?"

Oswald whipped his head around to me and we locked eyes. "No!"

I figured he was lying, but it seemed like a good question. Later this fat, pimpy-looking guy was working the crowd, handing out his card: "—you boys come by and see me." I took a card. Carousel Club, Jack Ruby. I didn't keep it. Diane was out on a flight, but when she got in I knew where I could get better stuff than that.

Let me conclude this "there I was in Dallas" aggrandizement with the decision I made that they had either already made a secret transfer of Oswald out of the jail, or they were going to wait to do it longer than I could stay. I had been down in the garage, leaning over the iron rail at the foot of the elevator shaft all day. Waiting right next to a TV camera crew. I gave up, flew to Beaumont, went to sleep. The station called me, "A guy just shot Oswald. It was live on TV. Where were you?"

I had one of my finest moments as a reporter during the Ruby trial. It was during the low, sagging belly of midtrial when Melvin Belli was covering himself with glory and losing the case by trying to educate a Texas judge and jury about the mysterious malady of psychomotor epilepsy which caused Ruby to suddenly go blank and want to shoot up Oswald. The judge was dozing, waking up to spit tobacco juice. The jury catnapped. All of us in the back row knew Belli could have saved himself all those headlines by just invoking the unwritten Texas law: Did the victim need killing?

Hell, everybody in Texas has always understood that. They would have let Ruby go on home because Oswald sure needed killing. But Belli was practicing Southern California law in Central

Texas and making the jury look like fools. Joe Tonahill who was
Belli's junior partner in this, got so aggravated that he stood up one
time and throwed his pencil at the floor and stomped his foot. The
judge woke up and fined him $25 and I grabbed the pencil and kept
it for historical reasons. Everybody went out and filed front-page
stuff about a $25 fine. I mean it was dragging that bad in there.

Well it was during one of these recesses that I filed my great "Face
of a Killer" story. The reporters were all in the back corridor where
the bank of phones was on the wall and some tables were set out.
They were lolling among the scraps and had nothing better to do
than overhear me as I filed mine direct to that little radio station in
Beaumont.

"I have seen the face of the killer. I have sat this long day in that
courtroom and brooded on the face of the man you saw step out into
the picture and, in cold blood, gun down Lee Harvey Oswald. He
stares back at us, impassive. He never shows a flicker of emotion in
his deep-set ape eyes. The jaw of a brute is covered with a thick,
dark stubble and sits unmoving on the thick, aggressive neck. He
sits by his attorneys who flutter, but his heavy body is impassive.
His face haunts me even now as I tell you this. Oswald, me, or you,
any of us, for good enough reason this cold-blue-steel man would
reach into his muggy coat pocket and pull out the tightened springs
of that snub-nosed revolver and pump bullets into you and extract
your life and see it as no more consequence than he sits there in
court day after day with his own life on trial, but in a civil manner.
I have looked into the face of a killer. I have seen one of the forms
that death takes when he comes for you. The heavy, blue-stubbled
jaw, the deep-set almost subhuman eyes . . . I shudder."

I hung up the phone, realized the press room had gone silent,
listening. Then they laughed and shifted and gave me a sort of
desultory applause. It is the finest thing one reporter can get, this
praise from another, for we are a jaded and cynical bunch, aren't
we?

Filing back into the courtroom, I encountered Joe Tonahill.

"Bax, you ever meet Jack? Ruby? You want to?"

I followed Joe to where Ruby and the deputy sheriff who always guarded him were seated at the table together. I extended my hand toward the brute I had just described. To touch the hand that had curled around the pistol, the killer.

The killer looked kind of surprised, so did Tonahill.

"No, Bax, my client, Mr. Ruby, is this one; that one is the deputy sheriff."

Ruby was a pale, thin, washed-out-looking little guy, sitting next to him. The "face of the killer" I had just described was the deputy sheriff.

Governor Wallace

I was in Tuscaloosa when Governor Wallace made history at the schoolhouse door. I was there.

I had climbed up on the side of that building to see.

Why there were more reporters . . . actually you get five hundred troops, and five hundred reporters, and one Southern governor and two Negro students, and you got the makin's for a good news story.

I had climbed up on the face of the building to see the schoolhouse-door confrontation, and I was hangin' up there on these window bars, and, oh, it was hot and it was tiresome, and I was on this little second-story ledge and I had taken off my belt and passed it from around my leg, and through the bars of this window to ease myself some. I had my Rollei around my neck and my notebook in my hand and was waiting for the action.

And somebody inside the window tugged at my pants leg and said, "You gonna fall off of there." And I said, "Friend, you do it your way, and I'll do it mine."

And this voice said, "Well, I'm gonna do it my way, don't worry." And I thought who's this smart-alec that I am talking to? So I hunkered down and peered through the bars into the dim in there, and there was Governor Wallace in the men's room.

And actually a governor in the men's room is just like anybody else in the men's room. I mean, there ain't nothing special about a governor. And it looked like a good time to interview him 'cause he wasn't doing anything else for a few minutes. So I did.

I interviewed Governor Wallace and I can honestly tell you all, in good faith, that this was one time that Governor Wallace knew exactly what he was doing, and was minding his own business.

Hurricanes

We lived in the hurricane belt. Ole man Neil didn't think we ought to be reporting our own hurricanes off the AP wire from Dallas. After Audrey, I flew over Cameron and Holly Beach, Louisiana, "—your KTRM on-the-scene reporter." I thought I had missed Holly Beach and circled back, flying low in sunshine. The day after a hurricane is nearly always beautiful. There was the road to the coast, but where was Holly Beach? I knew the little fishing town, used to play at Buddy Litte's honky-tonk near there. Nothing but smooth, cream-colored sand beneath my wings, a gentle mound of creamy sand, edging into the Gulf. Then I realized that was Holly Beach.

I knew that happy bunch of coonasses, with their laughter and cold beers and fishing offshore and their neat little houses among the oleanders. My eyes saw it all smooth, creamy sand. Gone. The whole town was gone. Just swept away. My mind tried to hold all that, it rolled down my gullet and balled up in my stomach. I held the door of the little Cessna 150 open against the prop blast and vomited. And my mind said you don't do that either. Holly Beach was like having someone slap his hands over both your ears. I flew across the pass to look at Cameron through the tears.

I used to come down to Cameron for the blessing of the shrimp fleet, the dancing all night in the streets, the fireworks and fistfights. One time we set the town on fire. One night there was a beautiful Creole girl who put a leg up on the hub of the flatbed the band was on and we pulled her on up and gave her a guitar. She sang, God, she sang, all in Cajun French with black ringlets matted to her neck, and her white pleated blouse sweated to her magnificent moonies. That wind-burned, salt-tough, shrimp-boat crew just jammed up to the edge of the flatbed truck body. Looking up with their mouths open. She did a little two-step, a little Cajun hop to her music, them looking halfway up her thighs. When she had done her number, she just stepped to the edge and spread out her arms like a swan and fell out into the flare-lit crowd. The fight was short, intense, the best man carried her off, holding her arched high over his head.

Next morning when the priest led the long procession down to the docks, there came the crucifix, the altar boys, the choir, all robed in white. She was there, raising her heavenly voice, a round-eyed glance of innocence for me.

You can get forgiven in the Catholic towns. That's why they have so much character. You don't have to drag the guilt of your fun along forever. Look at New Orleans, San Antonio, San Francisco, all the places that are vivid.

There were a few tombstone buildings left of Cameron, scattered in the sand; shrimp boats lay heeled up against them.

I flew back to Beaumont and got the news car. There must be hundreds dead there. There were. The survivors were still wading the ditches, pulling human corpses off the bob-wire fences, leaving the cattle.

The courthouse was still there, its high cement steps lined with shoes. I don't know why the shoes. Men were working with heat irons to seal the plastic bags before they went into the dump trucks for the trip up to Lake Charles. The heat seal was not working like it should, seams kept opening, an arm lolling out, palm up to the sky.

The older men who knew a lot of people were turning faces up and calling their names to be written in the book. Blacks on one side, whites on the other. The big black with the iron-gray hair and a face set solid in ebony called out strongly the names of a woman and three kids.

"How you know?" asked the deputy, big hat shading his face and the pocket notebook from the glare.

"Because this is my family," said the even strong voice. And we all looked down at the ground.

In hurricane Carla, Poppa Neil got me aboard a Navy hurricane hunter plane, and we flew into its eye.

"Commander, why do y'all use the Super Connie radar plane for this work?"

"Well, we first started out with converted B-24s, then when we got the Lockheed Neptunes, we used those awhile. Now we use the Connie."

"But why the Connies?"

He grinned and pulled the sack shut. "Because that's the only kind we ever got back."

We had to make two runs into Carla because we lost an engine on the first try about eight hundred miles out. After they got it feathered and the fuel dumping, the old chief looked at me. I was the same color as the green seat.

"Why would you do if we lost another engine?"

"I already done it."

Our skipper found the pilot who had brought the last recon plane in; he was at the bar in the officers' club.

I thought it was funny that we had to find him to ask him for the keys to his airplane. Like we were borrowing his Chevy.

"Awright," he grinned unsteadily, "but don't you guys break *my* airplane."

One arm of Carla touched Mexico, the other reached New Orleans. The eye was about thirty miles across and we spiraled up into it. The storm covered the entire Gulf of Mexico but was only ten thousand feet thick. On top it lay like a stirred bowl of whipped cream. A *Life* photographer asked if they could depressurize the cabin and let him hang out and shoot right down the eye. "That ought to make me a cover."

They put a rope around his waist and two men held him from each side, his orange flight suit molded and ridged in the blast. "God! That was beautiful!" when they hauled him in. I asked if they would hang me out too. The guy from *Life* looked like he had been to the river and been baptized.

I held my old Rollei camera and they hung me out. From the creamed-spiraled top it funneled downward, down through ever-darkening shades from palest blue to the black, roaring silent sea laced in whitecaps. I've never felt such a total moment of being alive. I would have pushed off and spread my wings and gone spiraling down down into it, yaa-hh ahh-ah, except that there would be no way to ever tell it.

"Hey, kid, whatever happened to yer old man, the one who used to talk on the radio and roped and rode hurricanes?"

"He shoved off in one . . . he liked it so much he just flew away in it. . . ."

The Connie pilot was not sure where he was over Matagorda Bay, that's way down the coast, almost to Corpus Christi. All the coastal nav-aids were already knocked out. High-frequency radio didn't do much in a hurricane anyway. Our reports back to the Miami hurricane center were sent by an old lifer radioman who still knew how to make the spark dance in a Morse code key. Dit dit de dah dah dah, the slow lightning flicked off the old-fashioned copper wire strung from wingtip to tail, and they could read it in Miami and tell who along the coast they ought to be moving to high ground. My family too.

The navigator laid down a clear acetate outline of Matagorda Bay but it didn't match the picture painted on the radar screen. Then, "Jesus! This storm is shifting the coastline. . . ."

I reported from the eye of nine Gulf Coast hurricanes, but Carla was the only one twice.

By plane, by train, by ninety miles an hour in the news car, I got from Pensacola down to Matagorda. Did you know that going downwind at ninety in a ninety-mile-an-hour wind there is no wind? Open the window, hold out your arm, it's stuffy inside. Did you know that a Ford wagon hitting a long streak of shallow highway flooding will hydroplane about a quarter mile? No spray at all. No steering either. I can still hear the tingling and pinging of driving through strewn and hanging copper wires. If you are moving fast enough it just bullnoses your car. Slicks off all the chrome, hood ornament, antenna. There is an insane euphoria inside a hurricane. A wild drunkenness. Nothing else in the world sounds like the full-throated, continuous roar of a Gulf Coast hurricane. The only people you meet are a few newsmen and drunks. The drunks are nearly always old wino fishermen who live in shacks that somehow never blow away with J. C. Penney, Sears and Texaco.

The old wino at Matagorda Bay asked me if I had brought any

cold beer. He said he had been perched up on top of his icebox when the roof went. "And you won't believe this, but when the clouds thinned one time I saw a big, black, four-engined airplane circling around up in there."

I told him he wouldn't believe my story either. That I was in the thing. He didn't believe me.

Coming out of the fresh path of a hurricane there were little indecencies. A home laid open, its yellow new wood showing, a wall slid out onto the highway, flat, but the curtains still in the windows and a tricycle, and little wads of all their clothes where they had blown away in the closet, the reds sogging into the blues. Personal. No man's home should be laid open like this and me seeing it a day or so before they could be let back in through the highway patrol roadblocks. Me knowing, and knowing what they had in their closet, and them off somewhere jammed in a brick schoolhouse and still hoping.

There was a special staleness about a refugee center. Half-lighted faces deep shadowed, nobody moved or spoke. The women sat and put each other's hair up in pink spiny curlers. The children were silent against the walls. There was no air.

I don't know if Neil knew, or just gut felt that hurricanes, like refinery fires, were a part of our culture, and we ought to be there, in it.

"For accuracy," he would tell you, but once when the press wire was reporting Bay City flooded and blown away, he sent me and they were just having a rainy day. I kept going down the coast, phoning in live reports of the sun coming out and people and their kids picnicking on the levees. The other stations were still gasping out the blood-and-guts wire stories in their newscasts.

Finally Jack got on the phone. "Listen, dammit, find me a hurricane. I don't want any more good news. I didn't send you down there to tell me how nice it is. The other stations are cleaning up on us. If you can't get me a hurricane, then quit now and I'll send out somebody who can!"

That senile bastard. There wasn't nobody else he could get to go out and play in a hurricane. I had already totaled out three news cars; one of them we put on display at the dealer he leased it from, and I stayed there with that paint-blown, windshield-gone, battered wreck all day long, soaking up the glory.

He wanted a hurricane, I'd give him a hurricane. I went to a shopping center and got into a phone booth; the winds were about thirty, gusting to forty. By holding the door just right, I could get a real shriek and moan out of that door crack. I went on the air live, and straining my voice above the terrible storm I was in, began to rock the phone booth back and forth on its bolts, slamming, kicking the inside of it. After we went off the news, Jack came on the line. "That's better." I knew he was grinning like a wolf. "Where'd you find it?"

"Same place I just talked to your whorehouse from a minute ago." Neil laughed. "Ahar, har, de har har . . ."

I looked up; there had been a lady coming out of the supermarket with a sack of groceries, holding her little boy by the hand. They were still staring after the performance in the phone booth.

"Sorry, ma'am, we had a hurricane in here; looks all clear now though." She grabbed her kid and hurried away.

Vietnam

It was Neil's idea to send me off to Vietnam too. "Nobody knows what is really going on over there and I wouldn't trust that left-sided bunch at CBS as far as I could throw them. We could really sell this thing too."

He didn't have to sell me. I was still wondering, as I had when me and Jim were kids, did I have any guts? Jim had gotten to meet some Germans head to head. He had sprinkled some tommy-gun bullets around, although he wouldn't talk about it. My war was impersonal. When warships meet, and one does not kill the other, the crew continues to eat three square meals a day and sleep on clean sheets. Deep inside I suspected that I was chicken. Would I stand or run?

All this was pretty unreal. They ran the same Doris Day virgin movie three times, Pan Am cabin service was immaculate and the stewardess stood in the door and wished us all a cheery good-bye, like we were getting off in Miami instead of Saigon. The only real thing was a haunting wall writing in the men's room at Manila. Someone had written, "I was here."

And beneath it another hand wrote, "And even I was also here."

At the Army public affairs office in Saigon the executive handed out my plastic badges. "What are you? Hometown news? Background? What are you working?" I just assumed that all war correspondents came to cover the war. I told him I had, and to put me in contact with the enemy. Several people at their desks looked up and stared.

"Any preference as to branch of the service?"

That one I was ready for. I had heard that the Marines, bad and bloody as they are, never ran off and left their wounded.

There is a terrible swiftness in a mobile war. A Marine helicopter hovered over an open field, the door gunner had his foot against my behind, he pointed to some deserted brush against a hillside. "India Company is over there, Lima Company is that way. When we get about three feet off the ground you better jump." I nodded, jumped. Turn right, turn left, live or die; I had read too many war stories. I ran ducked across the clearing; somebody stood up and motioned to me. Captain Lecky, India Company, Third Battalion, 1st Marines, shook my hand. They were moving out at midnight, Operation Double Eagle. Supposed to meet some heavy Charlies with automatic weapons. I was just what he needed, a middle-aged civilian. Nobody said it, but I felt about as welcome as a turd in a punch bowl.

The first little test was the sniper and the footlog. It was about 1:00 A.M., he had it zeroed in, popping with his U.S.-made carbine. We had to cross it one at a time. That was sort of zingy.

At daybreak we started moving across open rice paddies into the village of Tha Binh. Charlie hit the left flank, tried to roll us up. There was screaming. And screaming on the walkie-talkies about taking heavy casualties and send help! The old gunnery sergeant had been leathered in Korea. He looked disgusted. Over the radio he barked in a drill-field voice, "Awright, you guys, is that any way to make a report? Report like you were told to report, ya bunch of recruits. Get your stuff together and get on that radio and report right!"

That seemed to be the help they needed. The screaming stopped and the sound of rifle fire picked up from our side. They were right over in the next rice paddy. I crawled over the levee to go look. One kid was gut shot, another looked like a youth asleep. He had one neat hole right through the low center of his helmet. I was focusing on this for a picture when the gunnery sergeant called, "Move out!" He strode by me and kicked me with the side of his passing boot. "Cut that out."

"Move out!" he yelled, and India Company kind of went berserk. They arose in a rage and burst through the thin screen of bamboo on top of the low levee and rushed forward like wild men, abandoning the move-and-cover sequence of infantry in the open. Gunny stood up on top of the levee and bellowed at his runaway kids. You could hear him all over South China.

"Aw-right, you guys! Geddown! You hear me? Get down, or I'll put a round through your heads!" Brandishing his rifle against the sky.

India Company got down, and advanced in an orderly manner.

There was nothing to do but go with them, running, feeling very old and civilian. I got pictures of them rushing. Men crouching, running, M-14 rifles slanting. All my early pictures from that day have grass blades in the lower part of the frames. Even my shirt buttons were holding me up too high. As the sequence of the fire fight wears on, you can see what might be mistaken for courage. The camera is being held higher, pictures from bolder angles. At the end of the day we got ambushed crossing a shallow river and I got some beautifuly clear, backlighted pictures of our guys crossing the river, carrying the wounded, white spouts of bullet splashes between them. I was standing up on the levee out in front of them to get a better angle. A guy lying on the levee by me grunted, hit. I was on the verge of maniacal laughter, and I can remember thinking wildly that getting shot in the war is just random chance. A toss of the bright spinning coin in the air.

Later in the bar at Da Nang a reporter for the *Christian Science*

Monitor was being a friend, listening. "It's called battlefield euphoria," he said; "you were drunker then than you are now."

So do I have any guts? Did I find some great truth in that bottle that night in Da Nang? Well, perhaps, but the results are inconclusive. Any man who would go deliberately and do something like that isn't really scared enough to prove if he has any courage. Courage isn't something you can hunt for like dandruff. No matter how far in you go, you meet some guys who went farther. I know I would have run had the others started to run.

Was this for real? Or was this just more peeing off the top of the radio tower? I never got real excited about any of it, even then there was a feeling of being once removed but seeing it through a projector as I was to, many many times again with these pictures. The tour started at the Rotary Club and rose on upward to the Union League Club in New York. And that led to the book from World Publishing. The pictures are right here beside me now. And the book. It sold pretty good until that little teenaged girl came up and stuck a flower down the gun barrel of one of LBJ's soldiers and we all went home. I always felt like I had cheated. Me back stateside in thirty days, India Company slowly getting whittled away to ghosts. A book of young ghost pictures.

The only ones that carry anything now are the old man lying curled up in his garden with the top of his head blown away. He had run out of a hut, black pajamas. There was a lot of shooting in and out of the huts. Us and them. One of us took a wing shot at the old man and popped the back of his skull off. When we ran by the place the old man was lying there peacefully curled up on the hard-packed ground of his garden, among the yellow flowers. The blood pool from his head was a shocking thick red. His feet were toward us, the worn, leathery bottoms of an old peasant. In that instant I had wondered if the dreaded Vietcong were supposed to have good old feet like that. Or in haste and fear had we blown away an old man running through his garden? Some of our guys had been hit, there was lust and bullets in the air. Those of us still moving glanced down at the old man in his blood on the ocher earth of his pathway with a tight nod. He had paid his way. For what?

There is one other clearly remembered time. After the fire fight in the village, and before the river ambush, the old gunnery sergeant gave us a break. The men broke out canteens, flopped on the ground. The sergeant leaned back against a tree and I leaned back on it too, quartered around away from him. I had no web gear, no pack, no canteen, just the camera. He took a long swig out of his canteen, then wordlessly backhanded it around to me.

At least once, for a minute or so there, I knew I belonged.

There was another thing I knew, singing in my heart; I knew I had my story. When this day was done, if I could get my buns back to Da Nang alive, I had the story that was going to get me all the way to New York City.

A Coat for New York

I walked into Ducote's, into Ducote's my clothier, down by the railroad tracks, by the string-straight espee railroad tracks on Pearl Street. And I said, "Syl, I got to go to New York. To the oldest, most exclusive gentlemen's club in New York. The one where Eisenhower and Nixon stay when they are in New York. I have been invited there, to tell my Vietnam story, at the Union League Club. What shall I wear?"

And Syl grew as still as a stone. And all of his sensors and antennae ran out full length and sampled the environment around him, picking up little ethereal signals. And sensing that something important was happening, Honsberger, Ducote's understudy, dropped an oaf from the college, leaving him slumped there at the counter, and came silently to stand at his master's feet. And a drummer from New Orleans, with impeccable tailoring, with fine lapels and an iron-gray mustache, feeling the moment of drama in the air, came and stood. And a few idlers wandered in off the streets.

Ducote said softly, "What is the Union League Club?" I said, "Well, I guess it's what you could call Wall Street. Or the Eastern Establishment." Ducote said, 'Mmmmmmm." He turned to the racks, and the crowd shuffled their feet. A dog whined, and was smartly kicked. Ducote walked to the sports-coat rack, and every man held his breath, as he went like a sleepwalker along that row of jackets with his hand hovering in the air like a diviner looking for gold, or precious water in the desert. Then a gesture, his hand darted into that rack of clothing, and snatched out a sports coat, flung it out on the counter, as though he had flung down the gauntlet of his own good name and reputation! And a sigh of pent-up relief broke from the lips of every man there. Ahhh-hhh. A masterful stroke. The exact Jacket. None other could have done. It was as if this jacket had been cut and sent to this store for this historic moment on Pearl Street.

With the jacket as a reference point, Ducote began building. Muttering, clench-teethed, "Republicans, eh?" And he got a plain blue shirt. "No buttons on the collar. Republicans would get to staring at the buttons and wondering what kind of a fellow you really are."

"And you will wear this tie." And he handed me a rough knit tie. "That's a Swiss Grenadine." "What's a Swiss Grenadine?" "Don't you worry about not knowing what it is; THEY will know."

"Now," said Ducote, sweat beading his brow, "what else you gonna do in New York?" "Well, I'm going to take some of my writings and try to see some agents." "Aha! Agents! Publishers!" Ducote went back to the shirt case and got a shirt with buttons on the collar tabs. "Every man should have at least one Wing shirt. And when they come up to your room, leave the collar open, but with the jacket on, and don't lean forward in your chair. You hear me? Don't lean forward."

And then slacks, with a tab at the tip that reaches over and buttons over there, and another pair with a belt. "For the Republicans, the slacks with the belt. Remember."

And he said, "Wear this stuff, start wearing it now. Wallow around in it, so that when you go there you will feel like it's yours." Masterful! Everybody stood there in quiet awe. A few simple garments, and a country boy is armed to go forth into the World from his home hamlet, clad in shining armor and in Hope.

Martin Luther King

In 1967, during the author's tour to sell my Vietnam book, I debated with Dr. Martin Luther King on TV in Chicago. I asked King how he could reconcile preaching peace in Vietnam and war in Chicago. He told me that his marches were not war, but peaceful protests. I told him if he marched there would be war. He said if there was war in America that summer, he would not be responsible for it. I told him he couldn't duck the responsibility, why not settle it in the courts? He said, "Too long. Too long we have waited on the courts, the courts can delay a man's rights forever, but nothing can delay the tramp, tramp of thousands of marching feet."

After it was over I told him I respected his stand in the American Negro revolution, and that someday I would be proud to tell my grandchildren I had debated him, but that he was giving comfort to the enemy with his criticism of our foreign policy. He gave me the silent patient look and his eyes said, "I don't believe you." And I accused him of reverse discrimination. "Dr. King, you are judging me by what I look like and what I sound like, a white Southerner." He laughed and gave me a bear hug, and was gone.

I thought of that, now, as I thought of him dead, and I wanted to cry inwardly. The phone rang, it was the radio station, asking how long it would take me to be ready to go to Memphis. I told them I was ready now. An hour later I was on the plane. No plan. No instruction. The clothes on my back, camera and recorder, going to Memphis.

An hour out of Memphis I asked the stewardess to ask the pilot if there was any new word out of Memphis. She came back and said, "The pilot says to tell you, 'He's still dead.'" That, I thought to myself, is a poor start at reporting.

At the airport in the crowds I saw a Negro photographer and started up a conversation, my own camera being the badge to allow free conversation between us. He told me about Jesse Jackson, being in the terminal, catching a flight to Chicago. "Jackson was with him when he was shot." I found Jackson coming through the airport, blood dried on his green turtleneck shirt. I told Jackson I was sorry to intrude on him at a time like this but would he tell me his thoughts just now. Jackson eyed me and my microphone for a long moment, and then started talking. He opened up his soul, told of how the bullet sounded, how King dropped, how the wound looked, he went on and on, pouring it out of himself. At the end he said, "I don't know why I talked to you this much . . ." Jackson looked like a man in shock, unwinding by talking. I had my first break in the story, an eyewitness account.

What next? Get a cab, drive through the deserted dark streets of a strange town to the police station. If anything is happening, they know about it there. The cab drove off, leaving me in the dark street in the cold wind in front of the police station. I started toward the big brass doors; the only figure in sight that was moving was me. The doors opened a crack and a shotgun barrel leveled at my belly. I stopped, held up both hands and said, "I'm a reporter from Texas, ya'll." The door opened and in the dark a group of steel-helmeted men looked at my press card and let me on in. I got to the chief's office just as he started his press conference. More luck.

Next, find a room. A big old hotel on the corner; yes, they had a room. The desk clerk said the words that I was to hear so often in Memphis. "They shot the wrong nigger. I'm not surprised it happened. I'm just sorry it happened here."

The hotel later turned out to be the next piece of good luck. It stood on the corner between City Hall and the police station and the Federal Building. For the next three days it was the center of my ceaseless prowlings of trying to stay on top of the many sides of this story at once and being just one person. The networks, the magazines, the wire services worked as teams. I worked alone. Listening, sniffing, always moving.

Each night at my open hotel room window I heard the random shooting over the dark and deserted city. Each morning I went forth to scrape up the details. Some nights I sat up in a local TV station newsroom listening to police radio monitors. Each night we expected them to burn the town. Each morning we were surprised they had not. The Monday march, we were sure, would be a riot to end all riots. A detective offered to bet me cash. I refused. The city was a silent bomb.

I was there when the Monday march started. The silence of thirty thousand people marching through a deserted city between rows of fixed bayonets was like a dream. I put my microphone down to the pavement and recorded the sounds of shoes passing by. It was the only sound in a silent city. I thought of King in Chicago telling me, ". . . only by the tramp, tramp of marching feet will they hear us . . ." One man's words had stilled a city. One man's death had sent the nation's capital up in flames. His fellow black men misunderstood him as much as the white men. On my broadcasts I carefully restrained myself from too much emotion, lest I offend the white Southern listeners back home who could not see all this, or understand it. I toned it down; I wrote it like this for the papers back in Texas. I walked the fence.

Once the surging crowd around the marchers nearly broke. It was downtown, after the excitement when Mrs. King and the celebrities joined in. The tension suddenly filled the air. I could smell the fear, taste it. King's mourners marched on in silence, but the younger generation blacks along the sidewalks were laughing and capering. A holiday mood. They had come to the party, and they were anxious to grab the free prizes. A young slick-headed boy slapped a store windowpane; the glass quivered. His buddies looked at the rows of Guardsmen who were also kids, swallowing hard, knuckles white on their M-1s. The buddies said, "Don't do it, Ralph." I got up next to Ralph and I said, "Please don't do it, Ralph. Think, boy. Think." Ralph looked at me blank in the eyes, grinning. Ralph didn't know nothing about Dr. King. Ralph just wanted to break the glass. We hustled him on, laughing. And the breaking glass that would have been heard round the World did not break.

I watched the rally from a windowsill on the thirteenth floor of the hotel. A free-lance reporter rented me the window for five dollars. I figure he had thirty people in there. If he never sells a picture he can make a living renting hotel room windows. I set my Coke bottle down on the windowsill. A detective came in, saw the bottle balanced there and in a low voice said, "For God's sake, get that bottle out of that window. If that thing were to fall and bust in that crowd . . . that's all she wrote." I put the bottle on the floor, and listened to the roar of the masses below me. The peasants were in the courtyard and the king was not in the castle. They had City Hall, they cried out, ' "Oh, come down, Mr. Mayor, come down. Hear us!" ' But the patrician-faced mayor never moved. The silent white power that put him there sat watching him. There was no-place he could stand.

I left on the midnight flight, an extra full of reporters that Eastern had put on from Memphis to Atlanta. They charged us all first-class fare, and used an old prop-driven Convair.

In the airport at Atlanta, wondering what next. A youngster stood in the stream of traffic, handing out sheets of paper to each man. It was a directory from the Southern Christian Leadership Confer-ence. A list of phone numbers to call for food, lodging, transporta-tion.

Eager young hands and faces of students were receiving thousands of travelers into Atlanta and placing them in homes, hotels, gymna-siums, everywhere. They placed a half million of us without a fuss or without charging a dime. It was the first time that I realized that King's SCLC was more than just words, or a dream. It was people, helping people.

You saw the funeral on the TV all that day. You wondered, Why all this? Why so much? This is more than for Kennedy, what the hell? I was in that mob. Marching through Georgia behind that coffin drawn by two Georgia mules. Singing, they came up out of the cotton fields, up out of the trashy ghettos around the Ebenezer Baptist Church, up the roadway in the hot sun, up the hill to the city, the proudest city in the South. The governor remained guarded in his capitol, out of sight. Where else could he go? They passed for hours, following the spirit of the man who had led them in peace to the right to sit in the front of the bus, the right to travel and to eat wherever they could afford, the right to go to school, the right to vote. Martin Luther King, who was starting toward the last freedom, the right to earn a living wage.

That's what it was all about. Don't get sore at me for trying to tell it. I thought about it while Mahalia Jackson's voice throbbed out over the campus under the cherry blossoms and the budding trees, and the World wept and burned in confusion. I thought about it, and the only way I could make any sense out of it was to think, What if I had been born black? Go on, think it. What if you had been born black?

Riots

That was about as far as I could get into America's Racial Revolution. Neil didn't send me off to march at Selma; probably would have fired me if I'd gone on my own. The big, ham-fisted Irishman, weather-vaning his shrewd blue eyes behind a jibsail nose, was a pragmatist. On the Southern liberal scale he belonged in the "niggers is some of my best friends" category. Mainly he sent me to follow what would sell in Beaumont, Texas.

He sent me to Oxford. I was there on the square when the Union troops recaptured that Mississippi town again, almost exactly one hundred years after the first time. The soldiers marched around the square in a neat column to break up a scattering, rolling-marbles band of ragtags. Some of it was funny, although he only sent me there because they had killed a newsman.

A rebel in a long frock coat and top hat marched along backward in front of the Yankee column, waving a long stick baton and calling out cadence for the troops, which the mob picked up, jeering, cat-calling, Oh, how the stiff young officer heading up that column longed to get his hands around the throat of that comedian japing along backward just a few feet from his choking red face. The crowd loved it, and quit tumping over cars to watch.

The Feds got James Meredith enrolled at Ole Miss, and safely bastioned on the second floor of Baxter Hall. The rednecks, still in high good humor, but in a murderous sort of way, filled the campus under that lighted window. They began to chant, "Mr. McShane —come to the win-dow-w . . . Mr. McShane—come to the win-dow-w . . ."

It must have got to the U.S. marshal pretty bad, because after a time of this he jerked up the blinds, opened the window and stood full length in the light, knowing very well there were still plenty of loaded pistols out there in the dark.

"Wah do you want?!" he bellowed into the night.

There was a perfectly timed silence, then a rich Mississippi voice called out from below, "Can Jimmy come out and play?"

Oh, how they would have loved to play with Jimmy.

There is no time to rest following a story like this; I went to sleep sitting on the floor in a line of reporters waiting to file their stories on one of the few public phones we could find. Those guys were not even nice enough to wake me up, or at least shove me along. I ended up next to a crisp gentleman from the *London Times*.

"What are you guys doing over here just to watch us wash our dirty linen?"

"My good fellow, you seem to have not yet grasped the essence of this story. One of your states is in a state of open rebellion."

I realized again, as I had in Vietnam among other educated reporters, that they had sent out a quart bucket to fill up a gallon story.

But some of the stuff I could do good. The raw, while-it's-happening stuff. They were at it again in the town square next day. I was in a little half-high phone booth, one of those open jobs that reaches down to your waist, when some old gentleman of color drove his ten-year-old Pontiac onto the square, on his way to work. I described the gang who pried up a piece of curbing, and how it sailed out in a perfect arch and demolished his windshield. And what an everlasting tribute it was to the transmission builders at GM that this man shifted into reverse while still moving forward and his old, blind Pontiac screeched backward, gravel scattering down the street he had just come over, and how he must have been thinking, "Why me?"

And when I signed off, "This is Gordon Baxter, live and on the air, direct from the rioting in Oxford, Mississippi . . ." I looked over my shoulder and became aware that three really big bullies, shirttails out, unbuttoned over hairy bellies, bulging biceps, they were standing there waiting for me. They had heard it all, and me using my best non-Southern-fried broadcast voice.

What I did next was instinctive self-preservation. I swaggered out of that phone booth and said in my most cottonmouth drawl, "Y'all see that black sumbitch take off?" They melted away, to go give somebody else a concussion.

Next day in Beaumont, as I told this to my longtime broadcast partner Les Ledet, he listened to the end and then said, "And as you walked away . . . a free man . . . did you hear a cock crow three times?"

I only went out as a newsman on the big stories, and worked with real reporters from *Time*, the wire services and networks. I came to know them, and admire them, and was afraid they would find out that in real life I was not one of them, but only a hillbilly deejay from a little station in Texas. I told them I wrote for the *Kountze News*, "comes out every Thursday, ready or not." They would laugh, and drop the subject. The reentries were difficult, coming down from all this to go and sit between turntables again and solicit advertising from the local supermarket when I had been talking to Dean Rusk in the Department of State yesterday. Through nobody's fault but my own I have lived in radio station control rooms for thirty-five years.

That's over half the total history since Lee De Forest invented it and lived to say to a National Broadcasters' Convention:

"What have you gentlemen done with my child? . . . You have sent him out into the streets in rags and ragtime, tatters and jive and boogie-woogie, to collect money from all and sundry for hubba-hubba and audio jitterbug. You have made him a laughingstock to intelligence . . ."

I was sitting in the control room with my earphones on fore and aft instead of athwartships. One on my forehead, one on the back of my skull. People came in and whispered in my nose.

I was watching a control room roach, a medium-size one, dressed in a fine-tailored brown suit. He was quick in his movements. He had learned to trust me. He would whisker at me from under the control board, and in mornings past, had gotten bold enough to venture out and stroll around. He even rode the turntables sometimes and seemed to enjoy it hugely, but only at 33⅓. I decided he was old John Lofton returned. That when radiomen die they go to hell and come back as control room roaches.

A kid announcer came into the control room with his little chin beard wagging. Lofton darted under the control board and hid, just his whiskers showing, listening.

The kid asked, "Mr. Baxter, did they have engineers in your day?"

"Son, did we have engineers? We had engineers and firemen too. No tapes, no TV, no hot one hundred play list format, no jingles or jokebook subscription service. We had engineers and firemen too, the whole blasted works was run by steam. I had a big, black, greasy fireman, name of Ned, he stood right behind me and shoveled coal into those turntables until the control board was too hot to touch. When we came to a station break I would reach up for the whistle cord and quill it. That big, brass, three-chime whistle was beautiful. Moaning out over the river bottoms, through the fog and in the pines. Pregnant girls would feel their babies move within them, ole men danced and capered. We'd bawl and squawl and run up the wall, put our heads out the window and watch them drivers roll. You could bake bread by just putting it up against the radio. Ole Slimbeaux would holler out, 'Turn your damper down, turn your bread around, them's of you riding bicycles slow down to about ninety miles an hour, you know I don't like to ride so blamed fast. And don't touch that dial or I'll bite your finger!'

"The paint would start to blow and flake off the towers, and by sunset they would be all bent over like candlesticks at a Baptist Church wedding in July. The engineers had to go out and set 'em up straight again before the night air cooled them. They had to prune 'em back every springtime. Did we have engineers in my day? Son, we had engineers and firemen too. . . ."

—yah doggoned little push-button, cart-playin' automated peanut pusher. We ain't never gon' have radio!

After he left I sat there and studied the little gray plastic cable that comes off the mike and curves away somewhere down in the console. A lot of folks believe there is a wire in that cable. It's hollow, and actually it just leads to a hole in the floor and the end of it sticks out in the glom down under the radio station. A little drop of pearly fluid forms on the end of it and drips off onto the ground. Mushrooms grow there.

We ain't never gon' have radio. The Good Lord never intended for words and pictures to fly through the air.

Chapter 3

Mary and the Kids

I was out on the Interstate now, letting the big black Buick have its head. If it feels good at ninety, let it do a hundred. The Interstate, America's true cathedral, pave the forest, the farms, leap the rivers. The wind a solid substance of roar at the open window, pass the long-line haulers, vop! The heavy Buick busts the wave, darts a little. How many times would she roll over at a hundred mph? A pinwheel of parts going to hell across fields. Better'n cancer, or that one great stab in the chest of the all-American Heart Attack. Which will be your draw, ole man? Drink too much, smoke too much, live too hard, night rider, wind rider, hunched-up Buick a blur in the night. Ole man, why can't you be content with Mary and the kids? In little houses out there in the night, men sit content in front of their telly. (Their brains turned to jelly.) Loner, old man, you don't belong nowhere. Not in church on Sunday morning goodness. Not at the Rotary Club, that long line of bellied, balding prisoners under the pale lights of Wednesday noon.

What is this "ole man" stuff? "I look with young eyes upon these old hands and wonder—where has time gone?"

What would they put on your tombstone, ole man? That he was

a businessman and a civic leader? No. "That he never missed nothing." That he would still go the pit one more time to look at one more varmint. And get hit on the head and rolled one more time. Add, "He never learned nothin' " too.

"That's no way to run a business, sir. We must be five percent ahead of this same month last year."

"Well, you tell me, sir, did you linger looking at a sunset five percent more this year than last? Did you love a good woman who ain't yours, or really hear what's inside a song, or savor a good cigar or a glass of twelve-year-old whiskey five percent more this year? Or let out a fine car on a twin-row cement cathedral that is two thousand miles long and a night that is full of stars and life and death five percent more? Have you ever driven a hundred and ten mph in something that was carelessly assembled by a disgruntled worker of the United Auto Workers Union just to hear the angels sing at your elbow? Your belly is full of numbers, sir. I am not one of you."

The Buick driver was obviously crazy. A hundred years ago he would have come into town, shot up Main Street, then rode his horse into the hotel lobby.

Mary said, "You don't know anything about love. All you know is just sex."

And I said, "What do you mean 'just sex'?"

Then I told her I was sorry, I really was, that she was the queen of our castle and none of this ever touched her. She looked down, her fingers plucking at the sewn seam of the couch. Her head made a half a shake no.

Daddy's Home!

No matter what happened back in the dust of the day, it's like turning a new leaf in a big picture book to wheel the car off the main highway and start down the three short blocks of Highway 105 to home. Right into the setting sun. Everything squints up in a golden haze. I can feel the springs start to come untightened. One more block to home.

Then around the corner of Kreppers' fence, and there is home.

Always a fresh surprise at the comfort and beauty of the place. Always that little prayer of thanksgiving that we could ever afford to live here. But most of all, it's seeing the kids at play.

In the lingering sunshine and shadows of the Indian summer, the kids are out on the lawn, dotting it like bunches of bright-colored wild flowers. Some of them are whooping it down the driveway on surf skaters. Assorted kids. Mine, Kreppers', Jordan's. Beautiful children, faces turned toward my car, action freezes for a minute, then the call comes up— "Daddy! Daddy's home!"

Grinning and tingly, I ease slowly into the carport, line up fender to fender with Mary's car, and try to get the door open. Jimmy and Laurie and Martha are crowding up, reaching at me. No conquering hero ever stepped out of his *Spirit of St. Louis* or space capsule with a more joyous heart than mine at this minute.

Laurie's big blue eyes are anxious for a first hug. Laurie is a middle kid, needs much loving, lest she get lost in the shuffle between the big kids who are doing big things, and the baby, who does cute baby things. Laurie gets picked up and hugged and kissed.

Jimmy still has some of the middle-kid worry in his big brown eyes, although he is getting the confidence of a big kid nowadays. Jimmy wants to be hugged, kissed. "No, Jim, I hug and kiss all the girls; I shake hands with the men." Jimmy gets reorganized, and offers a stiff, manly little hand to shake. Then I pick him up and hug him anyway. Then there is Martha, smudged and sweaty, round and soft, under everybody's feet. The baby. She holds out a hand to shake.

"No, no, dadgummit, Martha, you're a girl. Can't you get it straight? Girls get hugged and kissed, not hand-shook. What's the matter with you people!" Martha giggles and melts to me like a warm salty oyster.

Now I'm out from between the cars, coat over my arm, tie loose, eager little eyes are checking me for packages and bulges. Sometime I have hidden goodies on me. And there are the shy little maidens. Marjorie and Bonnie. Marj, at eleven years, gives me a quick nuzzle and bounds away like a rabbit. Bonnie, tall and blond and sure of her place at thirteen, gives me the close hug of a confidante and old friend.

If the tall sons are there we give each other the knowing look, the fake punch. "Hiya, Dad." "Hiya, werewolf." "How's the wild ole man?" "Swinging."

Then Laurie is blaring into the kitchen where Mary will be, Laurie, the bellwether is loudly calling, "Daddy's home . . . Daddy's home. . . ."

Summer's End

I had told my teenage daughter Molly that she could not have sure-nuff boy-girl dates until she was sixteen. But when she started her tenth-grade year at high school this month, I relented and told her she could start having dates when school started. She'd be sixteen in January anyway.

So she put her pollen in the air and got asked for her first date on the first Friday night in September. Bob Kittel, a tall, blond South Park senior, picked her up at 7:30. I warned all those yapping little brothers and sisters to stay out of sight when Molly left. They try to make a Mexican fiesta out of everything. I stayed out of sight too. Mustn't be too much poppa.

Molly was a vision of light in a full-skirted, form-fitting, blue-flowered dress. She and Bob floated away like it was old stuff, like she been going out for years.

I believe in two things. Set a time for them to be home. Be awake when they get home. I think this is important to a daughter too.

So I had said, "Ten thirty or eleven," so all right. It was a long evening.

After the little ones were bedded down I made coffee, read, paced around the house, remembering all too well what kind of a guy I was when I was a senior in high school and hoping Bob was different.

I even sat down and looked at television (the opium of the ignorant), and suddenly the sound of a light footstep made me look up and there was Molly. Home already.

All shiny-eyed, and slightly rumpled. I wanted to ask her a dozen things. But I just said, "Hi, babe, have fun?" She said, "Oh, yes, we went to a movie, and the Pig stand, and then we came home. . . . What are you doing looking at TV?"

I went around turning out all the lights and closing up the house. I stood in the back door a long time and looked at the night sky and out over the fields behind our house. There was a cool dry norther blowing in. Summer had ended. Another year racing to its end. I locked the door and went into my bedroom and peered closely into the mirror. No doubt about it. I'm middle-aged and I look it. Hair thinning back at the temples, the marks of the battle set permanently in my face. Winter coming soon. Well, shuffle off to bed, old man.

Go On, Train

My son Gordon says he was born on an operating table in Montreal, Canada, at the age of fourteen. Ed Faulk was visiting me, sitting in the room where the gun collection of muskets wainscoted three walls. He was asking about where to find a good M-1864 Springfield when Gordon came in from playing out in the yard.

"What's the matter with that kid?" Ed is a neurosurgeon. A good one.

"He's on medication." Never talk medicine when your doctor friends are visiting socially.

"I can see that. What's he got? Spastic?"

"Epileptic. Since he was four. It's getting worse."

"Come here, kid, let me feel your head." To me: "He's had some bad falls, huh?"

"Some bad ones. He's on Dilantin. That's all they know to do." I didn't much want to talk about it either. "The sins of the father are visited upon the sons . . ."

"If he's got focal point epilepsy, and sometimes we can find out by tests, then he's operable." Ed went on to tell me about the new procedures developed by the team of Penfield and Rasmussen in Montreal.

A few weeks later Gordon went into "Jacksonian seizures." That's like pulling out the throttle, bending it down and letting the engine run full power until it flies apart. What if Ed had not been looking for a Civil War musket? What if Gordon had not happened to walk through the room just then? What if . . .

In the emergency room Ed pulled out a syringe about the size of a Colt Patterson and shot enough stuff in the kid to fell a horse. The seizures slowed and stopped. Ed had already made the calls to Montreal, I had sold a mint Officer's Model Springfield, hand-checkered stock and German silver forend, to raise the train fare. Gordon was too far gone to load onto an airplane.

The old Missouri-Pacific depot looked like a white paste building in the fog. Under a bare bulb the night agent was a picture out of a railroading magazine taken fifty years ago.

I carried their baggage up the steps and into the vestibule, suddenly sharply remembering how trains always smell, and other trains and the war and other good-byes. The sleepers stirred in their straight-up coach seats but didn't open their eyes. They didn't know what town this was or who comes. They were just enduring. Gordon sat beside his mother; somehow he had done most of the walking on his own. A quick brush of lips. I stood outside.

Go on, train.

We stared at each other through the window. The bad business of having already said good-bye, then waiting.

Go on, train.

I looked the coach over. It was an old cupola round-topper, painted silver to match the Budd streamliner cars. Route of the Eagles. This was a tired old Eagle.

Please go on, train.

The grime-streaked Eagle sits. But alive. Paused in its flight through this night. Steam tendrils curl warm from underneath it and mix with the fog. Wonder where they get steam from on a diesel train? A white lantern swings, a voice calls out, a distant word sung in the night. Silently the window is moving away. Our eyes lock, she forms a kiss. I raise my hand in a blessing.

So long, train.

Montreal

They called me from the hospital in Montreal. Women, his mother, have no legal right to grant this permission. They had found the inert mass operable, but in his speech center. "You have these choices, Mr. Baxter. His case is terminal if we do not operate. He will most likely be a mute if we do. The procedure will require about eleven hours in surgery." I said to go ahead.

Man's work.

At home I had the woman's work too. I had never cooked a meal, or fed a kid, or bathed a little bottom. I had also never missed a payday. When they fired me, I got another job before I came home to tell her about it.

I entered into the kitchen, a virgin.

On bacon and eggs.

The first egg I ever fried hit the griddle, burst, splattered, shattered and completely demoralized me. I scrambled it, and let the griddle cool down.

The second egg was carefully poured, assumed classic proportions, and was left to cook with slow dignity. While it was doing so, I found out that you don't crisp the bacon while it cooks. It crisps itself later. Or, as in this case, turns black and falls apart.

The third egg was launched in the bacon grease as a bold experiment. It immediately assumed the gaudy appearance of wearing brown lace panties.

Meanwhile, the second egg, upon being removed from its slow cooking revealed itself to be in a tough, indestructible, plastic condition. A beauty, but unapproachable.

I fed the first bite of one of these eggs to the baby, waited a decent interval, and offered her the second bite. By the way of reply she extended her tongue for the removal of the first bite. From then on, the kids asked for cornflakes at breakfast.

On Bed Making

You can save half the time and half the steps by making up the bed from one side. The bed looks a little lumpy, but so does my cooking. Also, sheets should be marked with a center line, so you can tell where you are.

On Mamma Sleep

I used to always marvel at Mary's ability to hear sounds in the night. The faintest cry from down the hallway would bring her pitty-patting to the child's bed. Now that she is gone, I find I have acquired the knack of Mamma sleep.

However, we had a quick, summer-night thunderstorm that nearly unnerved me. It rolled in from the northwest and suddenly blasted down upon our sleeping home at 2:40 A.M. Doors banged open, venetian blinds danced and cackled, curtains flew, I flew, sheet and all. Midst flashing lightning I secured the ship, and retired once more.

But an open door had admitted the silent tomcat. With padded paws he stalked along the baseboards into my room. A darker shadow, among the dark shadows. He sighted in on my blissfully sleeping foot which was poked out of the covers. He wound his silent springs and leaped upon me tooth and nail.

The tomcat was the clear winner in the scramble that followed this awakening, and when I pitched him out in the rain, he was still laughing.

On Grocery Buying

Each time I use up any item, I note it on a list, and replace it that day. In theory, at least, Mary will eventually return and find this place exactly as she left it. Except for me. What I'm learning about being a housewife should happen to every husband.

After Mary's phone call that Gordon's brain surgery was successful, her letters began to grow thin and vague.

I suspected that there was trouble of some kind, and it was being kept from us, and the number of things to worry about were almost without limit.

At last she wrote and admitted that she had been in the hospital for five days herself, and that our anticipated child had been called back by its Creator.

She had no complications, and had waited until she was up and strong again before writing me, to keep us from worrying! Then she advised me that she was living back in her second-floor boarding-house room near the hospital, and taking care of Gordon once more. Her letter was full of good cheer and optimism, and loving concern for my feelings. The fortitude of this woman makes me think of that hardy breed who crossed the Great Plains in the wagon trains and bore the usual burdens of womanhood while offering cheer and comfort to their men.

As the days dragged into weeks, I became better adapted to the strange world of housework, and came to know my remaining seven children better than I ever had before. I also learned some Great Truths about a woman's work, and vowed that Mary would never be so put upon by me and these children again. This experience should happen to every undomesticated male. I do not mean the tame house cats, who are tied into an apron early in marriage, but it is a seasoning experience for the old-fashioned Lord of the House-hold–type husband.

All the days were not sad ones. Take the peanut butter sandwich episode for example. The children were complaining about the reg-ularity of this food item in lunches. I assured them that nothing stuck to the ribs like a peanut butter sandwich . . . I whipped open my shirt and there was a peanut butter sandwich, sticking to my ribs.

Or the Hole in the Leotards Problem. Little Laurie, age three, had a nickel-size hole in her black leotards above the right knee. So I took the black shoe polish dabber and painted her skin around that area, pulled up the leotards and presto! An invisible hole.

And then there was Molly. This slim, fair, blond lass of only fifteen summers. This child assumed the responsible attitude of an adult, as children often do when needed. She had learned to drive, gotten a special license, and took the others eighteen miles a day to St. Anthony's. Then while I did my evening program, she bought the groceries and prepared supper each evening.

One night, when I was very blue about Mary's loss, Molly put her arms about me and said, "Daddy, you must pray for courage. I do every morning."

Mrs. Ruth Caraway, across the street, took care of the babies while I worked my morning programs. The house was left unlocked, and several times a week I would come home and find food or cake or pies left there by utter strangers. At the same time, in Canada, Mary and young Gordon were getting dozens of letters from utter strangers, and only God in His heaven knows how many prayers were spoken for us.

And so, in times of great stress, I learned of the fundamental goodness of people. People who not only keep His Word, but perform His Works.

Then came the letter in which Mary named the day they would be home. She said the great Dr. Rasmussen still had not told her how the operation had gone, except that they were coming home two weeks early, that Gordon was "just fine."

Our local Dr. Ed Faulk, who studied under Dr. Rasmussen, said, "He doesn't talk much. You just got your report in two words. Just Fine."

The day they were to get in seemed to drag on forever. I was cleaning the house for the third time when the phone rang. It was Molly. She had been in a wreck.

I grabbed up the babies and set out in the rain to find whatever this would bring us.

There, at a disputed intersection, was our poor, little, flat-faced Rambler. Mated with a Ford. Red fuses burned on the road in the rain. All my children sat white-faced, but unhurt, inside. An elderly lady, also unhurt, sat in the other car. An officer in a slicker came up and said, "It was just one of those things. Could have happened to any of us."

At home again, I held Molly while she cried it out. Then put her to bed. Then to the station, still in wet clothes, to do a happy radio program. The clown.

That night, after the program, with Mary's train speeding nearer by the minute, we crossed the last bridge. Little Jim, age five, turned feverish, and very sick, and we put him to bed.

I thought: one thing at a time, Dear God, not so fast. Not so fast.

Molly stayed by Jim's bedside, and I took the remaining children, in the one surviving car, and met that old train and had that woman in my arms before she ever set foot on Beaumont soil.

Young Gordon came down off the train carrying his own bags.

He was visibly taller, heavier and wore a quiet smile of absolute triumph that told me more than all the doctors' reports in the world.

He had a scar over his left ear that was the exact outline of a horseshoe print. And the same size, open end to front.

I said, "Did it hurt?" He said, "Nah, I just worried about where the sawdust was falling." We hugged each other again.

Mary was more vibrantly beautiful than I could ever remember. She swept her eyes over me and my ragged little band and laughed and said, "You look like a bunch of refugees. Let's go Home!"

They made a lot of comparative tests on Gordon after he got back. "No loss of IQ. No loss of motor control. No relapse." Ed shook his head and grinned. "Man, you really got off scot-free." He and the people in Montreal seemed proud of it. They kept up anniversary tabs on him for years. I would send them photos of a young man getting brawnier, sprouting up to a broad-shouldered six foot two. There was one Sunday morning I wish they could have seen, it would have told them everything they ever wanted to know.

Gordon had gotten his driver's license. I had asked him to deliver the news car back to KTRM. Some irate listener had called in about the KTRM station wagon doing figure eights in the high-school parking lot in front of a bunch of hopping cheerleader girls.

"Kid, how could you be such a nurd? That thing with our call letters written all over it in red letters a foot high?" He just hung his head so I couldn't see the grinning. The kid is not gabby.

I grounded him, but let him off on good behavior after forty-five days. Couldn't stand to hear him baying at the moon at night.

On his first date he made it home about 2:45 A.M. instead of midnight. Some story about a very long movie. Surely you remember when movies were that long?

I didn't have the heart to clip his wings again, so I asked him to hand over his driver's license. I carefully put it into a watertight plastic bottle and wired a weight to it and dropped it into the deep end of the swimming pool. The temperature was 38 degrees.

I said, "Son, you have had your fun, and I was uncomfortable. Now I will have my fun and you will be uncomfortable. You can have your driver's license back anytime you want to pick it up . . .

by hand. It's only eight feet away, right there under all that ice water."

The word spread. All his brothers and sisters came whooping out on the deck, the savages. Gordon appeared in the door, stripped to white skivvies. All he needed was the music of the "Toreador Song" for his march around the pool. He knifed cleanly in, I saw his watery image pick the tube up, then frog-kick strongly flat along the bottom. At the shallow end he flipped a racing-turn kickoff, and still not letting out the first freezing gasp, he stroked smoothly along the bottom, using his surfacing buoyancy and an arm press on the edge to land smartly on his feet at the spot of his departure. There was applause, general cheering. He bowed deeply. I bowed. I may have lost a round in that one.

Soon his younger brother Roney had been invited to his first dance. Roney came to me for advice. Roney too was to grow well above six foot tall, with crispy blond hair, oddly set off by an olive, swarthy complexion. Roney always seemed to have a burble of laugh barely swallowed. With him it would always be Saturday Night. But this was his firsty.

He took a bath three hours before it was time to go, and spent nearly an hour combing his hair. He said he was going to dance with his girl every dance, and kiss her before he left. The fact that he had never danced, or kissed a girl, didn't seem to worry him too badly.

His big sister showed him how to dance, and he asked me about the kissing. "Should I ask her, or tell her?" I advised him, "Don't talk, just kiss." He asked, "What if she hits me?" I said, "Life is full of uncertainties."

It was a church-sponsored affair. The kids were about twelve years old. All the girls fluffed and primped at one end of the hall, while the boys twisted and sweated at the other end. The matrons gave up trying to get the dance started, and called out, "Girls' choice." From this the boys had no escape.

I asked Roney how he felt during his first dance with his girl. He said, "Brittle."

Nobody had told Roney about cutting in. He was dismayed the

first time that he lost his girl during the middle of a dance, but he soon learned the rules.

At one time Roney said he danced with his girl's sixteen-year-old big sister. "And how was that?" I asked. "Too much," he said, "too much."

Roney and his buddy Larry observed that when there was a shortage of boys that the girls danced with each other. So they assumed that the same rules applied to boys. When their dancing with each other drew laughter from the crowd, both these clowns started a new game.

One would dance with a girl, and then the other would come out and cut in. The girl would turn, expectantly, and the boys would dance off with each other, leaving her standing there.

The dance ended at ten, and the mothers were outside to get their children, and this kid of mine was still trying to plot a way to get a kiss from his girl. There was no chance among the laughing, shouting boys and girls, and he saw her going away to her car. And then he saw her returning.

In final desperation he croaked her name aloud: "Frances!" She came back and said, "What?" He kissed her swiftly upon the cheek and then sped away to where his own mother waited in the car.

The Death of Mom 'n' Dad

My own mamma and daddy never lived to see these kids unfold into the flowers they were going to be.

Daddy died violently, and that still doesn't seem right. He was such a quiet man. Careful as a cat about where he put his foot next. He only made one wrong turn in his whole life, and that one killed him.

He was diabetic. Alcoholic too, some said. "He never went to work drunk, he never went to bed sober." Daddy's fatal miscalculation was the day he ran out of gin and insulin at the same time. Measuring the closing time of the drugstore and the liquor store against each other, he decided to make the gin run first.

He drove an old '53 Dodge sedan, the one that had the hemihead V-8 in it that is still a favorite of dirt-track racing-car builders. Daddy never thought of it as anything but "Dependable Dodge," their old company slogan. But when he slumped unconscious over the wheel on Procter Street that hemihead opened up with the first howl of its life. It missed three lanes of oncoming traffic, crossed a churchyard and stacked up a pile of about six cars in the parking lot.

He was the only one hurt. And Johnny, the ambulance driver, found the gin bottle with the seal still unbroken. He gave it to me quietly and I still got it, put away with the things that people keep for reasons that are hard to describe. I labeled it Daddy's Last Gin Bottle.

Daddy hurt for three days before he died, but I don't think he came to enough to realize what had happened. He could barely see and any of us who stood by his bed and held his hand he called "baby." I could comfort him by laying my head on his chest and he would softly pat me and say, "—everything's going to be all right, baby." He was talking to Mamma.

She was there when he died. His heart just quit. He relaxed. He was still like that when I got there. Asleep in a hospital bed. I pulled the sheet up gently, knelt and tried to pray and kissed his brow, but you can do that stuff and still not feel real about it. Something comes down and sets it all on a quiet stage.

The minister on the other side of the bed asked me what church my father belonged to. I said his church was inside him.

The last time I had looked into my daddy's eyes they were rolling darkly and I have never been able to put away the feeling that Daddy knew, and he died hating me.

Don't ever carry around something like that.

Mamma quit. She didn't go to his funeral, and she didn't make it through the year.

It still sounds too easy and too stagey to say both my parents were drunks. Except for a few Christmases you couldn't tell whether ole "Pappy" "had his little fire going" or not.

When we were kids me and brother Tommy either kept up the family fiction that Mamma was "sick," or we just didn't talk about it. Gentle Tommy was her soup bringer. He worried and took care of her.

I rescued her once. Came home from school and sensed the dreadful stillness in the house. I called, and looked, and finally broke down the bathroom door, and found her lying unconscious in that awful red bath. I used my boy scout training on both her wrists and called the ambulance and was sort of proud of myself.

When I was about ten my aunts and grandmother invited me over to go to church with them. They all hovered over me to tell me my mamma was an alcoholic. I went home and told Dad what had happened. He never said a word, just looked. But next time I went over there, he said, "Son, don't let 'em pump you."

That's it. No right or wrong of it, just, "Don't let 'em pump you." My first concept that there was going to be an "us" and "them."

Whatever crisis went on in the house, and I kept track of the twenty-five different houses we lived in before I was eighteen, my folks kept it pretty much to themselves. What they did let us in on was the good-bye and hello kissing and hugging, the handholding, and if Mom could stand up, she always prettied up before Dad came home.

Tommy remembers Daddy for his saying, "Don't worry, everything's going to be all right by September." I always suspected he might have been mocking us; himself too. I use the saying sometimes now. I sure wish I knew if Daddy really believed in September.

I never really knew what he was thinking. After I got old enough to try a little "man" talk with him, and would get exasperated at his clamming up, he'd smile at me and say, "Big coon walks just 'fore day."

To hear me and Tommy talk about it now you would think we grew up in two different places.

Tommy always said that they had a symbiotic relationship. That they were too close for love, entwined around, choking each other to death. I don't know. But every time Daddy would put her away to get her dried out, she would start a stream of "Daddy, take me home" letters. He would go get her, and they would stop off at the first liquor store on the road.

I guess Tommy and I both knew that she would tap herself out now that Daddy was gone. Now it was my turn to get into the "Daddy, take me home" game. I put her in Rusk, the state mental hospital, and while I was filling out the forms the lady asked if my mother had ever been a patient here before. I said, no, I didn't think so. The lady got up and walked smartly to a gray wall of file cabinets and looked under *B*.

"Mr. Baxter, according to our records your mother has been a patient here five times before."

Mamma sort of ducked and grinned at me and looked at me over her shoulder.

"Gotcha."

I stood the letters long as I could. She could write beautiful stuff, could pick locks with it. When I came to get her, I flew up in a beautiful rented Cessna 182 airplane, still showing off being a pilot.

With the bags aboard I asked if there was anything else to do. "Yes. Could we buzz that place on the way out? I told all my cellmates to be watching for me and it's about playtime right now."

Well, I dived at it, buzzed hell out of the Rusk State Hospital, breaking about a dozen sane FAA, state and local ordinances. All those crazies were down there in the yard, running, waving their arms and white handkerchiefs. I wagged me and Mom's wings, us laughing and hugging each other.

That's leaving the crazy house in style, the big Cessna bellowing away, climbing free.

Back at the airport they said, "Bax, that was crazy." I told them I wasn't so sure of what was or wasn't crazy anymore.

The next time Mom OD'd, Johnny, the ambulance driver, picked her up and called me. Mom was not pretty. Old at sixty-one, toothless, sacked, but Johnny loved her too. Johnny's a city judge now. He took her to the emergency room and the doctor gave it to me straight. "Her system won't stand another go-round of this."

What we did next I'll never know the right or wrong of. Tommy had always tended her. I think he grieved more. "Gordon, I can't let her do it." He and our family lawyer brought her into court to have her declared noncompetent. He believed he was saving Mamma's life. Saving her from herself. And he was right.

I stood before the bar as my mother's only legal council and won the case to turn her loose. The judge, and what was left of Mamma, looked each other square in the eye. She nodded as I testified that Mamma had always been a free bird, and to cage her up now would be less humane. The judge asked her in judgely tones if she understood all this. She said she sure did.

He turned her loose and she made it on across in about two months.

I thought of one of the many little poems she had stored up in her ragbag mind when they called me and said she had just died.

> Once there was a grand old man,
> Who was so wondrous wise,
> That he jumped into a bramble bush
> And scratched out both his eyes.

Mamma died in what we call the "funny farm," the psycho ward of Baptist Hospital. That was home. They loved her there.

Her doctor was building a new clinic next door to the hospital and told her that he was going to need her for an assistant when the new clinic opened. They put her chair over by the window so she could watch the day to day of the new building coming up out of the ground.

I stood beside her as she told me all this: "—son, what in the world could I do there?"

I put my arm around her skinny little shoulder and peered seriously out the window with her. "They are going to keep you as a 'Before' example. When they get some really hard case they can't crack, they will say, 'Send for Mrs. Baxter,' and you come shuffling through. You won't have to say anything. The doctor will just wave a hand in your direction and say, 'You see there? Now if you don't straighten up and listen to me, that's what's going to happen to you.' "

Mamma leaned her head on my chest, laughing, and I went on, telling her that on the weekends she could subcontract out to haunt houses. "Real moonlighting."

"Son, I thought I'd never laugh at anything again."

That was our last visit. Me and Tommy went out and bought her the cheapest coffin we could find. Mamma taught us that death worship was both pagan and commercial. Me and my brother carried her. She bore us into this world, we carried her out of it.

They left me alone by the grave. When I finally turned around, the bunch of them were going away toward the cars. I stood a moment, feeling the separation. Then I hurried after them, head down, so nobody could see the clown mask both laughing and crying. Mamma had said, "Son, you don't have to march along with the herd. That way you can only see their behinds. Go upstream if you want to . . . you can see their faces."

Molly's Wedding

The marrying and the burying. I was thinking of that when Molly married Alan Rayne. He had been a friend in broadcasting before he courted my daughter. We had a unique privy council about the lady. He claims he won her at one hundred mph on a winding road, her a banshee standing up holding to the windshield of his Austin-Healey.

We shared the morning show. Some mornings he came in with his beard flattened with the look of a wet owl.

"What happened, Alan?"

"Your daughter, sir."

"Care to talk about it?"

"Picture if you can, a man who thinks with pure logic, married to a woman who thinks with her bloodstream."

I remembered their wedding.

We stood in the back of the church midst a moving crowd of our dearest friends as my two grown sons ushered the guests inside with big-footed solemnness. Molly champed at them at every slow return. "C'mon, you guys, get them going!"

At last Mary was ushered in, and I was alone out there with my daughter for the last few moments. Her bridesmaid, Juanita Dailey, lovely as a yellow lily, fussing over Molly's veil. Juanita is Molly's first cousin; they have loved each other since they were roly-poly infant girls. Now tall and beautiful, they were about to walk together in the first steps of their lives as women.

"Trish" Tydlacka, herself a bride of less than a year, fluffed and rustled at the back of Molly's full-trained satin wedding gown.

Molly: "I wish you two would leave me alone!"

Trish: "Hush up, whose wedding dress is this?" (It was Trish's.)

Me: "She's perfect; what's all this about? Why are you doing all this fussing?"

Trish: "Hush, Mr. B., brides are supposed to be fussed over."

Over our heads in the choir loft Warren Clover's voice floated down, delicately and perfectly phrasing the Lord's Prayer.

Molly: "Shh, shut up, listen to Warren, isn't he wonderful!" (Warren was my youngest apprentice DJ; I had no idea he had a trained voice. He had a crush on Molly for a while, and told her he had dreamed he had sung at her wedding. Molly said, "Why not?")

The music had stopped, the church was nearly filled, and all astir. A few latecomers hurried by, eyes lighted up by the white castle of loveliness that was my daughter. Molly was bursting with her great reserve of energy and boldness. Standing at my arm, stamping and snorting under her breath, "Hell's bells, let's get this show on the road."

Me: "Shut up, they can hear you all the way to the altar."

Molly: "Let 'em. I'm ready!"

Far down the aisle, between gleaming tapers, Father Montondon appeared and looked at us. Now Juanita was starting. I noticed that her ankles trembled. Molly lashed out with one more stage whisper: "Slow down!" Juanita's pace slackened a little.

I stood numb and dumb, Molly gave my arm a squeeze. "Let's go."

We moved in perfect step. No bobbing. I whispered, "I love you." A squeeze on the arm. Halfway down the aisle I said, "Can't believe it." Molly breathed back, "Me either."

Now we had stopped before Father. My eyes were blurred, but I took a deliberate slowness in lifting her veil, and looked clearly into her shining face. I brushed her cheek with my lips, and whispered again, "I love you, baby." Then I turned to Alan at my right. Our eyes met for just an instant. He stood tall, bearded, handsome as the young Confederate officer of his ancestry in ancient Natchez. Our hands met, and I stepped back, drawing him into my place.

Me: "My son."

Alan: "Thank you." And then I passed behind their backs, and faded away to Mary's side.

The wedding words were half Catholic, half Protestant, like the couple themselves.

Now Father Montondon lowered his gaze to Molly's and blushed. For a moment I was afraid that the entire affair was going to dissolve in giggles. His face was wreathed with smiles and love. Then he started talking to Molly and Alan. And then he was saying the words in English, and rings were being exchanged, and I felt the tears burn down my cheeks.

Then Molly and Alan crossed over to the statue of the Blessed Virgin, and Molly left flowers there, and bowed her head briefly, while Alan stood. I still don't know why I was crying, unless it was just a man's heart brimming over.

Now they were leaving the altar. Man and wife. Mary and I stood, moved out to the aisle and genuflected before the altar. My eyes looked up into Father Walt's. He solemnly winked.

Tonight the house seemed empty. With nine of us in it. But every room shouted Molly is Gone. One had flown the nest. A great leaf of the calendar had slowly turned and fallen silently into place. Now we were starting down the other side of the slope. The diminishing began. Mary caught my mood, and called me to the window.

Mary: "Look at that moon. Just think of how happy they are now. They should be in New Orleans by now." Even the little ones felt my emptiness; Marj said, "You still have us, Daddy."

Mary was right. She saw this not as the ending of a time, but the beginning of another time. And she enjoyed the swift passage.

Roney

Then we sent a son off to war. Then it was Mary's turn to go stand out there in the night. "I knew it was going to be bad. . . . I just didn't think it was going to be this bad."

Fresh out of high school Roney went Navy. Volunteered, U.S.N., Regular. "It's the best deal us Vietnam kids can get, Dad." It was 5:00 P.M., the mantel clock was ticking steadily. At 8:00 P.M. the bus leaves. In a few hours a big ole kid would walk out of the house. He might come back, he might not, but he never would be our big, old, big-footed kid in the house anymore.

Mary was laying on his favorite supper, the house was rich in the smell of cutlets. Do you know there were ten of us when we were all at the table? I had built the table years ago because nobody sells a table like that with bench seats. Built it out of two-inch pine, bolted together. It had taken on a warm worn tone of kitchen browns, all but the new plank added after Laurie and Martha. It never did take on the same patina. I always thought of it as the new plank.

They all turned to me to say grace. I said to Roney, "You do it." A regular Norman Rockwell scene. All stairstepped down, heads bowed. Well, I bought Rockwell's whole book.

So we are middle class. And schmaltz. It's the middle class who feed their kids to the war.

The talk was light. About what the little kids did at school today. Roney piled his plate high as usual, except for one thing—he couldn't eat any of it.

He said if it would be all right he didn't think he could stand any good-byes. He went to his room a minute, then came back down the hall wearing his paisley shirt and tan Levi's and carrying a blue canvas bag. He never broke stride going by the table; he just said, "Adios, group," and softly closed the door.

There was a silence at the table. When I raised my head up they were all gone. Each one had gone off to a separate place to be alone with it. I wandered down the hall to the room Roney and little

Jimmy used to share. Jimmy was in there. He had room all to himself now. Right now it looked like it was swallowing him alive.

Roney volunteered for 'Nam, then volunteered for an outpost on the DMZ line. Then volunteered for what he called the "skimmer run." This was after the Vietcong had made the Khe Viet River too dangerous for the Navy's regular river patrol boats and my kid ran a plastic Boston whaler skiff up to the Marine outpost once a day.

"Don't worry, Pops, I got my flak vest, an M-16, a sack of grenades and the little boat runs too shallow to set off the mines. Even if it did tick one, I think it would go up in my wake. . . ."

He talked to us on tape. You remember those treasure-yellowed letters sent back from Hood's Texans during the War Between the States? Well this tech generation saved tapes. He was talking to us one night when they sounded a red alert; we could hear it too.

"Excuse me one, that's incoming. I'm headed for the bunker. I'll bring the tape. . . ."

We got to listen to the rocket crumping in.

"Hot damn! That one got the officers' quarters; them Charlies ain't such bad guys."

Another time: "—I'm in the bunker now, and you won't believe this, but here comes a guy running across the compound . . . incoming hitting all around him . . . and he's bringing his portable TV. No kidding. All I can see out there is that picture tube bouncing along. . . ."

Another tape: "Last night they had the bunkers pretty well bracketed. Lots of dirt and crap falling off the overhead, smoke, stuff breaking up, and this one guy starts screaming, 'Oh, my God,' and for his mamma. It was dark in there—but we know who he was."

Roney had the night communicator's shift awhile, alone in a shack high atop Monkey Mountain. He sent long rambling tapes from there, passing the long hours. Once he yelped, "You won't believe this, folks, but a mongoose just stepped in the door. Really. A mongoose. He's just sitting up there staring at me. . . ." then a long section of the kid calling the mongoose like he used to call the kitty.

Roney kept assuring us it wasn't so bad. But he asked me to send him a short-barreled pistol. "We got Charlies all out back in there and I think they are running an infiltration school and this place is the final exam for graduation. We flunk a lot of them. Enlisted men don't get pistols, and I need something close and quick."

Roney got into some kind of plea bargaining with the Navy, got his tour shortened for re-upping for Vietnam and a thirty-day leave home for sweeteners.

We were out at Houston airport, watching the smudge in the sky of the big bird bringing him in. I remember thinking, Please, God, don't drop him now. . . ."

He swaggered off, seabag on his shoulder, full of beans, but there were new fine lines in his face. He was all over the house, went into his room and got silent. Not a word, he just moved around touching things. The everyday things that had been him.

Said he couldn't tell if he was here, dreaming of 'Nam, or still in 'Nam dreaming he was here; "—and old Dan, still out there on Monkey Mountain, rotting his behind."

Roney made it through the second tour and back to the living room fireplace. We sat by the embers sipping whiskey and speaking of our wars as Southern men have done for generations.

"What about those draft dodgers in Canada . . .?"

"I think they ought to let 'em come home."

"Jesus, kid . . ."

"I know how you feel, Pops; I used to feel that way too. I volunteered like you did, go save the world for Democracy. But by the second hitch I knew this was a rip-off. A political war. A no-win war. Hello, suckers. Now the whole country wants to forget Vietnam, right? We admit we were wrong, all we want is out. So ok, those guys who said, 'Hell, no, we won't go,' they had it right. Now the whole country has come around to that, why not let 'em come home? Treat everybody the same. That's America."

"Well, gahdamn, kid . . . suppose the Russians were right down the road at Sabine Pass. What would you do then?"

"We'd fight, we would all fight. Sometimes I think a good clean war, right here stateside, will be the only thing to ever unite this country again."

Silence.

Then Roney spoke softly. "Dad, how would you feel if I was the last guy killed in Vietnam? Some mother's son is going to be just that. How would you feel if instead of me sitting right here, all you had was a little box with a bronze star in it and a triangle-folded American flag?"

Long silence.

"Dad, I was only one-quarter click on some Charlie's mortar tube from being just that."

There was no more war talk.

Chapter 4

In an Empty Room

In the Beginning

Village Creek, ten thousand years old and how I love her. Sweet Sister Creek, where my father brought me as an infant in his arms. That was back before too much of man and we would huddle to hear the panther scream in the night. Village Creek, where I brought my sons and daughters in turn, and let them learn the lessons of beauty and of courage and to hear God's peace.

As a teenager I built a canvas canoe and strapped it to the top of the Model A Ford and drove up from Port Arthur to where the old iron bridge crossed the creek. There was a favorite place a few hours downstream that I called my secret sandbar. This distance was far enough paddling down from the bridge to have earned a rest, a cool swim and drink from the creek. I would belly flop on the untracked crescent of sand in the shade of the small willows and squint across the white glare to the wall of the forest.

With my mind I would try to penetrate the gloom of oak and pine and try to picture what it would be like to live here all the time. The vision was so hallowed that I could not give me permission to cross the hot sandbar, actually go inside there and turn round and look out. I knew that someone must own this place but it was beyond me to imagine such. And the fantasy of finding such a man, and asking him if I could buy this land, seemed as farfetched as speaking to the queen of England. And yet as I lay there, daring not to dream it, I was equally certain that someday I would own this place, and would be sitting in my house back there, looking out through the cool trees and remembering me as a kid dreaming of it. And that I would always tell it that way.

The years had rolled me along smooth and tumbled me as a slick river rock in the stream bed, and now I knew from some inner timetable that it was time to go and ask.

The land belonged to the Barry family, and good ole Doc Dudley English. Some of them still lived around here. Good and decent people, they had settled this part of the creek in the early twenties. The last time they sold off a parcel of creek front was twenty-five years ago.

Now there are customs in deep East Texas. You don't just walk up to a man and offer him money for his land or his dogs. First you get to know him a little. You visit and hang around now and then and talk about other stuff. He knows well enough what you're there for. You never had showed up before, had you?

I got in touch with ole Huck and Wallace Barry and the doc. Got permission to camp out on the sandbar. Met them in town now and then. They got used to seeing me and my kids on their part of Village Creek. One day I told them I sure would like to homestead that place. They solemnly agreed that sure would be nice. Said they would think about it.

Ten years rolled by. Whenever I saw the Barrys I would indicate that I was still thinking about it. And they would acknowledge, without so many words. And then one day me and Wallace Barry and old Dr. Dudley English were stepping out of a boat and pushing our way back into that very forest and pacing off the yards and acres. It was floodtime and the sandbar was under water, but we knew where we were. And I was so dazed that when they named the price for this tract that they held in common that I was not sure if they were talking about all of it or that much per acre, and I wasn't sure how to phrase the question. I would have given all my treasure for this.

And later in the office, with the surveys and plats curling up on the table and the lawyer's papers signed and the solemn ceremony of standing up to shake hands all around, I asked them, "Why the ten years?"

"We wanted to wait a little and find out what kind of feller you are."

In July of 1968 we had a picnic there. All of my grown kids on the sandbar, under the little willows beside the stream of the joy of my youth. And I told them the story. And then it was time to enter into the woods and see where the cabin would sit.

We opened the dream and went into the tangled cool darkness. Within a few feet we were out of sight of each other, shouting. We found there was a narrow ridge facing the sandbar, dropping off behind into the spooky dark waters of the still cypress baygall. What I was looking for was the high ground, room enough for the cabin, but laid out so as to not cut any mature trees. I started from one giant oak, left a kid standing there, paced away fifty feet, another tall oak, as if planned. Left a kid there. Thirty feet toward the creek would leave a screen of small trees. It was a kind of ritualistic thing I will never forget, calling out to each other, hidden in the trees. We came back later with the crew and sunk the four foundation pilings where those living corner posts had stood.

Now I had my site, but no road to get there. Part of the deal was Wallace Barry said he would hire a Cat and build one. The trouble was nobody knew how to find Barry. An elusive old bachelor, a tree elf. Grinning in old clothes, going to great pains to conceal his classic education at the hands of the Jesuits. Kids and stray dogs follow him. Some said the only way to find Barry was to go out in the woods and think about him and then look behind you and there he would be. I went out and conjured up Barry and asked him how about my road.

The way I like to tell the story is that our woods road was built by a drunken Irishman on a D-6 Cat with a bottle in his hand. The crews that followed it later in the cement trucks swore that it was about a two-pint road. The truth is that Bob Harris is a pretty steady, good old Christian boy, and the reason the road looks like that is because Barry told him to stay on the high ground, miss all the mature trees, and a D-6 Cat is perfectly capable of making a right-angle turn with a blade full and your car can't do that.

When Bob got to the end of the road, he had built a sand bridge over the baygall, and lifted his big, shiny blade at a beautiful cypress tree. That's where he stopped, right behind where the cabin was to be. When I first drove down the road, bumping over the Caterpillar tread marks in the sand and the clay, it was at the end of the day and there was, or seemed to be, some strange marker in the cypress. I got out and came up to it real slow. A 4 X 4 of redwood, about four feet long, was stuck clean through the trunk of that cypress. Something was branded deep into it. It said, "Barry Done It."

I conjured up ole Barry. Pointed to the 4 X 4 stuck through my tree, asked him what the hell that was.

"That, my friend, is the answer."

"Well, what, my leprechaun friend, is the question?"

"You'll find out."

And he was right. Ever since then, as people have found their way to our place and see that sign that bars the end of the road, they cry out, "What's that? Who did it?"

And the answer is staring them right in the face, that wry joke left by that Irish elf in living wood to outlast us all:

"Barry Done It."

I came there a few days after the road was new, the still scented windrows of brush piled up higher than my reach. I walked and looked at it a little while, then took my ax and stone and honed as fine an edge as I could get.

Then I hefted the ax and began to clear the land I was going to raise my cabin on.

Try Me, Test Me

We started building the camp in 1968. I knew Village Creek flooded, that she was frolicsome. That she liked to hike up her skirts and run bare through the woods. I knew that at her worst she would be four feet deep over my cleared site on the ridge and over my head where we parked. And when she is up and running like that she is five miles wide and forty feet deep and I could launch my boat at the highway and make the whole two-mile trip setting high enough up in the woods to look into squirrel nests. And if she ever got any deeper than that, she would be knee-deep in the bank vault in downtown Silsbee where the congressman stores his money and that would never happen.

So I built my floor eight feet off the ground for the part I was going to live in, with the understanding with the creek that she could have the downstairs part back again anytime she needed it. I got the idea from the Venetians. They don't even give the ground floor a number. The second floor starts with one.

I bought nine big black telephone poles and hired Casey Jones to set them in three rows of three, eight feet down in the ground and eight feet up in the air. Casey contracted to set my pilings and hang my timbers on them, leaving me a frame level and square.

Now Casey belongs to the Full Business Men's Gospel and he will not drink, smoke or swear. Not even the day he trucked in the "three sisters," the three main beams that were all sawed out of one fir timber that was 14 X 14 X 50 feet long. The three sisters would span the pilings across notches at the top and we would build the cabin on them. He got the long load jacked in between the trees on the road, and his truck was ranting, and the tandems were digging into the sand, and lurched and wiped out his fine set of California West Coast mirrors; not even then did Casey swear. I don't think the Lord ever wanted that much from a man.

And when Casey got the pilings set and the timbers hung they were not square or level and I told him so, and still he didn't smoke, drink or swear. He set a tape recorder out on a stump and ran a loudspeaker and made us and the crew listen to about an hour of what sounded like Oral Roberts and Jimmy Swaggart, until the squirrels were trembling and covering up their ears and rabbits were coming out of the brambles and shaking their fists at us. Then he rehung the timbers.

I built the whole place out of used lumber. Brought it up from town sticking out of the back of an old VW we called The Woods Bus, and lying across an eight-foot trailer made of loose iron, we called it "Bang-shang-a-lang." The trip was a twenty-mile, second-gear episode with the long boards hanging off the back of the trailer and striking fire off the road from the bent nails in it.

Hauling the lumber only used up a couple of years and a couple of engines. You know the VW engine is not iron-bolted to iron like a Detroit engine. It is more woven, like a wicker basket. If you carry enough rocks in a basket it gets real tight and solid. That VW engine was so gaffed that it was silent as a Rolls-Royce. It only burst into flames once, and one time fired a piston out through the side that went out into a pasture and killed an old red cow. I convinced the farmer she had been hit by a meteorite. Showed him a piece of the melted slag.

I bought all the lumber from J. R. Samford, whose card says he is a "demolisher," but that's not so. Samford is an antiquer but doesn't know it. He was taking down some old mansions in Beaumont and he did it just like they were put up: one board at a time. He saved elegant staircases and mantelpieces and old brass light fixtures and word about him got around and he sold a lot of that stuff to crazy rich widder women that came down from Jasper. For two years we did business out of his hip pocket, standing at the curb. He kept track and his word is his bond.

Samford wore an old felt hat pulled down low over his eyes and never said anything. Big hulking man. Wore a white shirt taking down houses. One time I asked him what kind of a man he was. Said, "I'm a wolfer."

"What's a wolfer?"

"Back in the old days when the frontier was moving West the first ones you would see would be the mountain men, riding way out in front. The last ones were the sodbusters, the settlers and their kids. And there were a few men who kind of drifted in and out along the edges of it. They called them 'wolfers.' "

So I bought a lot of clear, long-leafed, yellow pine from the Wolfer and drug it back into the woods it had come out of about

1900. Samford was also dismantling an old two-story, brick whore-house. Samford pulled out some beautiful clear pine 2 X 14 floor joists that were twenty-four feet long, and I used them for floor joists in the cabin to tie the three sisters together, and their long solid span made the cathedral beam ceilings inside. Sometimes on a still, clear night you can listen and still hear high heels tapping in them.

The family was still full of enthusiasm about The Camp back in those early days, and we got the rusty nails all pulled out, and the old boards air-dry stacked, and the copperhead snakes all got settled down under there and began to suckle their young, and Village Creek started in on the worst cycle of floods that anybody could remember.

In February of '69 it rained for seven days and seven nights. Gentle Sister Creek became awesome, moaning round the bends in whirlpools, carving into her banks. In my bed in distant Beaumont I listened to it rain. I could hear the great trees scream and fall as the creek in her madness chewed at her banks.

My clearing is on the inside of the bend, the eddy side. Here she came up softly, covered my ridge, rising an inch an hour. First the pale sand would stain dark, then the water would tickle the edge of a leaf for a time. Then the leaf trembled and was lifted, still dusty dry on one side. When the creek went down, the leaf would be deposited back on the forest floor and the sand would dry out and there would be no trace of what it had been like.

Millions of gallons of water came up and stilled the land, and the same gentle power that had lifted the leaf found all my lumber, lifted great stacks of it, waltzed it gently around the foundation site. I came out and staked it, waded through the floody forest, tied it to things. And at nights I had visions of a grand regatta of all my lumber coming downstream and into the Neches and passing Beaumont on solemn review.

I could just see the headlines in the *Beaumont Enterprise:* "Mysterious lumber jam clogs river . . . elderly disc jockey found still clutching old boards. . . ." And I consoled myself with the oldest of homilies, "The Lord giveth, the Lord taketh away . . ." At the worst the flood would not take away the trees and the land, and I would still have my little clearing and I could start all over again.

I was being sorely tried and tested by the wilderness I was seeking to enter. In March the floods cut my sand bridge, washed it out, and the earth was too soft to bring back the Cat and fix it. I stood there at the rushing-waters gap and thought so hard it brought old Barry up out of the woods. "What you need is some gringos here."

Barry, don't play with me, goddammit, I'm uptight as spider claws. "And what, my scholarly old faker, are gringos?"

And while I stood there wretched and itching to do something and watching my world washing away, I had to be polite enough to humor him through a long soliloquy about how during the war with Mexico our troops marched in singing a popular song of the times, "Green Grow the Lilacs." Only the Mexicans heard it as, "Gringo the lilacs," and that to this very day is why they call us gringos. And then he faded off into the forest. Senile old bastard.

And I stood there, gnawing on my own liver and too full of myself to hear the voice of a child that came back to me much later and I went out and planted "gringos" along the shoulders of the sand bridge and it's been under and swept by current many times since then, Barry, and still there. And one of the gringos is a pine tree and it's six feet tall now, and it is yours and may it live a hundred years and grow a hundred feet tall and perfume the air around children yet unborn. I will tell them the story, and teach them the song.

All that year it rained and Village Creek rose and fell and sobbed and moaned and I would come out and bring my ax and my maul and my son Jim and we would round up the floating piles of old boards and stake them down again.

We met Sister Creek when we turned off the blacktop at the old Silsbee Highway, a foaming sheet of water, sluicing over the road. And we would take the pirogue out of The Woods Bus and ride down the water road in silence and in awe. The forest was a floor of dark rushing water, chuckling and burbling through the corn at the Dean place. Only the Starks were dry; Wladyslaw and Veronica Stark, who ran the Dutch Lake Egg Farm for the Barrys, their knoll was an island where five thousand white leghorn laying hens and a few milk cows roosted in pastoral comfort while the current tugged pine needles away from the Starks' doorstep.

Birds sang and flitted through the trees while all around them the creatures of the earth fought and died in unseen little struggles. We saw how fire ants survive, floating islands of them, squirming and glinting in the sun. The top of the red mass was dotted with their own eggs they were saving. Food came to them, spiders and beetles that boarded the raft to keep from drowning and died twisting and turning in the agony, and were devoured. Jim said, "Daddy, the ants on the bottom drown so the ants on the top can live." And we thought about that for a while. Jim was thirteen then. Eight years later Jim had gone West to seek his fortune. He got off the bus in Los Angeles with nothing but his dreams and a cardboard suitcase. We got a card from him after a few months. "Dear Dad and Diane, I have held my breath as long as I can, I am not going to be one of the ants that drown on the bottom of the raft. . . ."

Jim and I rode the flood down our road, laughing at the Keep Out signs which were up to their chins in water. We came to our place and rested on our paddles and gazed at the foundation structure, the stout black pilings still holding the floor timbers steady. We gathered up some floating boards and built a platform up on the floor joists and thus became the first inhabitants. I had just loaded my pipe to rest a bit when a soft rumble announced the fact that a ton of 2 X 4s, stacked ten feet high, had just floated up, turned over and begun their journey to the sea.

We worked shoulder deep, rounding them up, stacking, sharpening long stakes and driving them in. We worked out of the boat, heads up in the tree limbs. So many creepies and crawlies got off and rode around in my hair and on my neck that I quit brushing them off. I'd just check to see if they were the man-eating kind or just wanted a free ride.

Weary and scratched and bruised we left, rafts of lumber tied out in the thicket. We stopped at Stark's on the way out; Veronica made us hot chicken broth and Wladyslaw towed us as far as he could with the tractor. I asked Veronica if she needed anything. "I just miss going to Mass, and I miss not getting the Sunday paper." Next

Sunday I flew low over their place in a little Cessna 150. Veronica and her kids came out on the island, waving at me. I shot a rolled-up copy of the *Sunday Enterprise* out the window in a plastic streamer, saw them run and get it. Later she said, "I was thinking it was like when I was a little girl in Poland in the war and the American planes came low and dropped leaflets to us. And I was just as excited, the memory coming back, only the Nazis would shoot at us for doing that."

In the fall the creek went down and stayed that way. My road emerged unhurt except for the sand bridge washout. The foundation site was intact; even the plastic sheeting and the iron mesh and the little border ditches cut for the footings when we pour the concrete were all still there. The structure had been proven.

I walked around amongst the slippery wreckage; I had some fine lumber hanging in treetops but it was all still there. Nothing to do but let it dry out and start over.

The stacks had been five months wetting, drying, steaming; I began to think I might have a cabin which would rot down before it ever got built.

I guess the all-time low point was when I went out into the baygall to bring up the rafts of shiplap lumber jammed into the thicket. I waded out into the black cold waters, beneath the dim vaulted roof of the cypress trees. Their knees prodded and poked me beneath the water, my feet sank into an ageless muck, I gathered up arms full of wet and slippery boards and staggered back to high ground with them, panting, ignoring the spiders and the red crawfish backing off with claws upraised. I would dump the board, pick the black leeches off my body in the naked smear of mud, and go back endlessly for more.

Quit, my body screamed, quit, you are beat and you don't have sense enough to know it. I was staggering around in a kind of slack-jawed madness. Somehow I knew this was the moment of something or the other. Like a man seeing his madness in a dream, I tied my nail apron round my naked waist; I was panting, shaking, beating inside of me. And I hauled some of those long, red, slimy boards up on top and carefully forced my mind to measure and my saw to cut.

Now. It had to be now. Never mind the folly of nailing up wet boards. It will be worse folly if I don't. Now. The saw was binding and bending, all the universe was focused on the bent back of a man. Now. I drew the old Bluegrass hammer and felt it sliding in my grip, wiped a hand clean of mud in my hair, dad-gum savage, ignorant board. I set the nail and drove that sonofagun in until it left a round dent and a shiny head and the juice splashed and filled with water. By the living God in heaven I was building. Not beat, you hear? Not beat! The fury lasted long enough to drive in a swatch of boards about six feet wide, and I folded down on my floor, knees against my chest, cheek to the wood and shook and shook with tears till there were no more, just the shaking.

Try me, Sister Creek, test me. I come to you with my ax and my maul and my muscle and my sons. Try me, you are ten thousand years old and at every springtime you will frolic in wild beauty and carry off all the old and the unfit and sweep out the garbage from the city people. But I have not lost a board, or my faith. I am as primitive as you are, I will not resist you, oh, Sister Creek, but you will not dislodge me here!

And back in the baygall spirits howled.

A Lizard Tale

Nothing went right during the time of the plumbing. The creek flooded, spreading cold and black, whispering right up to my door. My road was a river happy with fish. But the cabin was dry, and I was in there alone at my plumbing.

I would run a section of plastic pipe, do the magic thing with the cement, dibblin' and dabblin', cram it all together and pray while it set up. Then flip on the pump power switch and dash back to see the new squirtings and sneaky cold drips. My world was cold and wet. Discouraging. I would cheer me along with an Ivan the Terrible, my winter drink invention, hot black coffee and vodka.

And then suddenly I had a string of pipe that didn't leak. The sun came out and shined in my breast once more. I opened the faucets to test it. No leaks. Also no water. Ah-hh.

I traced the no-water out to the pump which was standing up there among the trees on its above-the-flood, eight-foot-tall well pipe. The tracing led to some scary tests for power and ended at the little box that goes "click" when the pump comes on. No click.

Don't like that little box, or understand its terrible secrets. Last summer it housed, along with its deadly 220 volts, a family of red wasps who chased me all around the place. So what now? Trembling, high atop the ladder, one arm hugging the pump head, I eased off that tight little metal cover. Scream!

A family of sixteen lizards leaped out! Leaping lizards! Ran down my neck, up my sleeve, through my hair. All but one. He was bridging two bare brass terminals carrying 220 volts. He just lay there starry-eyed.

I gave him a Christian burial, had another Ivan the Terrible in his memory and tried the pump circuit again. Dead. I thought of calling Bellinger, the Pump Man, last of the Great American Tusch Hogs, but the creek was over the road and Bellinger, the well digger, don't like water in any form. So back up the ladder, hugging and shaking and peering in. That's when I saw a tiny little something holding those relay points apart. A li'l ole bitty piece of lizard tail.

Now that lizard had got away. That's the part of the tail that comes off, never miss it. She's fine, wherever she is. I got the pump running again and sat down, sharing the only piece of dry ground with some friendly-looking copperheads, and a great truth came over me out there in those lonesome floody woods: If a man ain't careful he can get his whole plant shut down over a little piece of tail.

I had it on my mind. Every time I sat down to think I thought up another morality play.

When the driller had brought in the well and tore down the rig, I thought, Suitcase sand. That's what they call it in the Eastex oil fields when everybody knows by what's coming up that it's time to tear down the rig and go. I was bringing water to the house with leaving on my mind.

Make it cheap, Bax, you gone lose it all for a little piece of tail. You couldn't possibly be thinking right, could you?

You keep on reinventing Eden, Eve and the apple, and you bring your own snakes.

In an Empty Room

"Charlie! Come in this house." They were yelling at my grand-son. And he came right in, right where the door was going to be. It meant a lot to me. I just stopped right there and thought about it. Not that the kid was minding his mamma, but that she had called it a "house," and he had recognized it as what she was talking about. A house, this thing we had been working on for the past year. So it ain't just pilings standing forlorn on a sandy ridge on Village Creek anymore. It ain't just a collection of old driftwood that's been rained on forever and floated all around in two or three floods.

She had called it a house without thinking. First time anybody ever did that. By golly, if it's a house to a mamma and her kid, then it must be a house.

The bottom half was finished in 1970. We had lights and water and an indoor toilet. We had worked on it as a family. Bob Hayes and his son too. Bob is a real carpenter. In the heat of the summer he said to his son Howard, "Boy, the only thing that is keeping me cool is the wind off your hammer, but the sparks are setting my hair on fire." We finished up the bottom half with coffee over the camp-fire.

We camped out weekends, and on Mondays I would wonder where I had put my watch and my wallet and my shoes three days ago, and could I fit back into the real world again? Or worse yet, why?

Two more years drifted by and we worked on the top half. Hayes, hanging way out on a scaffolding high up in the air, tugged at his power saw. "Man, I hope if I ever fall out of an airplane I can grab onto an extension cord . . . it's bound to hang up on something before I hit the ground." But his kid Howard wasn't there, and neither were mine much anymore. The campfire pit was gone out. Cold ashes, sand was drifting in.

During those two years the tight flower of my family had opened fully. Petals fell away. Strange breezes unknown to me came and carried the seed afar. As my obsession with Village Creek filled up more and more of my life, discontent drained in and puddled where I was leaving. The kids quit coming. "Hell, it's no fun at the camp anymore. All the ole man wants to do is work on the building." And I finished up the last part with my hammer ringing in an empty room. I had done it myself.

And then on a perfectly ordinary day, the camp was finished. I had nailed up the last board. And the time of the discontent had begun.

One of the last things we did as the old family was the claiming of the land. My brother Tom, doing research on the old Church customs in England, had found these rites and we did them, and filed this document in the Hardin County Courthouse:

The Taking of The Land

I, Gordon Baxter, in the presence of witnesses of my own blood kin, my sons, my daughters, my brother, The Rev. Thomas R. Baxter, did take possession of this land, this homestead, as described in the warranty deeds in the records of the Courthouse of Hardin County, Texas.

We did walk the bounds as described by the survey, the limits of the metes and bounds of this tract of land, loudly announcing the distances and bearings and landmarks, thence to a clearing at the cabin site on Village Creek, I did heap up dirt and vegetation and sand with both my hands, four times, heaving it in turn to the four compass points and heartily stomped the earth four times, I did then proclaim in a loud and ringing voice before God and man, child, bird and beast, "We take possession of this land! This land is our land!"

We then did enter into the home, built by our own hand with sweat, blood, curses, tears and treasure and offer up prayers and thanks to God, and we did shout and sing and drink and rejoice much!

Signed by my own hand,

Gordon Baxter

The next documents I put into the courthouse were the divorce papers. I gave her all we had gotten together in our lifetime; she gave me Village Creek.

Hello, camp, it's me. Are you something of wickedness? In building this dream have I destroyed something? Is this evil? The reason for the camp on Village Creek had disappeared as fast as the camp appeared.

Spirits howled round this place. They came up out of the baygall and rattled the boards and laughed with glee. And some whispered the name of Diane. I made a date to see her in Dallas. Cratered out and didn't go, afraid of what I would know. Made another date to see Diane.

Who is Diane anyway?

Chapter 5

Diane and Ace

Ole Ace

Diane was a beautiful and sensitive twenty-two-year-old when I first met her ten years ago. At that time she was waiting at home for her call to be an airline stewardess. And she was about to meet Ole Ace, a famous, if not fictitious World War I fighter pilot.

Ole Ace was lean and courageous. He might have won the war single-handed if only the old fat major behind the desk had understood him. Ace flew alone, flouted the rules. Rules are made to protect the slow.

Ace lived by the code. Never desert a buddy, never gun down the Hun when his guns are jammed, and die bravely. When the sheet of flame gouts from under the engine cowl, stand up in the cockpit, scarf streaming, and toss off a salute.

Nobody could handle the delicate little French Nieuport fighter plane like Old Ace. He was a born pilot, flew with a touch at the controls usually reserved for women.

And there were women in Ace's life. When once again he had cheated fate and returned from Dawn Patrol, guns blackened from the kill, fabric trailing from his machine-gun-tattered wings, Ace rewarded himself with the very best of Cognac and the most beautiful of women.

There were always women in Dawn Patrol. None of them had a speaking part.

Girl in a Bell Jar

When I met Diane she was in her high Kahlil Gibran, Ayn Rand and Sylvia Plath period. "I was like the girl in the bell jar, I could see them out there, faintly hear them . . ." Her classmates from those kick-pleat, saddle-oxfords and bop days of high school in Beaumont remember her as "—that quiet girl." She said, "I thought being intelligent and being a girl was some kind of a curse, that I had to choose one or the other. I wanted to date the football star, but when we parked and he started fumbling with me, he got disgusted because I kept pushing him away. He said, "What do you want to do, run me a footrace?" I told him I thought that would be a good idea. And we did."

Diane thought she was dowdy. "Mamma was making me a dress; I was just starting to fill out. My aunt looked at me and said, 'Poor baby, your bottom looks just like mine.' I was always self-conscious of having a big behind." We had been married a year and she was thirty-three years old before I was able to reach her mind about that. I had her stand in front of a white wall in the bedroom and made pencil marks at the broadest point of her hips, then at the broadest point of her shoulders. I let her take the yardstick and do the measuring to prove that she is nearly two inches wider across the shoulders.

She has the true Scandinavian build, flat, tapered, the prettiest fanny I ever saw on a white girl, and breasts that got a head start standing up from her deep rib cage. "No, I've got Jewish boobs."

"What? Like what?"

"Like avocados."

I am more and more convinced that women don't know what they look like. Or that the men who love them see them as they want them to look like. Diane is classic. Golden tones in her skin and in her green eyes, and in her thick mass of auburn-in-the-sun, shoulder-length hair. In profile she looks like a struck Grecian coin of herself. Her fine, high-bridged nose says "Lady of Athens." Once, during her flying days when Braniff had all the girls in those harem costumes, she tinted her hair lighter. She looked like a commercial. Stunning, but hard. All the harmony of the golden tones was lost.

I spent a lot of the early times trying to guess what was going on inside her head. Once we were at a little newspaper staff party and a preacher's wife was weaving in front of me. Roy Dunn, who got to be the publisher by paying attention to little details in people's faces, wrote a column about knowing Diane by watching her eyes. Her eyes are like cathedral windows, with clouds or sun passing by outside.

After high school Diane went on reading heavier and heavier books, in and out of college, knew she was withdrawing, and went to a well-known psychiatrist. He made a pass at her.

She was twenty-two when I first met her, and already had her application in to go fly for Braniff. "I had come to a place where I knew I would have to take direction of my life. I knew I was shy, felt awkward. Being cooped up in an airline cabin full of people was meeting it head on." Diane is capable of giving herself ice-water cures.

Fay Abood introduced us; she said she did it "just to see what would happen." Fay had been the "big sister" next door to Diane in her teens, and she worked with me in the radio station during my reporting-out-of-the-eye-of-hurricanes-and-meeting-chicks-behind-the-supermarket period.

I was controversial. "—tell it like it is, Bax!" threatened with firings from the Establishment. I think Diane saw me as an Ayn Rand figure, standing naked and defiant on the mountainside. I know I did, and I hadn't even read the book.

A very young Diane lifted the edge of her bell jar, stood there trusting. I still remember the beads of perspiration on her lip. "—take me . . . do with me as you wish . . . you are the most sensitive and alive man I have ever met. . . ."

What she had met was Ole Ace. Me, I lived at home with Mary

and the kids. Ole Ace had just brought his fighter plane back from behind enemy lines and was doing victory rolls over the base. The night announcer had just knocked up my cousin and left town about two jumps ahead of the hounds, taking all the good Kingston Trio albums with him. My cousin turned to me for sympathy and compassion, and while I was consoling her, she gave me the crabs.

First the blue ointment, then Diane.

The affair with Diane was intense. Our first romance. And lasted about a year and a half. I think I was in love, but had lied about it so much I couldn't tell the difference. She was based out of Dallas and flew Denver, Memphis, Chicago, Cleveland, Minneapolis. I told her I didn't even know which way to face when I went out in the backyard at night to look up into the sky and grieve. I came clean with her and told her about Ole Ace. She said she knew about Ace the minute she met him, but she also knew me. That's further than I ever got with it.

She bid for the little forty-passenger, prop-driven Convairs long as Braniff flew them. "I like them. One girl, one airplane, my airplane. The guys on the regular business runs got to know me, and I remembered how they liked their coffee. The nicest thing that ever happened was once two of my 'regulars' were seatmates, flying another airline. They got to talking about the best cabin service they ever had, and after a while both of them realized they were describing me. They sat down and wrote a letter to the company about it. That was back when the company circulated 'sunshine letters.' I still got it."

We lived on letters, and no matter where ole man Neil sent me on a news story, I seemed to be routed through Dallas. He would read over my expense accounts and shake his head. "Your coverage of hurricane Flora made the AP wires, but Haiti, via two days in Dallas, Bax, that's creative."

Once Diane smuggled me onto her flight. That's when the Electras were falling. Those people were her friends. She smuggled me onto her Electra for an overnight in Kansas City, when the last trace of me would have shown that I boarded an American for Dulles. If that Electra had shook a wing loose, me and Diane, and all those good folks we didn't even know, would have been part of the aluminum scraps lining of a big smoking hole in the ground somewhere in the Midwest. A real "Judge Crater." I would have vanished in thin air.

But that's not what I was thinking. I was watching her twinkling ankles and trying to secretly pat her fanny. With her eyes, next trip up the aisle, she traced the route of the steaming pot of coffee on her tray to my crotch. I kept my hands to myself. She would have done it.

We had outrageously good luck during the Ruby trial. I was posted in Dallas, and she came back from a midnight flight with red spots all over her tummy and back.

Measles! You must remain quiet with measles. You must stay in the dark with measles. You must not go fly public airplanes with measles. But you can make love with measles. Measles is the ideal disease for lovers.

I took her to the swank hotel suite where Melvin Belli and Joe Tonahill and all those fake doctors who were making headlines defending Jack Ruby were having a little PR party for the network and wire service guys. I introduced her as an SMU journalism coed, and she called them all "dah-ling," and gave them big hugs and went around secretly licking all the glass rims.

She said, "You may have to introduce me as your 'uh-h,' but if I give all these guys measles and cause a mistrial and blow up this whole circus, someday you'll have to write about how I changed history."

But mostly letters kept us alive. She wrote: "—you have reached into the muddle that I am, the drudge, the idealist, sipping the wine of dreams, and you have found me. You have given me a most priceless gift. . . . But I am so terribly frightened when I realize that for me, loneliness will be the eventual end. Gordon, just love me, trust me for the woman I am, not the child I seem to be."

"Diane, I'm no longer sure I can love in two worlds and survive in either. There is no free love."

"No free love," she wrote for Christmas; "how bittersweet this joy. You are probably with your family now, kneeling in worship. I know that I am in your heart, perhaps in your prayers. . . ."

I wrote:

What flight? What city? I whisper your name to a moving star.

I went to communion Sunday. Attempting to take over the spiritual leadership of my family once more. Herded them all along, son Gordon saying, 'Thanks, Dad, I feel so much better. . . .'

In church, looking at the cross, looking into the ages, into eternity . . . and into my own death and judgment before God. Prayers came easily . . . but badly scrambled. The Christ on the cross over the altar became you, wearing a crown of thorns. . . .

You, fragrant, holding out your arms. I closed my eyes. Prayed. Please, no, oh, please please, and it became your voice saying, "Please, please, I want your baby." I opened my eyes and stared. Church. Family. All in a row. Clean. Dressed. Sunday clothes. This is madness. Must not think about Diane during Mass. Am pure. Am about to go to communion. Will the Body and Blood of Christ be the body and blood of you? Oh, this is the red Devil himself, straight up from hell, arm wrestling with me at the threshold.

My eyes swim in and out of focus, the cross is Christ, then you, then Christ, alive, looking into me. . . . *God*, I love you.

God, I love *You*.

No, its supposed to sound like *God*, I love you. How easily it transposes. Around and around in my heart.

I must not lose the Church. To whom else would I turn, Lord? I must not lose you, Oh, Lord. . . .

Electras Always Look Like They Are Dying

By the springtime of '64 we had strung this thing out for a year and a third and we knew we were reaching our limits. I was beginning to prepare Diane for the cutting of the cord by writing stuff like this:

> I was a doorway
> Through which a little girl passed
> On her way
> To becoming a woman.

We were giving each other cues, and Diane was beginning to build and broaden a life structure of her own. Instead of being glad for her, I could only focus on the simple fact of life which is that if I could not keep her covered, I would release her right into the arms of some horny old airline captain. I began to set hooks to stay into the bait to go. She was in touch with what was real; I was writing this:

"I must preserve myself from ruin. Like the aces of old, my only real choice is in the manner of how I die. I can ride the flaming plane to earth, or I can just step over the side and die quick and clean. . . ."

Diane was not above a little gamesmanship of her own. I asked, "Are you late?"

"Three days. My breasts are tender."

Ah, so. Main thing, keep cool. I must come up with some workable plan even though I am learning she is a most unworkable human. If the shadow of God has passed over our love, then so be it. Many choices lie before us, but two things seem certain. "You want my baby. Your utmost cry of passion, your final expression of our lovemaking is always, 'Oh, I want your baby!' And I will help in any way, but I will not help you abort!" And so I made her two promises, that I would support the child, that I would be with her at birth.

Weeks dragged by. The classical timeless question, is she or ain't she? If she ain't, I think I will just be her good friend, starting now. I told her that too.

She flew home on a pass to break the news to me. We drove out along the highway, speaking calmly but breathing from the tops of our lungs only.

"Are you?"

"Nope."

"Are you really not?"

"Really not."

"Then why in the hell didn't you tell me?"

"Wanted to let you dangle awhile. See what you really would do."

We carried on jaggedly a few months more. In early summer I was in Washington, out on the eighth-floor balcony of the State

Department watching the Lockheed Electras inbound to Washington National, flying the Potomac. I was thinking of the metal plate Braniff crew members are required to carry. It is a deeply engraved ID card in metal. Diane said they call it their "spin crash and burn card."

Electras always look like they are dying. Coming down out of the mists over the Potomac, one from the right, one from the left, with too much nose in front of too little wing. Like a wet mud duck the Electra comes dying down to cross the stone arch bridge, whistling her dying dirge, laying her four-striped shroud of kerosene behind her. The Electras come out of the clouds to die silently, one by one, right at the threshold of life.

Poor dying Electras. Filled with pulpy passengers about to be omeleted together. And beautiful hostesses with grave eyes and passionate breasts and hurting feet, flying out of the crash and into the front pages. You never see a picture of a live airline hostess on the front page of the paper. And they look at you forever with silent reproach for not having loved them enough.

But should a man's thoughts be filled with flying buttresses when he is all alone in an economy-class, Washington, D.C., hotel room? Let him take stock of himself. He has filed his story, he is indoors, drinking modestly from his own jug. He has done his laundry and it is hanging in the closet. The drip-dry Dacron items are hanging between the woolen suit and pants so that the moisture given off by the one is absorbed by and straightens out the wrinkles in the other.

Such a man cannot be all bad, although he has done some moderate cheating and lying to get where he is tonight, and he finds himself lonesome to be in at least two other places. Do not flog yourself, old man, just because you cannot decide who to be lonesome for in this little green clutch bag of a hotel room.

You, who only this day did shake the meaty hand of the President of the United States while you and the other reporters trampled the sacred grasses of Lady Bird's Rose Garden. And looking just past the President you met the slitted eyes and the uniform trench coat of the Secret Service. Him just itching to snatch out that snub-nosed magnum and bark you into the sod, and you just itching to whirl and stab a finger pistol at his chest and go "ka-pow! Where were you in Dallas, buster, when we needed you?"

So much for the affairs of state. Come on, settle down and be longing in just one direction. You can't go mooning after the whole lot. There is just not enough time for that. Try this for a test. Who would you miss the most if they were all departing forever? Dating all the way back to 1940 when some of the starters were not finished yet and some of the finishers were not even started yet. Who would you miss the most?

Diane once said that she was only a necessary accessory to a man such as me. Not fair then, not fair now. "Q" in this exchange is an imaginary authoritative figure who has had me hauled in for questioning:

Q. All right, sir, let us take inventory of what you are lonely for.

A. The orderly certainties of home.

Q. And where is home?

A. My house.

Q. Do you miss the people that your house always seems to be filled with?

A. I'm sorry, no. Not very much. Nor do I think they miss me.

Q. Do you miss anyone there at all?

A. Yes, I miss my wife.

Q. Commendable. In what way do you miss your wife?

A. Well, I am doing my own laundry, eating out of vending machines. The comfort and routine she surrounds me with are gone. They were good. Like well-worn gears, smoothly meshed.

Q. Do you think your wife knows that you regard her as a well-meshed old gear?

A. I am afraid she knows exactly what I think.

Q. Do not be afraid, we are only trying to help you. Do you miss your children?

A. Only the oldest and her husband; they are my kind of people.

Q. What are your kind of people?

A. Well, you know, a little nutsy, warm, expressive, emotional, the stargazers.

Q. Isn't your wife one of these?

A. Oh, no, sir; if she were the house would be a mess.

Q. Hmmm. Are you lonesome for humans or service?

A. Both.

Q. Do they not live in the same place?

A. No, the humans I am lonesome for were never intended to live anyplace, I don't think.

Q. Who are these persons you crave the company of, these transients?

A. Well, I see them now and then, but they are beyond approach by the very nature of what identifies them, and the things I miss most about them.

Q. And what are these unique identifications?

A. Well, to coin a phrase, they are big-breasted intellectuals.

Q. Someone to curl up and chew the fat with, as it were.

A. Sir, I am in no mood for frivolous carnality.

Q. Very well, when are you in such a mood?

A. When I am with the people I miss.

Q. Touché. Is this a large group or exclusive?

A. Very exclusive. In fact, one. Now.

Q. Commendable. How so?

A. Oh, there would not be even one if she had not allowed me to approach her. These rare people have so much to offer that they go about with the blinds closed lest they pick up a howling mob of hopeless addicts. Even then they tend to gather a few silent worshipers.

Q. Are you one of these?

A. Never. It is a most delicately balanced, mutual relationship. If either of us so much as gives a flicker of wanting to terminate it, the other vanishes. Forever.

Q. Formidable. How do you manage?

A. By being at all times equal and honest with each other.

Q. Are you honest?

A. I am not capable of being honest. But the idea is vital.

Q. Why?

A. Because we have no claim recognized by society. No civil, no religious claim. All we have is a mutual offering. A reciprocation which cannot become unbalanced or impose, or it will destroy itself.

Q. Sounds like a perfect marriage. Any hope of that?

A. I doubt it. Neither of us has the advantage over the other just now. People can only be married if one thinks he has a slight edge over the other.

Q. Are you a cynic?

A. No, Catholic.

Q. How does the Mother Church view this situation?

A. With all the respect due an older institution.

Q. Now who is being facetious?

A. Sorry, but I am starting to feel much better now.

Q. Do you think we may have solved the problem?

A. Yes, home during the weekdays when I can work steadily and look my best to my dependents and reassure them. And to the ethereal one on weekends, where she will have the security and satisfaction of knowing she is fulfilling all my creative needs and I hers.

Q. Do you think that this untidy scheme will please either of your partners?

A. No.

Drifting off to sleep, mumbling:

> It is springtime again, and I am not yet dead.
> Nor any older, though aging.
> Nor any wiser, though experienced.
> And they all know more of love than you.
> Good night, my love,
> Whoever you are. . . .

Blossoms in the Surf

By midsummer of 1964 Diane was raising the pressure to resolve what she accurately perceived as a "half-life" for her. I was reacting like a rat inventing the maze.

I took her down to my secret sandbar on Village Creek and pulled the pirogue up under the willows and went on and on about my dream of living here someday. I bought her a little solid-gold wedding band and we sat up in bed and I slipped it on her finger, trying to finds the words to go with it that not even I could understand. So I just said, "Before God."

She wore it on her right hand on the airplane, on her left hand on the ground. Stewardesses could not be married back then. No matter where she wore it she knew it was against somebody's rules. But she wore the plain gold ring. All the ten years we were apart after I left her. All the ten years of the other men. All the ten years while I built the cabin on our sandbar, she wore the ring. She still does. When we were married ten years later on the front porch of the cabin, standing and looking out over the creek, I took it off her right hand and put it on her left. It was hardly worn down at all. My own wedding band that Mary had given me, I cut off with a pair of pliers in a filling station.

Ole Ace staged the going-away scene for her. He couldn't shoot his wife and kids in the back. In his own dim way he had come to know the depth of Diane, that she was too valuable a person to wing on with him and his going down in flames. He set up the scene on the beach. The Gulf of Mexico is only about fifty miles on down from Village Creek. He was going to cut her loose to go fly with a safer squadron than Dawn Patrol. He was concerned, oh, yes, he was concerned. He was even hurting. What he was hurting about was the image of what was sure to come. Sooner or later, after her grief, some dumb guy will come along and be lucky enough to find the right combination. He will be gentle and quiet, and they will talk about good books and psychology and all that stuff. He will be her friend first. Oh that hurts to think about. But be real, Ace; that stuff's too good to be left uncovered. Somebody's gonna cover it for you when you are gone. She'll go out and find a friend. Damn! Man, think about something else. Think about what you got to do.

Ace was all heart.

They walked hand in hand beside the low surf on the packed, wet border of sand, walking toward the sunset. In the twilight he scooped out two shallow places with his hands, right at the edge of the surf ripples. He placed a red carnation in each one, side by side. Then the camera pulls back for a long shot, showing Ole Ace leading the Sky Goddess slowly away. He is pointing back at the two points of red blossom about to be devoured by the surf. On the sound track his voice floats down to us on the wind. He is telling her they will always be there, blossoms in the surf. Really, he said that. Dear God. The wind is blowing her hair, she is walking head down, leaning forward a little.

The send-off was a catastrophe for Diane. She took sick leave from flying. She turned to her parents. Her dad took her out into the open country, to the rocky, sandy part of Texas, to Llano County in the sagebrush sea. They walked among mesquite and over the rocky ground. He said, "I know you must talk about this to someone, and you can't talk about it to me."

Diane went back to the airline and she worked. "I always knew it would happen. I always knew I would have to build my own life. I would have to make me a whole person again."

I went back to meeting chicks behind the supermarket. I had saved the marriage.

I never quit thinking of Diane. I never had the decency to leave her alone. I sent little short notes, little cat's-paw touches from afar.

Diane,

Skirting hurricane Hilda in the Cessna 150 on low-level beach patrol I saw an unbelievable sight—two red blossoms
growing in the sand
at the edge of the sea.

Always,

Gordon

And she touched back. With letters, sometimes a phone call to tell me she had decided to marry the guy, and what did I think of him? "I wasn't trying to hurt you, I was really trying to get my life together and thinking of marriage. I wanted to check with you before I made the final step to see if there was any hope for us. I guess I wanted to hear you tell me not to do it."

I never did. She never married, and somehow the years went by. The cabin on Village Creek was finished. And so was my marriage. My place was swept clean and my flock was scattered, like it says in the Bible.

Emancipation Jeans

I remember when I made the conscious decision. I was standing in the Galleria, the new leisure, pleasure-spending city they had just built in Houston. It was about 1972. In the center courts beneath the beaded curtains of light, ice skaters were a slow ballet of moving color. Indoor ice in South Texas in July? We can afford that? And all these lovely people drifting by endlessly, rich with purchases, sloping along in sandals, turning their heads to each other, laughing. Flare legs swirled romantically. Warm breasts mooned against thin tank-top material. All so rich, so free, so casual. You just know they had probably been smoking dope and screwing. Probably don't even know each other's last names. And laughing about it.

End flicks of my movies ran by raggedly, in black and white, superimposed, with the blurred numbers running off the ends. Nobody cares. Movies of John Carradine's finely boned face and Henry Fonda, *Grapes of Wrath*. Holding up the Bible, "How can they get so much hate out of this book?" Before they smashed his fine face bones with the ax handle. White hickory.

The film flicked on, white hickory, black Bibles, old Ford cars coated with dust, my daddy at the supper table leaning forward intently. "Son, don't waste bread. Never."

My movie. At last I had gotten my hand on the girl's thigh. We were parked in Daddy's '40 model Ford waiting for Cecil B. De Mille to announce Pearl Harbor. The girl squeezed her knees together, no longer panting from the kissing. She said, "Take your hand off of that. It's holy." And I groaned, thinking, What kind of a church does she go to where they got religion all mixed up with lovin'?

This is no way to send a young man off to war. "What if you never see me again?" I asked. "Would you send me off to war like this?" For one thing, I was thinking, they would never get a pair of pants to fit me. But I kept still about that. Get people to giggling and you'll never get any.

They had loaded our crowd up pretty heavy. "Make the World Safe for Democracy." Then, "Make the World a Better Place for Our Kids." And now the stone ache. We left a lot of kids to make the world a better place for. It is a flinch reflex of young men going off to war.

So my postwar movies ran on, now in color, but the way was straight. Get into the traces and pull a Chevrolet, and if you could outpull other guys also harnessed to Chevrolets, the winners got to pull heavier cars. Pontiac, Buick, Olds, on up to Fleetwood Cadillacs which would cause you to double up and drop dead at age fifty-three.

By the time I got to the Galleria on this epic night, I was towing a four-hole Buick. That is the long one, with four mouse holes in the hood. General Motors knew me, understood my needs. The gold-crested Cadillac lay just ahead. The bumper guards of a Cadillac were shaped just like big female breasts.

I deserved all that, I had put in my time and fulfilled the contract. I had made the world a better place for the kids. And just look at them, shuffling by, free, laughing. What the hell has gone wrong here? These kids got no sense of values. Perish. They will all perish like grasshoppers when winter hits this place and they have dug no warm burrows and stored no grain. This place will be littered with their flimsy husks. It ain't right, I tell you, it ain't right. Look at their carmel lips. Gahdammit.

It ain't fair.

How I envied them.

Secretly I was getting old. I had been watching me get old in the face, but that part is ok. After forty everybody makes his own face. Mine showed the road I have been down. The war, the dangerous curves, some carving from facing hurricanes, some fine lines from caressing the controls of the plane while flying into the sun. An old hawk whose steely eyes could go tender. I was satisfied with the way my old face had turned out.

Then one day I saw my back in the mirror. An old man's back. Creases, and all that. Now I was up there on the balcony of the Galleria, leaning against the railing, dark suit, white shirt, leather shoes, executive socks, leaning there hiding my old man's back, lusting after the kids, hating the world I had built, and not a part of any of it. Had I done all I was going to do? How much of the stale marriage was my doings? My income was in the top percentile, my mistress was young and beautiful, I steadfastly sheltered my wife and kids, carried heavy insurance, all the right stuff.

Standing there in the Galleria, leaning on the railing in my suit, a fake, watching the kids laughing and drifting by, I decided one of us had it wrong. And I made part of the decision. I swore I would never put my feet in leather boxes or my back into a cloth black box again. Except for wakes and weddings. State occasions. I would keep one suit for contempt. I went out then and bought me a set of flare legs. Denims. And I turned my face toward Village Creek.

I still got that pair of jeans. I call them my emancipation jeans.

Ten Years Later

There was never a time when I had not thought about Diane.

I called her. No, she had never married. "I would find some reason if they got too close. There was the danger that if they got too close they would find out some awful truth about me. You are the only man who has seen into me, you already know all of that. Seen into me and thought I was still good. You made me feel beautiful. I felt safe with you."

We made a date, I chickened out. Didn't go. Then I called her again. I think what I was afraid of was an intact Diane. She sounded so grown up over the phone.

I kept the second date, went out to the plane and put on my helmet and goggles and adjusted my long, flowing, white silk scarf, and took off for Dallas.

Ole Ace had a rare human faculty. He could grow older without aging.

We were going to get into that stuff and take up right where we left off.

Hello, Dallas, Would she be waiting? Who would we be this time? Can you expect to come crashing down out of the sky and through the crystal skylight of her life and land munching on her table again?

I was shocked at her beauty. I don't know what I expected ten years to do. Frump? Scales? She was still the classic Grecian carved marble, her eyes still the luminous cathedral windows of her soul. I stood around and gawked.

Ten years. Thomas Wolfe said you can't go back. I am not sure of exactly what I had in mind, but coming back was a part of it. She stood in the arbor, beyond the latticework of her life. Wary of Ole Ace and the time she had stood outside his walls and threw a rose over that he never heard.

We were being careful not to tear open well-healed scars, but our minds grew close. Hurrying across the way stations of what we have been, of what we now believe, amazed at our parallel growth apart. I was so happy. No yesterday, no tomorrow, as consenting adults we could now . . .

Suddenly she was telling me soberly, most sincerely, "I could never be a corner of your life again. . . . I am worth more than that." I was backing off, confused. It isn't supposed to be that way. We had just toured our personal museum, and now here she was going round briskly snapping the locks shut on all our recently opened cases of treasure. It isn't supposed to be that way.

I was backing up in small steps. She held me, and said through tears, "I love you. I always have. If you want me, come and take me. But all of me. Now."

I took her out to Love Field to make her flight to Seattle. I was thinking. Thinking hard, and thinking that thinking has ruined too many lives. She boarded the 727 and was out to the Pacific Ocean and back before the scent of her ever left my clothes.

What had happened to this lush little girl who ten years ago had said to me, "You, with only a few words, have awakened in me a life that had been sleeping. Do I love you? The question is too great. There is so much I would say, but the words are held in captivity by awe and fear.

"Who are you? And what is this temptation which tastes of limitless freedom and hopeless confinement at once? How shall I restrain my soul from touching yours? You will know that one woman has loved the silent sorrows of your soul and loved the pilgrim in you. I am one of many, and you are one of few. Take me, do with me as you wish."

I had been suspect of that much love. Diane was operating with no Plan Two. Leaving no back doors. Because it never happened to me, I doubted its existence. I asked her. "Why me? I am old, not pretty, much married. Why me? Maybe this is just storybook romantic love."

And she had answered, "Oh, no. It is you I love. And I can see the difference between Ole Ace and Gordon. I don't see them as black and white, as two separate characters. They mesh. Even when you are coming on as Ace I know Gordon is down in there somewhere, and I love him. Come on, admit it, Ace didn't have all that much fun, did he?"

I had to think about that one, and admit to her that in the bedroom Ole Ace worried about hell, and in church, Gordon could not keep from fanny-watching girls going to communion. That neither one of us ever felt like he was where he belonged.

Sure I worried about this conflict. It was a lot of not liking who I was and how I was living. But what I was wondering the most about right now was what happened to that little hush puppy I had so gallantly set free because her life was too valuable to be messed up screwing around with the likes of me? About the last thing I wanted to hear from her was that this was true.

I ran the "ten years later" reunion scene over in my mind again. She had the opening lines right. I said, "You look so great! Tell me, what have you been doing?" And she said, "Waiting for you."

But it was the stuff that happened right after that which made me think maybe I had wandered out onto the wrong set. Instead of pouring the wine, she sat right down and crossed her legs.

Maybe she was not fully aware that things had changed. I told her the cabin was finished, that I was getting a divorce and living alone on the creek now. Still no wine. So in all honesty I added that tearing up of the roots was pretty painful, that nobody just turns on the cold water and washes twenty-seven years down the sink. Maybe a pat on the head for that.

She said, "Let me tell you about pain. Because of you I am a woman. I wanted you, needed you, the man, not the parent, not the friend, and oh, no, my love, not the physical need, far worse. I thought of you safe at home with your own children, with your own woman to stand beside you. When we parted there was the realization that with a whole new world to be explored I was alone. There was no one, not even you.

"Flying was my lifeline. It was satisfying, it was emotionally safe. I threw myself into it and it threw itself back at me. Forty meals in twenty minutes on the Convair. People dallying with their food, no time to get the trays stacked and put away and us on final for landing. I set them down and strapped me in. Better they should bounce than me. And bounce they did. The galley was ankle deep in syrup.

"And in Wichita, leading thirty-five passengers out to the plane, I found the only patch of ice on the ramp, slipped and fell on my behind and watched all my boarding passes blow away. And landing at St. Louis we lost all our hydraulics and I was standing up advising all the passengers to remain belted in and we came bucketing onto the runway and I was thrown all over the galley. And I thought of you and wanted to say, 'Thanks, it was all very educational.' And I shook my fist at that toothless, smiling deity who moves me about on the game board of life. Have a good chuckle, old god, you are at your peak today. I knew the answer. That I would rise up and look that toothless, sneering power in the eye and I would say, 'No more. I have beaten you. I shall be in control. I shall live.'

"I got sunshine letters from passengers and some of the old senior captains said I was the most efficient hostess they had ever flown with. Then I began to explore the reasons why I am who I am and not functioning as a totally effective person in my personal life. I began to do a lot of reading.

"During this time I met a guy who was really a kind of a nurd. We had long philosophical discussions. This was during a time when I would stay up all night and discuss philosophy with anybody who would listen. But he gave me a turning point. He said, 'Diane, you will never be happy until you accept the responsibility for your own life instead of trying to discover reasons for everything, or to place the blame.'

"After that I went into a period of total independence, total responsibility. But I was still scared all the time, and I went too far with this. I tried to accept the responsibility for other people's happiness. I overdid it.

"I knew I still didn't have it right. Just always doing the 'right thing' and my overblown independence were really a wall between me and other people. The bell jar again, but more acceptable. People saw me as aloof. I was still a scared little girl.

"I finally recognized this walling-off and started the pendulum swinging back the other way, seeking that middle ground. I had found out I could be responsible; now what I had to learn was that I could relinquish control, take chances. That I might look silly, and there would be some things that I might have to back away from, but at the worst, I could live through it. I could survive.

"Gordon, in my growing up I never quit loving you. The calls to you over the years about the guys I was going to marry, and the hope that you would tell me no, should reveal everything you need to know about that. But I have come to question what there was between us, how much of it was the dreams of a romantic, very young girl. I have carved out my self-esteem. I still love you, always have, but as you sit here and tell me you are not sure you can live without your family it's ok. I can live without you. I have done it."

And with that rap across the mouth, and the "take all of me or none of me, I could never be just a part of your life again," she had boarded that big green 727, looking as smooth and intact as an egg, and she left me.

Leaving me I could understand, but all the rest of that heavy stuff she had laid upon me I couldn't seem to get sorted out. I sure wish we'd had time to pour a little wine and give me a chance for a little eloquence of my own.

She still looked like Diane, only finer. But she didn't sound like Diane. I think I liked it better when she was a silly, romantic young girl; at least I knew who was in charge here. I was pretty certain that she still loved me that much, and nobody had left any marks on her, but it was plain to see that we had two different ideas about what was love. She was capable of expressing her total feelings standing up. I began to get the creepy feeling that she might have outgrown me, or she knew something about love that I didn't, or the part of me that drives me and the part of me I think with are located in two separate places in my anatomy.

The discourse in Dallas had sure shed a lot of light on whatever happened to Diane. Now what we needed was to find someplace where we could lie down and talk things over.

What I had in mind was to lure her down to the creek for the summer. Only a suitcase move-in. She would commute to the airline and keep her apartment in Dallas. This is what is called a Free Home Demonstration, or, If there had been a back door in the Alamo there wouldn't be no Texas. The sort of thing the average fly must be thinking when he lands on the lip of the Venus flytrap. "Just one little sip of this. We can always quit and go home, can't we?"

Among the other follies of such thinking, living together will teach you nothing about being married. It is trendy, and you can tell your friends, and get caught up on lovin' and try to think straight, but living together is no crystal ball into marriage. Both of you are still being company, trying to be quiet in the bathroom.

Being better armed than me for such a contest, and being equally certain I was not aware of this, she agreed to bring her suitcase to Village Creek.

Chapter 6

Spirits Howl

Spirits howl back in these woods. Huddle close round the cabin some nights and shriek and moan up under the eaves. Restless spirits that sway the tall cypress where their columns rise and arch out to form the cathedral roof over the dark waters of the baygall behind the house. Spirits grown cold from the primitive campfires that remember the awful things the Indians did out on the creek front. Spirits of the early logger and the cork from his whiskey bottle buried beneath the sand there.

Spirits decided that people should live here again. Entered my heart and found its inner compass always pointing back to this place. Commenced the upheaval of breaking up concrete sidewalks and the family circle and brought me alone to this wilderness. I raised old wet boards and began to hammer together a cabin. Only the nights were bad.

The spirits brought Diane down from distant skies. Her books lined the walls, her bright Braniff cabin costumes slept in surprise in covered closets.

The spirits tried us and tested us with mud and floor and discouragement. With garlands of vines blooming spiders and a few grinning snakes. Found us worthy of such a place, decided to reward us.

The spirits said, "What they need now are creatures." Rummaged their inventory of who was wandering hungry and cold in the woods, and sent us Pearl, the pregnant woods cat. And a week later sent us Wolf. Noble dog Wolf, the half-crazed shepherd who ran in circles, eyes gleaming like the coals of hell, and seemed to hear and bark at earthworms.

Then the spirits drew back, quarreling some amongst themselves. Springtime was overriding them. Even the darkest spirits lean back and admire springtime as she comes and touches the woods. Blythe little spirits peeked out of the wild orchids and jasmine blooming. The red dash of cardinals lighted the dark green tangles that hemmed us in. There was fresh creek fragrance in the air and at dawns the great blue heron made her slow wingbeat way down the creek. So majestic her blue among the shadows that she is to us the very Holy Spirit, moving.

In the creek-bank cabin, Diane looked with luminous eyes at the garbage I trail from the winters of my life, and softly said, "I wish people could leaf out anew at each springtime."

It wasn't the garbage I was trailing that bothered me, it was the leafing out each springtime.

When I was still Daddy and head of the flock, we would come up to the creek for a weekend, all the kids in The Woods Bus, singing, "Do Lord." We would go by the old Dean place, the cabin crumbling back into the earth, and his corn coming up green.

Dean's cornfield became my dreadful time clock. One more springtime and the corn is green again and I have already seen more springtimes than I am going to see.

At midsummer the corn was tall, rustling with its burden. Mature and full and the harvest coming soon. Have I been all I am going to be? All I could be?

In the fall the stalks were brown and going back into the ground. I would avert my eyes, I knew what I would see. Winter was coming and I hadn't done it yet. Another year is gone.

The kids were singing "On Top of Old Smokey" and The Woods Bus was warm and moist with them. Then what are these cold, formless shapes pushing against me?

With Long Backward Glances

There were no guidelines for divorce back in my family. I grew up watching the other things you could do. You could faint, go crazy, get cancer, sink into the bottle and stare out with fluid eyes and keep saying, "I love you, my darling," while performing the long, slow, hatred ritual of death by drowning in the sheets.

Grandpa had "Aunt Ruby." That ceremony began with shouting echoing in the house, the door slamming, then Grandpa would pack his suitcase with his bottle, his pistol and a clean white shirt and go catch the train to Houston.

But Grandpa always came home again to Grandma. I don't know what they said to each other next. She would bang pots and pans in the kitchen, he would sit and rock and spit in the fireplace. They played it out, with him dying out with the coals and her buying a new dress and a broad-brimmed hat and becoming a Christian. The ladies of the First Baptist Church who looked like her would flock around her. "Your grandmother is a pillar of this church," they would say to me. They all went with her out to the cemetery to set the stone over Grandpa's head. And to set the silence over whatever happened to Grandma and Grandpa's marriage. Grandma went to his funeral in a red dress, green perfume and that broad-brimmed hat.

I even went to Houston during the war and looked up "Aunt Ruby." She was behind the counter of a big downtown department store, the kind where the ladies wore pince-nez glasses. Her hair was silvered up in a bun. Her breasts were high and full in a somber-buttoned bodice. She had deep eyes, and they caressed me, but she spoke of Mr. Owens as though he were a business associate. "Fine man, your grandfather was."

My generation was surviving the sausage mill of the war with barracks humor. One-liners. For Grandpa it was: "The anvil wears out the hammer." But I never got beyond such simplistic thinking. I never learned the language or the customs of infidelity and divorce. I was never sure of how to feel about what I was doing.

To Mary's early rage and, "Aha, I got you, you son of a bitch!" I would withdraw and think, Any good folly is worth whatever you are willing to pay for it. A saying originally intended for sailboats, I think.

Later when Mary had no tears left and no rage left, but simply looked into my face and pronounced, "You are a liar. A liar and a cheat," I had graduated to Pope's "You purchase pain with all that joy can give, and die of nothing but a rage to live."

Always the actor, the comedian, full of good one-liners. Always able to buck-and-wing it off the stage and leave them laughing or crying, but this time the curtain was stuck hanging open. They were watching the set tearing down. "All that talk about his family on his radio shows . . ." "They used to come into St. Pius and he would lead them all down the aisle, down in front, they would fill up a whole pew, and he would lead them all to communion . . ." "He had a woman on the other side of town, you know . . ." "Yes, and that airline stewardess in Dallas too. . . ."

My cute-trick mind could only give me more one-liners.

"You ought to see an old lion thrown to the Christians . . ."

"Never leave home in the wintertime."

"A man can be married all his life, and carry out his share of it in his two arms."

And to anyone who would listen, I needed to explain. To tell of how I gave it all to Mary. "Twenty-seven years and eight kids, she was never anything but a good wife and a perfect mother. She deserved more than that. I gave her everything. She's set for life. All I took was Village Creek."

Village Creek, the final irony. The cabin we had built for all the kids and grandkids to come home to. Jim, the serious son, had painstakingly branded it into a broken canoe paddle blade that still hangs over the downstairs door: Tribal Longhouse—1968. Outside my window Village Creek flowed like gray lead.

I walked around in the cabin, wondering what they were doing at "my house." Made a Spam sandwich, poured whiskey and tried to get drunk. The whiskey was only bitter. The "No fault" thing in front of the judge had been so quick, so cold. Mary and I sat stunned. The little hatreds sputtered and died out. The enormity of this. God!

No fault. Twenty-seven years of no fault? No man should try to peel that back. Flip back the pages, little scenes stand out. After the war, Molly was just over a year old, I had steady work, Mary had the next baby in her. I remember that speech. "There is man's work, and there is woman's work. I won't have no babies, you won't bring home no paychecks." That's the way Daddy did it, the way his daddy did it. What else did I have to go by?

No fault. I never missed a payday; she made perfect babies and took care of them. I never fed one and held it, never washed a little bottom, but a lot of times I worked night jobs too. No problem. I figured I would get to know them after they grew up and became human.

Sure, I went outside the marriage. But why? What did I go outside looking for? Whose fault? We couldn't talk about it then; nobody should talk about it now.

Then suddenly it's twenty-seven years later and they are mostly grown and gone and we are sitting in the living room of a big fine house, looking across at each other with nothing to say. How do you think successful people can do that?

The last night at the supper table I told the two young daughters still at home. They never said a word. Laurie formed a tear, but she never let it fall. Martha was silent.

On the phone Bonnie, the Houston daughter, was silent for a moment, then all she said was, "Go. And find love." I saw Marjorie to tell her. She just hugged me. Her voice in my ear was her little-girl voice. "I love you, Daddy . . ."

And so I went, stowing and hiding all the guilt. With long backward glances going out the gate where the honeysuckle grows.

Later Diane said, "You don't even know how to have a good divorce. Divorce should be more like war."

No Hands

Knowing better, deep in my heart, I brought Diane to these woods. We burned the bridge. She quit Braniff with regrets and we emptied out her orderly little apartment in Dallas. Bags, bundles and boxes. I asked her if she understood that a woman's place is in the bed and that she would be expected to walk ten paces behind me and carry the baggage on her head. She laughed and kissed me lightly. "If you can keep up, you can walk beside me."

We got to the cabin site at floodtime and stopped where the road dipped down into the water. The cabin stood green, hugged in the green woods, an island. "How do we get there?" I had a boat, but I might as well find out about her now.

"You shuck off your drawers and you wade in, carrying the baggage on your head."

Part of the Eastex tradition of the Big Thicket is to find out what you are made of. Find out if you are fit to stay. Halfway across the shallow brown waters I called to her and told her that Snavely the snake was right behind her, grinning in a little vee wake. She not only did not stampede in a foaming rush for the cabin, she did not even look back. She would, as folks say here, "do to go to the woods with."

I installed her in the cabin. Rowed in her bags and bundles and boxes and installed her in the cabin. But things did not go well. The pile of old boards had been five years of mud, flood and blood becoming a house. Now could we stand to live in it? She who had never been married, I who had never been single?

There was comedy. And tragedy. And endless little earthquakes. Putting the pictures back up after one of them, I said, "Damn, gotta go below and get my hammer."

"Use mine, I brought my toolbox."

"Look, there is a difference in hammers. It has to do with casting, forging, weight, balance and a subtle curve on the hammer face. I would rather make the trip downstairs than try to use some light-weight, discount, two-dollar hammer. Someday, when you are older, I will let you use my Bluegrass. I built this whole house with it, including throwing it a time or two. Maybe you could feel the difference of an eight-dollar hammer." I did not pat her on the head, but might as well had. She got up with that little smile again, dug out her hammer and handed it to me. It was a Plumb, a nine-dollar Plumb and an ounce heavier than my Bluegrass. Ace, I said to myself, you're in a heap of trouble, boy.

We were not easy with each other. The smallest thing became a point of contention that needed proving far into the night. "Age difference," I decided; "apples and oranges arguments." In truth I had no idea of what she was talking about, or why. It seemed perfectly reasonable to me that I should be the captain of this vessel, and solely responsible. We got down to carefully choosing words. Bad.

Across the supper table, far into the night, while Village Creek passed outside, unsung, she confounded me with speeches. "I love you, Gordon, the human being, not a newspaper clipping, or a framed testimonial. I am proud of your accomplishments, but they do not replace the contact of a real human being.

"I want you to love me, the human being, not a young chick to show off, or any one of the component parts—but the total me. I want you to be you, and me to be me, and for us to share as much as possible in the process.

"I wish that we were steady enough to be at least gently honest with each other without having to weigh words. I wish that we could disagree without fighting, and that when we must fight, we could do it fairly."

Mother of God, what is the fight about? I arm myself each morning before break of day and go forth from the cave to join the hunt. I am a good hunter. I never fail to return to the mouth of the cave before dark and lay down great portions of choice meat. She is warm and dry and safe. As my old pappy used to say to complainers, "Nothing to eat but food, nothing to wear but clothes, nothing to spend but money."

What then is all this crap of coming home, tired but triumphant, and instead of getting my just rewards from her choice and nubile body, we are sitting in cigarette smoke across the table corner and forcing my mind to listen to her hours of intellectualism while I am thinking about her mouth.

Catering to her, being nicer than I can be, pretending we is equals. Yeah. Equals my hairy ear. Now she is off on some long soliloquy that ends with, "I am torn between a desire for independence and a wish to be dependent. I want to feel secure in your affection. I don't like feeling that if I make a mistake I will be abandoned."

Jesus! If she would just shut up and come curl up I could give her some affection she could feel secure in. I liked her better before the word Love got so awful. Then she was saying, "I am a high-class broad, a pretty good copilot and the best you ever had."

Ain't that the living truth. Why is it that all the really good ones are about half crazy?

She is not really a militant or a marcher, and I don't think a castrater. And she knows I am just kidding her about tying her to a post. She is a good-headed woman but she is going to analyze us to death. Right here in our Eden I come home to a fresh apple and a new snake every day. She is so intent, so serious, she thinks all will be lost if we cannot communicate. I think all will be lost if we can't laugh about it.

That is when I challenged her to the Great Sandbar Peeing Contest.

"All right," I agreed, "we are fellow humans, but we are man and woman, and we are not equal in every way. God never intended it that way. If you will follow me, please, I will make for you a small, harmless, but graphic example of men can do some things women cannot do."

I lead her out onto the sandbar. With a stiff, extended toe I drew a line in the sand. Like Travis did at the Alamo with his sword. I asked her to toe this line with me. I had already given up telling her. I had learned to ask.

"What are we going to do now?"

"We are about to have a peeing contest. Drop your drawers."

She thoughtfully moved hers away. Looked at me with the satisfactory amount of submissiveness. Asked, "Same rules apply to both of us?"

"Of course. What kind of tyrant do you think I am?"

"Ok, then, no hands, just like me."

Tight Eye Thicket

Trying to talk out the reasons for our summer of discontented paradise brought more discontent. Once so independent and active, now she was idle in the daytimes. I decided maybe she was starting to rust. Everything else in this Godforsaken floody wilderness does. When it was not raining the temperature and the humidity were both 98. You could breathe it or drink it. We explored endlessly the ideas of her going back to the airline, commuting out of the nearest base, Houston. That would be a mess. Or perhaps going back to college. That sounds fulfilling enough, doesn't it, for this opaque female cat mind I was trying to cope with? You want in the door or out? What DO you want?

"For openers I would like to know where I am. We came here down winding, twisting roads through the forest. I have no sense of the distance or the direction. All I know is that I am alone somewhere out here in the big woods. The sun seems to be coming up in the wrong place."

Here at least was something I could solve. We rented an old Cessna airplane and I flew her over the land, pointing out what landmarks we could see beneath the dense, double-canopied rain forest and calling the compass headings to her. Her fine sense of airmanship from the years as aircrew made her at home and gave her a quick, easy grasp of this sort of orientation.

We flew almost north out of Beaumont, following the Eastex Freeway toward Silsbee, then cut eastward at the bridge and followed the loopings of Village Creek, the inside of her every bend marked with a long crescent of crystal-white sandbar. Found our sandbar and the string of willows that stand out along the creek front, circled over the shiny broad expanse of our tin roof, and I pointed out the scratchings of the trails that led upstream about a quarter mile: "That's Tilley's place." And the other way across the broad finger of water where the creek had abandoned her bed centuries ago and left the false river now called Dutch Lake, we could see the broad pastures of Wladyslaw's cabin. We live on a narrow peninsula. a densely wooded ridge surrounded on three sides by water, and still more water in its center. The nearly landlocked dark and mysterious baygall, shaded by tall cypress, and nudging at our cabin from the rear. Beyond that, stretched the unbroken forest of the Big Thicket, reaching eastward toward the River Neches, then across no-man's-land, the traditional hideout of outlaws and deserters from the Union Army, to the Sabine River, and still more treetops on into the distant haze of Louisiana.

In the springtime this carpet of green is dotted white with magnolia blossoms and dogwoods in bloom. At night only the booming of the hoot owl breaks the stealthy silence where the predators hunt. The place is an ecological masterpiece, a crossroads of the wildest variety of plants and trees where the warm, moist tropical zone overlaps the system of the dry mid-Plains area, and orchids and cactus can be found growing within sight of each other. There are only four brands of poisonous snakes on the North American continent, and all four of them happily share this land with the alligators. But the most dreaded viper is the Big Timber companies. The romantic lumberjack is no longer economical. They come now with dozers and shove down vast acres, pile it up in windrows and stain the skies with its burning. Then as the homeless coons and bobcats sit and watch, they come and set plantations of quick-growing pulpwood pines in rows. These grow up in the gray, shattered battlefield that once rang with berries and the nests of millions of rare and exotic plants and birds.

The Big Thicket, the Tight Eye Thicket, the early settlers called it, and the explorers turned their trade routes to pass to the north or south of it. Even the Indians shunned the place of bogs and bears, pumas and the fevers of a billion flying insects. Everything in it would bite you, sting you or stick you. So dense a man could not walk through it. And yet to some of us this great wilderness holds its charm, draws us in.

Ole Archer Fullingim calls it the "Holy Ghost Thicket." Claims that when he is out and among it, he can speak in tongues. Ole Archer spoke best in hot lead. He published the *Kountze News*, came out every Thursday, ready or not. He composed his columns sitting upright at the Linotype. Wrote justified type right out of his great shaggy head, casting it in hot lead. He was the first man to hire me as a writer. Paid me in mayhaw jelly and gourds.

The printer, as Arch called himself, was among the first to see the irreparable damage and sorrowful loss to the nation as Big Timber diesels moaned their dirge far into the days, shoving down the forest. His cry of rage was a part of what caught at the heart of Senator Ralph Yarborough and started the decades long, and not yet finished, business of saving the Big Thicket by declaring it in Congress as a national park.

I wrote then, and I say again now, that the Big Thicket National Park is a near impossibility for the same reasons that make it imperative: the meanness of the country and the orneriness of the critters that live in it. Kountze and Silsbee are mill towns, and if the saws don't sing there ain't gone be no payday. The very people who live in the Big Thicket fought saving it like a dog with a stick in its mouth.

If an area was about to be declared a park site, the owners would spite-cut it. When the record-setting largest magnolia tree was pronounced, the old nesters went out and felled that ancient beauty. "Ain't gone be no tourist here if they ain't got nothin' to come and see."

When the first sightings of the thought-to-be-extinct ivory-billed woodpecker were reported, and college teams and photographers searched the woods for that shy giant bird, a redneck brought in a fresh-killed one and pitched it on Archer's desk, saying, "Was that what you're looking for?" Nobody has seen another one.

These are some of the tales of the Big Thicket I told to Diane. Giving her plenty of room to run. She went to her books. "Here in *Future Shock* it explains how people can expect stress with any change of their life-styles; read this. . . ."

"You mean the shock of coming from first-class cabin service on the JFK-DAL jet to being a redneck princess with feet of bare?"

"No, I was thinking more of you. Of being alone here after having built this place from the center of a big family and then having them grow up and go their separate ways. That's really best, you know."

I had been expecting her to not adjust, to be out running up and down the sandbar barking at airliners, when it was me who was glomped back in my workshop fashioning a new ironbound oaken chest, this one marked Father Guilt, and packing it carefully full.

And trying to get in touch with what was real, we would walk the sandbar while Village Creek blushed to summer thunderstorms, her breast rising and falling over the sands.

She would leave clear tidal pools and the creatures caught in them were doomed. We would dig channels to the sea and watch the fingerlings and tadpoles skitter free. But we had to rescue the clams. The clams would sense the pressure change and spiral in to the central deep and bury themselves in dark panic, waiting for the water to shrink away and death.

We would walk the sandbar in quiet, looking for the blowholes and scoop up the little fellows and set them back out in the mainstream shallows and they would breathe thanks to us. "Pshh-Thlanks-sss."

And in such twilights the blue heron would wingbeat slowly by and circle and perch in the Lookout Tree and fix us with a disapproving eye. Taking care of slow-witted clams was her business, as evidenced by the stately handspan of tracks on the sand each morning and all the dirty dishes of opened clamshells she left.

"Do not be selfish of the shellfish, oh, mighty bird, do we not protect thee too?"

And she would stretch her yard-long neck, whet her bill a time or two and say, "God has given you two plenty to do minding your own untidy affairs. You keep minding mine, and what you are going to get here is a whole generation of inept clams."

And Diane was thinking of generations. She wanted to talk about babies. I absolutely balked. I think I said something as unfortunate as "messing up my playhouse." I know I warned her that this was how I lost the first wife.

"I'm sorry for you," she began; "you're an emotional parasite.

You prey upon the love of others, but you don't know love. You can't return love. You are only a technician at bringing forth the response you need. I am sorry for you. You have used me, and all the others, but mostly I am sorry for you."

What is this crazy woman talking about? Any one of them would give their front seat in hell to get me back.

She was going on: "I give up. The situation is impossible. I'm not angry. I'm not hurt. Each of us needs something the other cannot provide. It really is best that we stop right now before we do more damage to your comfortable life-style and to my future happiness."

I felt only relief as I went around emptying her piled-up ashtrays. In my mind I was conjuring up her replacements. She would be middle-aged, placid, an excellent cook and housekeeper and have a stunningly beautiful eighteen-year-old daughter. The only requirement before I moved them in would be to confirm that neither of them could read, write or speak English.

We slept in separate rooms that night. An armed camp. I pictured the inside of my skull as the control panel of the Apollo spacecraft. I was familiar with it from the assignments. I reached up and methodically powered down. Snapped off each small chrome microswitch in an orderly manner, leaving only "automatic hold." Everybody should work out a way to preserve his sanity the best he can. I could hear her in the other room, tossing, turning, lighting cigarettes. Poor kid. Suddenly she was standing there beside my bed. Moonlight filtered through the trees. "I won't fall for it again. Enough is enough," I calmly told my spacecraft.

Then she opened her robe. Held it open, arm's length. Stood there. "Take one last good look," she said, and was gone.

DAMN, woman can play hard games.

It was the time of the boxes again. Boxes, bundles and bags, up and down the stairs, strangers passing. But the work cooled us. When it was time to get into the truck, I couldn't find her. I made the rounds. There she was, a little form huddled down on the creek front at the edge of the sandbar. I stood behind her. She scooped up the water of Village Creek and held it in her hands to the tears. Then she looked up at me, made a jerky gesture that included our willows, the great silent face of the forest on the other bank, summer sail clouds moving overhead. "Will you please," she said so low, "explain to all this why I am leaving?"

Gone. Safely delivered she was, back into her life. Ole Ace standing up in the cockpit, smoke and flame curling. I drove back to the camp. Peace and quiet at last. Peace and quiet fairly shouting at me from the empty walls. I did not dare go look out at the creek front for fear she would still be there, huddled. I mixed a tall, cool one, a "Moontang" (my summer drink invention; Tang and vodka), lit up a good cigar and leaned well back in my favorite chair. Above me, written in black wax marker on the wooden beam, right where she knew I would lean back and look up with the comfort of good drink and cigar, she had printed: I, DIANE TITTLE, LIVED HERE IN LOVE. JULY, 1973, NOV. 3, 1973.

I fled. Routed. Rolled into bed, looked up from my copy of *Hustler*. There on the beam it said, HERE TOO.

I called a conference of me. Bax, this is serious. You may have to have this place exorcised.

It had been bad enough just driving in, knowing she would not be there. The woods closing in on me, coming into this house, just emptied out in shouting and tears. White mists were rising like ghosts of the damned off the face of the Village Creek, saying, "Bax, you sorry son of a bitch, we rise up as wraiths, we dance about you and we cover you. We are the witches' broth of all your rotten sins, the face of every woman. We surround you now, shut up in your cabin of tears and echoes; what streaks that windowpane is a tear from Diane. You will never know how wrong you were for turning away the one woman who can ever know and love you."

Gone. I had sent Diane away. I wonder what would have happened if I could have been honest enough with her to tell her what was really eating on me? That with all this paradise, I couldn't get rid of wondering what was happening back at "my house"? Was ole Mary all right? Was she taking this ok? What the hell is the matter with me? This ain't the way studs are supposed to think when they make their breakout.

Daylight came. Was that butterflies or dry leaves blowing past the window? Is this the end of summer, or the beginning of winter? I just can't peel off twenty-seven years of marriage. An ordinary snake can. He just wiggles under a tight rock and leaves the whole thing. Dry as a husk, head to tail. You can find a clean snakeskin and it tells you two things: The snake is gone. And he don't fit in there no more.

It's daylight and they are gone. All gone, my tribe, the whiskey bottle and Diane's sweet young face.

I came out of the woods, two red eyes, around the curves, between the trees, out into the clean Sunday. Maybe I could just go over to Molly's. She and Alan were having a little party, just some of their friends over. The young people came smooth and unmarked. I stood around awhile, looking down the muddy road of my life. I felt a thousand years old.

I went home to Mary. Had to stand outside and ring the doorbell. I remember the day I hung that door. Bright brass new screws. We had worn out the old latch and the hinges. That's a lot of kids, fanning in and out. I had a key, still had it, but it didn't seem right to use it now.

We hugged each other standing in the door, and crying. Then we stood apart and looked at each other. She invited me in and I complimented her on the new carpets and the way she had done the den over. We did what you might call "visiting." The kids looked ill at ease too.

"Hi, Daddy . . . we, uh . . . miss you."

"Well, you guys are welcome up at the creek anytime. What you got now is two homes. One in town, one in the country. Pretty lucky, eh? Ha ha."

I knew I could never come back here.

I knew there would be a full moon on the creek tonight and I would sit alone where Diane and I sat catty-cornered at the kitchen table. One cup of coffee, deep in the belly of the night. Maybe this is what they always talked about as hell.

You go to hell for fornicating, Ace. You did it to them all, and wasn't that a ball? Now you have made the grand, ultimate conquest; you did it to yourself.

The car took me down streets. Alone, you wretch, alone. You really don't belong anywhere.

Maybe I'm hungry? I pulled into one of those ghastly carnival-painted Bogus Burger places and went inside. So warped up that I could see hell in a hamburger joint.

The Bogus Burger

I looked at the first young fellow frying the patties. A pleasant, round-faced oaf, spotted with blond pimples, not a flicker of thought within his eyes, just standing there, putting in his hours. I thought of him as a tiny, kicking, squalling baby, his mother dandling him on her knee and saying to admiring friends and neighbors, "He's going to grow up and be a hamburger cook as soon as he gets his pimples."

A well-dressed lady behind me made the error of asking the griddle man to "Leave off the mustard, please." Griddle Man put her in her place and reassured silence in the line with a jerk of his head toward the next man on the assembly line. "Tell him whatcha wan onnit."

The next man, the accessories man, was a tall brunet, almost handsome, but with a very shallow head, and his eyes were vacant too, like the second-story windows of an empty rooming house. I pictured him and the girl he was having an affair with. Together in her little apartment, staring silently at the TV. He will knock her up, and in a few years they will have a little house on Easy Down Dale, and a little child to sit and stare with them as they drift slowly down the tepid, turgid stream of TV.

Next in line, at cheese or not to cheese, was a dark girl. Our eyes met, then darted away. She was people watching too. Like burglars never steal from each other, people watchers never watch each other.

Now the lines of people and food were about to merge, but first had to ooze through the fat girl at the cash register who was stoppering up the whole thing. This girl wasn't just fat, she looked like an air hose had been connected to her navel and she had been in-flated all over. She looked new fat, like she hadn't been wearing her fat very long and hadn't gotten used to it. She had a slow, fluid movement, like a very large catfish inside a small aquarium.

Her head was large, round, and made larger by the teased-up bleached white hair, it sat upon her shoulders like a pumpkin half covered by hay in a frosty field. When she bent down, the black roots, grown about a half-inch long along the crown, provoked the imagination.

She bent down to get a fresh roll of pennies. Most cashiers rap a roll of coins smartly against the edge of the cash drawer and the coppers spill smartly into place. This girl, with people stalled on one side, hamburgers on the other, slowly unwrapped the pennies, carefully put them in the drawer and then seemed to be perplexed about what to do with the wrapper. I could almost see her going over in her mind the company regulations about what to do with the wrapper the pennies come in. Not being able to reach a decision, the fat white fingers simply released the paper and it drifted down to find its own place.

Then she asked the company questions to the man ahead of me. "Do you want french fries?" He did. I watched in happy, horrid fascination as she slowly turned to the bin and started dredging up french fries and putting them into the sack for the customer to eat, using the pennies fingers, giving the man ten million exciting new germs and the zingy taste of copper. Halfway through the operation she sensed that her hair was rising up in back and reached back with the pennies and potatoes fingers to smooth it down, leaving a slick swath in her hair, and then contentedly going back to dredging up french fries.

I drove back to Village Creek with the hamburger squished up against the steering wheel, mustard and mayonnaise and soaked pieces of paper between my fingers. Everything about the cabin said, "She's gone." The walls I had built in sunshine looked darkly down, accusing me.

I was like an old gray cat, keeping close to the walls. Then I began to find her notes.

With the key: "Welcome home! I leave this building, our home, in your care. Be good to it. Be happy here. Here is love in every corner."

In the mailbox: "There are no words for my love."

In the washing machine: "½ cup soap on top of the clothes."

Desk drawer: "You are free. You can leave me and travel forever —but you will never be beyond the reach of my love."

Peanut jar: "You need food! You cannot think and work on peanuts, and I just happen to know a teachable cook."

Coffee jar: "No, no, let me get up and fix it."

In my shorts: "My bottom misses your bottom."

Stove top: "Love does not cause cancer."

Toothbrush holder: "I don't want to taste toothpaste, I want to taste you."

The mirror: "Look close. I am here."

And she left a pair of her panties under my pillow.

I was starting to reel. To stagger around the place. On a creek-front window: "The misty morning creek is so beautiful. The air is thick, a brightening blue, everywhere. And from here the silhouette of the wintering trees. I love you."

More notes in the bed: "I have placed my heart in your hands— my life within your reach—sleep tight."

On a headband she had left: "Keep this for me until I come home."

Booze was not the answer. I could not even get drunk. I just lay stupid abed and looked at the winter trees etched against the stars. The rotten-notes campaign was bad, but what made it double bad and funny was I had done the same thing to her. In her boxes and bags and bundles. She said it was like a Jewish mother giving her only son a lifetime subscription to *Reader's Digest* as a wedding gift. Every month for the rest of his life, here comes Mamma.

I got the giggles and started trying to sort out why I was planning to see if I could go bring her back when I ought to be celebrating being free. I went over all the possibilities. A few really great fantasies. Why Diane? What was I missing the most about her right this minute?

The only thing that confounded me the most about her: her mind.

Next day in the mailbox:

Dearest Gordon,

It is early. The time of the false dawn. Twenty-four hours ago I was seeing these glories across the mist-shrouded creek.

I'll bet when you brought in the mail you saved this for last, like you do the funnies with the Sunday morning paper.

No plea in this one. Just that I miss you. We were good together—good for each other—with each other. You bring me a spark of life I found nowhere else.

You are so fine. I wish I could ease some of your suffering. If you could accept yourself as I accept you, you could know peace.

You are a most human man, with human failings, far outweighed by your goodness and strength. I am a high-class broad of impeccable taste and generally correct. And I love you. Diane.

My letter to her said:

All of today was nothing but things to save up for telling to you, and now I am home and the evening light change over the creek has started.

I brought your letter in from the mailbox in my shirt. I wanted to keep it warm. My endurance of my personal hell is running out. My brains are wrecking my body. I may settle for just a gut feeling in lieu of a thunder-clap. Marry for love I don't understand and let the future work itself out. I am going to stay on this creek forever anyhow. I was wrong. But I don't know how to handle you.

I brought her back, and the wildwoods rang all around, all around. But after the passions, there was still something of us that was like a grenade with the pin pulled. We decided to go for outside help.

The shrink was an old friend who had known me most of my life. We were in his warm living room. I had never noticed how sane he looked. He heard us out. We tumbled it. Did poorly. Handed the grenade back and forth; neither of us could recognize what it was. Neither could he. He looked at my savaged old face, and then at fresh Diane. He ran out all his sensors, got back, "Does not compute." He said to me, not unkindly, and in truth, "Baxter, you are crazy as old Hogan's goat." Then he turned his professional skill to Diane. "He is a dirty old man. And you, young lady, must be a dirty little girl."

We decided to get married.

The exact way that Diane phrased it was: "Bet your heap, sleep in the street." My ole pappy used to say it just like that. And I always knew then he was drawing to an inside straight and I had him sure as hell.

Chapter 7

The Wedding

30 December 1974.

The Wedding was held at Village Creek, and the creek rose to the occasion. For the twelfth time in twelve months Village Creek rose and flooded the roads, leaving the cabin an island.

The groom arose early and went out into the floody forest and called, "Who will come and deck my halls to welcome the coming of the bride?"

"Take me," cried the youpon, "my berries are bright and red!" "Me too," called the holly, "my leaves are Christmas green." "And me," said the big bay tree, "and crush some of my bay leaves and fill the house with the smell of spices." And they all crowded eagerly into my arms and I decked the house in living green. Made arches and arbors over the windows and doorways. And there are wild flowers that bloom in the wintertime on Village Creek. These I gathered into a bride's bouquet, full and bright and laced with fern, and I took the scented moss from the oak to make a place for her hand to carry it, and borrowed from yesterday's garbage bag a wire tie to bind it all with love.

It was a High Church and solemn Episcopalian wedding service, with a few elements of situation comedy. The wedding party could be roughly divided into two groups, the "straights" and the "freaks."

The bride's family, geologist, schoolma'am, all properly suited up, were rowed to the cabin by the groom who also served as ferryman. The groom's family, miscellaneously employed or unemployable, came in jeans, sandals and Mexican flower sack shirts. Eddies of smoke curled up out of the beards, and some appeared to be walking across the water and flying in the windows.

This group, warily lined up for the wedding picture, would have confounded a caption writer trying to sort out the goes-withs. The father of the bride and his prospective son-in-law are of the same generation, both in their fifties. The bride and the groom's oldest daughter, both lovelies in their early thirties. The priest, grandly vested in best robes, was the groom's only brother, Tom. The best man, Alan, was returning the favor; the groom had handed off his own daughter Molly to Alan just a short ten years ago. Ring and flower bearers were assorted grandchildren of the groom. Hello. You still there?

The bride wore a two-piece outfit of ivory lace, full-length skirt and long-sleeved blouse, bought at Neiman-Marcus. Her beige sandals were found on the $2 table at the Fair Inc. of Beaumont. The groom wore his cast-iron marryin' and buryin' suit of navy blue, and a look of surprise.

The marriage license was stabbed to the cabin door with a Buck knife, the handle garlanded with an ornamental bow of red velvet. The ceremony was performed in the hushed whispers of Village Creek, the party grouped out on the open rocking-chair gallery whose low open banisters and broad stairway led down to the rushing, muddy waters and the broad vista of midstream willows and the somber silent forest beyond. At the prayer, while the wedding party knelt on the bare porch, a flock of southbound Canadian geese flew low overhead. Wedding music was the cry of the old wild goose, whose symbolism caused the groom to begin to secretly weep.

Alan filled two new wedding glasses with old wine afterward, and the newlyweds drank a toast to each other, then hurled the glasses at the wall, lest they ever be used for some lesser purpose. The right smart crack and shattering of the two wineglasses hitting the wall caused some of the wedding guests to instinctively duck, well thinking that the fight had started again already.

Wine *botas* were lifted high, grandchildren formed hands and danced a circle of delight around Diane, shouting to her, "Do you live here now?" My daughter Molly answered, "Yes. She is your grandfather's bride." She and Diane looked at each other and laughed at how that sounded, then Molly uncovered the ceremonial pot of chili. The two young women looked into each other's eyes for a moment, then closed the short step between them in a long hug.

I rowed them all ashore with a broken oar and we began our life as man and wife. I sat at the table and she, who has served ten thousand cups of coffee down the pitching and heaving aisles of jet transport planes in the dark and storm of night, did walk to me across an absolutely flat and still cabin floor, trip and spill a scalding hot cup of coffee right into my lap.

And howled with mirth while I was up, doing a wild Zorba wedding dance, coffee running on down my leg to boil my foot in my shoe. I danced, screaming and vaulting into the bedroom closet, began to ferociously throw out all her clothing into a heap on the floor.

"What, for God's sake, are you doing?"

"It's over! Finished! You woman's libber. You will never convince me that wasn't planned. It's back to the Boeing 727 for you!" We collapsed in giggles, and she let the toast burn.

Still Got Everything?

We had been married for six round-eyed days when Diane found a lump in her breast. In my rutting I was resentful. "See there? Love does cause cancer." Either that, or reading too many books. We went to see Cliff Dunlop and he listened to Diane's history of cancer. Cervix, 1970, found early, successful surgery, no recurrence, and she could still bear children. But she must now go to the hospital for a breast biopsy. That's where you go to sleep and wake up not knowing if you will have one breast or two.

I was surprised at how badly I was taking all this. The dull rage, the bitter prayers. "Dear God, spare us." Dear God mutilates. "Cliff, does it have to be like this?" "Yes, Gordon, there are always alternatives to medicine, but statistically this is best. It doesn't feel like cancer, but with her history I must be sure. I do think you got a ninety percent chance that it is just cystoidal."

I beat against the doors. Diane consoled me, but softly said, "It's me who should be getting the sympathy." And I took her in my arms. But could I enjoy both her breasts again? Both of us knowing that each kiss might be a good-bye to the doomed right one. What would she look like? Do they just toss it? Why not take it to a good taxidermist? That is crude? So is being thrown out with the garbage crude. Diane crept close, whispered, "Hold me. Just hold me . . ."

We tried to talk out the shock. Will I love her with just a solo tit? When I reach for her and my hand comes to a flattened scar? Much holding close and thinking, Farewell, little perfect breast. The day came to go to the execution.

Cliff was two men; he was my friend and he was our doctor. We talked of airplanes out in the hall, then he went in and marked her breast with an X. "Cut along dotted line," Diane giggled, and I held her and felt her teardrops fall, the doomed little breast nuzzled me, so warm. She fell asleep, like a child, her thumb tucked protectively into her fist. Twin brave mounds breathed beneath her blue flannel nightie. I stood watch. How do they do it? Will he lift it off tenderly? One long slice or lots of little whittles? Will they just chuck it away, flopping, nipple weeping? She stirred in her sleep, tucked a hand under me and murmured, "—now I'm safe." Dear God. Oh, dear God!

They came and got her, rolled her away on the gurney, looking up at the lights. The swinging doors barred me. I stayed rooted to that spot. Never moved. Go on, thirst. Go on, feet, hurt. I made my eyes go away. People came and went, whispering, "That's Gordon Baxter standing out there looking like that." "Yes, they are cutting off his wife's breast. His second wife, y'know." "My, doesn't he look fierce?" "Yes, he is trying to suffer pain. He should."

I stood out there a thousand years. Tears came, tears dried. I rummaged through my soul. Nothing.

The swinging doors burst open, he was holding something, actually holding it up in a jar for me to see. He's grinning. "She's ok. It's benign. Cystoidal. She's ok." Why me crying like this? Go on, y'all, stare. Goddam you, stare.

She's waking up in her room, talking woozy talk. "Um-m, we still got everything?"

"No. Your breast was ok, but they took your ass."

Soft, hurting laugh. "Oh, no they didn't, you wouldn't be so calm." Feeling herself feebly: "What is this?"

"An ice pack."

"You sure there is something under it?"

Then she wants to know if she has clean sheets and if they brought her any ice water. Then those long butterfly lashes come to rest on her cheeks. "Um-mmm . . . clean sheets, ice water, and I got my man. I'm back in business."

Next morning I shared this on the air. What I don't tell they make up for themselves and they get it wrong. Tell it all, take your lumps. This right on top of just having told them I was remarried. I only got a few hate calls but those are the ones I keep. Suffer, Bax. "You heel, that girl will leave you in a year. . . . God will punish you . . ." The Old Wives' Union, checking in.

If only they could see the goddess of their venom and fear when she is casting her magic spell.

Diane in the Mornings

> She arises like the birth of Venus from the sea,
> Stepping forth from her opening shell.
> She awakens with more beauty
> Than most women can paint on in a day.
> And I'd never grow tired of marveling at her
>   in this unposed moment.
>
> It is not yet 5:00 A.M., I have brought her first coffee.
> Soon she will be in there fixin' me a field hand's breakfast,

But for now she is standing there asleep,
Holding that faded, familiar favorite robe,
About to raise her hands and let it fall around her
In a quickness that is all beauty and grace.

Each morning I nearly hear her mumble the same thing
As she lifts the garment high,
The other morning I listened close and heard the faint phrase
That she starts the day with. . . .

"Pockets go in front."

Anybody Remember Tittle?

There is a real streak of meanness that runs here, through the Bible Belt. The Old Wives' Union saw me and my fresh new bride as a threat that should not go unpunished, nor allowed to spread unchecked. When they recognized Diane in the checkout line at the supermarket, they would stare long enough to burn in eye contact, then snap away, "Hhumph!" lifting their noses and shaking their wattles. If their husbands saw me and Diane alone, they would let their eyes drift over her, meet mine, and silently go, Heh heh heh.

The radio show drew hate calls and mail: "You lecher, it won't last 90 days. Think of po'r ole Mary. . . ."

Diane was furious. "Go public with me. Write me up in your newspaper column. Go on the air with it. Own me. Quit reading all that hate mail out loud on the air. You ever consider just throwing such a letter away? You don't have to wallow in it. You ever think of just telling some of those old biddies on the phone to just go to hell? Say, 'She's my wife and I'm proud of it. Bug off.' Own me, and make me a part of your public too."

I did it, and it worked. I worked her into some of my TV stuff so they could see what she looked like. I encouraged her to call in on my talk shows with her own opinion so they could hear what her mind works like. That was almost too good. Before long I began to get sympathy calls. "Bax, we been listening to Diane on your show. Boy, you may be overmarried. Haw haw haw." But it was good-humored, and I began to realize I was tapping a response from a whole new segment, the divorced people, who had never faced up on the show. I guess they had been hearing me holier-than-thou all these years. There's a lot of them.

I also began to encounter another silent weave in the American social tapestry. Other men, usually in the business world, would let it out through conversation that they too had quit old marriages. It was almost like a secret lodge handshake. The fraternity of those who had made the mid-life bailout of an old, dying marriage. We mostly talked in low voices about how much it cost. All agreed that they had been Solomon wise in the choice of new wives. All of us had married younger women. "Chicks," the term used by those still in their original traces.

My chick was besieged in her cabin during a cold and bitter first winter. The creek was still flooding over the road most of the time, the forest was bare and freezing. I was delighted to come home to this warm cabin and satiate my lust; she seemed to be demanding something out of my mind, some unfulfilled sharing that neither of us could put into words very well. She was alone, and in a hostile and strange land.

We began to see sides to each other that neither of us had been aware of. The "compared with first wife" bomb sat big and black over there, ticking away in the corner. That I had sense enough to tiptoe around. But the tiptoeing was just as bad to her. I tried obvious, easy outs; we talked again of the idea of her going back to college. She could warm to that until her logical mind got to the "college for what?" part. College as a coat hanger? Someplace just to be for a while?

The Crisis of My Kids never developed. They floated in and out with natural casualness. "What we like most, Diane, is what you've done to the ole man's outlook on life. Look at his face." "Diane, he was scripted to double up and drop dead of a heart attack at fifty-four. You gave him life."

Some natural closeness and friendships sprang up; they would just as soon come visit Diane as me. Others came and went with no more or less in the relationship than we had ever known. All of them were smart enough to not carry dirty sacks of "he said, she saids" back and forth.

But Diane became more and more inconsolable. She wanted to talk it out with me at night. We would sit catty-cornered at the kitchen table again, with endless coffee and cigarette butts a growing pile. Her leaning forward, intent. My looking at the thrust of her breasts, wishing we were in bed. Me worrying about having to get up at 4:30 and go do the morning show. "I get up too and fix your breakfast, don't I? Please listen to me."

I labeled this chewing of some unfathomable discontent as "The Midnight Rambles," during which I sometimes had the misfortune of going to sleep.

My attempts at waving off her anger with, "Just come get into your nest . . ." showed me that this woman had a really quick, vicious and blazing temper. I told her that this was unbecoming in women. What she did next I labeled as "Door-slamming, tire-sliding, gear-crashing mad." And telling her that after she came back was like putting out a fire with gasoline.

She wrote me long epistles, met me with carefully-thought-out speeches. She was trying to communicate with me. I was trying to survive her.

"You married me for all the wrong reasons. For my tits and ass. Now you have found out that you have a woman who thinks in bed and you are terrified."

I couldn't understand what all this was about. I treated her just like I've treated all the other women I knew, better in lots of ways. I never carried out the garbage before in my whole life. She would glare at me during morning farting. I tried to explain to her that my father had always said that was a sign of male authority in the house, and I had told her that before we got married. What's the difference between a fart at the Ramada or a fart under my own roof? Was she going to be one of those women who marry an ideal, then try to make the man fit it?

My discontent began to seep into the morning show. What Diane called the "B team" detected it right away and began to cat's-paw me. I told Diane all this. When each ex-girlfriend called, I told

Diane. Secrets in a marriage are like ringing the bark around the trunk of a pine tree. Nothing happens for a while, then the whole thing begins to die at the top. That I learned from last time.

"Get rid of them. Blow them all away." I did. She had too. She sent a note to each man in her past life when we were married. It was all civil and final.

"I feel like I'm swinging on a vine over a pit full of grinning alligators just waiting for me to slip."

"Get rid of them; I did," she cried.

I explained that I had tried to, but I didn't want to hurt anybody's feelings. That they had been very understanding.

"Well, by God, let me handle this." She sent each one a letter edged in black. And a form letter at that, with their names filled after "Dear Miss ———."

Diane got even with me on the "B Team" episode after a trip I made and came back to tell her of boarding a Braniff 727 and playing "Does anybody remember Tittle?" again. This was a good game that would usually win me the favors of the crew and as part of the "family" of airline people. They would sometimes let me sit in first class and give me free whiskey.

On this fateful day I boarded the ramp, said to those crew members within hearing, "Does anybody remember Tittle?" The reaction was the same, always good, she had been well known and senior with the line.

"Yeah, we used to fly Denver together, great girl. . . ."

"What's she doing these days, I heard she got married?"

That's my cue to draw myself up proudly, poke one hand inside my coat like Napoleon and say, "She did. To me."

And the flight engineer leaned out and heartily shook my hand. "Well, congratulations! You must be Curtis. . . ."

Diane, still laughing after I told her this, invoked what we call the "Rover Rule."

Rover was a good ole dog, and he was getting it off in the front yard one Sunday afternoon. All the ladies were lined up in rocking chairs on the front porch, and embarrassed, hiding their faces with their church fans. The men yelled at Rover, threw sticks and one even went in and sloshed a bucket of cold water from the well over Rover. Ole Rover kept on getting it off.

Then one of the ladies got up, reached inside the hallway for the broom and approached Rover with it, handle first. She jabbed, Rover screamed and ran for the trees, tail tucked under him. She turned to the admiring flock and she said,

"Ole Rover, he can dish it out, but he can't take it."

Diane was dynamiting a place for herself in my life on Village Creek. I liked to tell folks that when she moved in I carried all her clothes upstairs in two cardboard boxes and the rest of the two-ton U-Haul truck was full of her books. What I was saying was, "—see, she has a good mind too." But in private when I asked her, "What is the tie that binds?" she would pat her own fanny and say, "That's my tie," just like I taught her.

The cabin actually shivered with her library installed upstairs, and I had to go below and add a center pillar and corner diagonals to the frame of the house. Her precious volumes march around each room, spaced up under the ceiling beams, resting on 2 X 12 shelves of dark ancient pine. "Auchincloss" to "Zarathustra," plays, poets, psychology, philosophy, she spent weeks cataloging. When she unpacked the rest of her stuff I realized she was a "Saver." A pack rat.

"What are you staring at?"

"I'm waiting to see when you dig down to the Teddy bear." And she did too.

I was starting to be afraid we might have to build a second cabin. One for us, one for the museum. She invited me to come downstairs with her, into my shop.

"What's that?"

"My sea chest. I brought it home from the Navy."

"What's in it?"

"My war stuff."

"That was 1943, wasn't it? I was two years old then."

"Ok, ok, I . . ."

"And in that drawer?

"All the bolts and nuts."

"Why not in that other drawer with the screws?"

"Aw, c'mon now."

"And why all the separate trays?"

"Well, to separate the SAE Fine from the CAE coarse . . ."

"Any more, Rover?"

Thus we established the set piece of their being only two categories of stuff in the house. "If it's yours, it's treasure, if it's mine, it's trash." I began to wonder what happened to this hurting little hush puppy I had brought home. This broken bird who had said her life would only be complete if she were married to me. Wasn't I the same great guy who had come dashing down and rescued her from out of the sky? My act hadn't changed at all. Now how come she's got her knees jammed so close together and I'm hearing the hollow sounds of me explaining being me?

I had always been proud of my "trophy corner." Autographed pictures of LBJ, Dean Rusk, Minnie Pearl, Arthur Godfrey and Roy Clark and all the good ships and planes I had ever known.

It's true that all this hangs in the corner where her desk is, but one day I came in and there was our marriage license framed and nailed to the ceiling beam right over our bed.

"Don't you think that's excessive? That almost looks like a trophy."

"Don't complain, or I will have it tattooed on your behind."

Then softly, "Don't you see, Gordon? I'm a person too."

So she did all the walls. Hung our art, the paintings by Frank Gerrietts and by her daddy and all the others and the objects too. But she left my trophy corner. And a creek-bank neighbor's kid was heard to tell his folks, after a visit to our house, "You ought to see the place. They hang stuff on the walls we'd throw away."

And a town lady said, "You have some good art, but what Diane has done with it makes this whole house art."

"Yes, she's quite a person," I heard myself bragging.

Chapter 8

The Nesters

The Tilleys

During these sharp and early times a few good things happened that laid upon us like a healing balm. Most of them originated from our fellow nesters, our Village Creek neighbors. When I first moved Diane in here during the springtime of '74, we went down through the woods and presented ourselves to the Tilleys. Not that we were close to Tilley and Norma Jo at that time, but for the practical reason that there are few of us who live back here in these woods and it is better if we know who is coming and going.

The Tilleys were enjoying the twilight out under the trees in front of their cabin, and here we came, gawking. I didn't know them well enough to make proper introductions, and Norma looks young and pretty as some of her daughters and stepdaughters. So I just went through the "Uh, this is Diane. She is going to live with me awhile." That is not a bad breach of manners in East Texas. Most folks here are uneasy about making proper introductions, and rather than risk getting it wrong, they just don't. We leave folks to sort it out by themselves. Last year when we went to the wedding of

Tilley's son down at the Gulf Service Station in Lumberton, nobody knew anybody and we just all grinned around and shook hands and had a good time. I had to explain the custom to Diane, who felt uneasy.

In time we came to know all the Tilley clan. Her kids, his kids, their kids. Owen Clyde, Joe Dane, Laqueta Monett, Lonnie Lou, Leslie Earl and Grover, Jr. But for this one evening, standing out there in front of all them and laying us on the line, that's how it's done. And Tilley, God bless him, beamed his Saturday-night smile upon Diane and said something like "Hit don't make no never-mind to us."

And not long after that, during one of the worst of the floods, we heard a motorboat, and it tied up to the porch railing, and here came Tilley and Norma Jo. She was carefully carrying something which she brought in and presented to Diane. It was a pan of hot, home-made buttered bread. All the way down that flooded creek. If you were an East Texan I would not have to tell you what all that said. We were home.

Another East Texas custom is to be deadly polite with folks you are not sure around. When Tilley started calling Diane "River-mouse" I knew it was going to be ok. He explained to her: "I call you Rivermouse 'cause you ain't big enough to be a River Rat yet."

Me and Tilley had come a long way. When I first got my land it was him, as president of the Circle G Club picnic grounds that blocked my getting an easement for a sensible road that would have followed the high ground along the creek-bank bluff, out of his acreage and into mine. In every other instance here the giving of a road was the custom. Tilley only knew me by reputation and had said, "Hell, no, we don't want Baxter up here, throwing them wild parties and driving like a drunk madman through our picnic and campgrounds at one o'clock in the mornings." And that's why I had to get the dozer and build the sand bridge and the crooked slick road down through the swamps and damps. It went around Tilley's place.

He never said anything about it, but he came down and sat on his tractor and watched me work on the building, and during the high water I sort of punched through the bushes and made my way across Tilley's place which was a good four feet higher ground. He never said a word about it, and later, when somebody did, he hauled in the membership and got out a vote and gave me a piece of paper that said I could cross his land when my road was unusable. "You ain't got no road anyhow." That was as close as Tilley could come to saying, "I might have been wrong about you." What he did was better than the words.

The Starks

Wladyslaw Stark is the most mild-looking man you may ever meet. His faded denims are the color of his eyes, his seamed face and slightly stooped back say "of the field." When you hear the Polish brogue and see the wreath of smiles, you almost expect him to touch his cap. A good man, this gentle Polish immigrant, perhaps a contented peasant before coming here to the land of the free.

He was a highly trained military man in the regular Polish Army, in command of a machine-gun outfit. They met the panzer divisions first in 1939. The chances of his being alive today are as thin as you can slice it.

From the German side of Poland, he was six years a slave, assigned to a large German farm family. He saved all their lives on the last day of the war.

When the familiar sounds of battle told Wladyslaw that both sides were about to sweep across him again, his military mind understood the great risk of being casually killed in the confusion and haste of either the retreating German Army or the advancing Americans. Soon random shells were dropping and the advancing lines were near enough to hear small-arms fire. The German farm family headed for the cellar.

Wladyslaw moved out into the open fields and dug slit trenches, enough for all. Then explained that the very strength of the big stone farmhouse would be its destruction. That a Tiger tank would drive in the back wall and conceal itself with a forward field of fire out the front window for the advancing Americans, who would then recognize this as a strong point, call down enough artillery to blow the farmhouse to dust. The tank would drop into the cellar.

From the slit trenches the family watched the gray-clad German infantry come out of the woods, laying a heavy covering fire. If they could survive this, and the shooting of the advancing Americans, it would all be over. Then a young and very zealous German machine gunner dropped into the slit trench with Wladyslaw and his huddled flock. Wladyslaw watched in dismay as he opened up on the first line of Americans coming out of the woods. Mortars would be next, dropped into the slit trench to silence that machine gun.

Wladyslaw says he was thinking, —to live through all of it, and then get killed on the very last day. He says he picked up a heavy piece of cord wood and hit the machine gunner. "But how? Wasn't he wearing his steel helmet?" I asked. Wladyslaw grinned mildly, made an abrupt chopping motion at the back of the neck.

Veronica was taken very young as slave labor to build Me-109 engines. For German fighter planes. She has very little to say of those years except that the bombings were bad.

After the war some American families were great enough of heart to sign for displaced persons and bring them to this country. The Barrys did this.

This you should know in case you are a historian in later years trying to figure out why, along a short stretch of Village Creek, pure Polish is spoken in some of the warmest of homes. And why some of the outstanding honor students at Silsbee High School have such funny-sounding names when the rest of the roll call sounds like morning muster for Her Majesty's Massed Pipers and Drummers.

Veronica and Wladyslaw Stark had been good to us during our first winter of discontent. Like the Tilleys, our only other neighbors on the river had sensed Diane's isolation and welcomed us warmly. I had held back from taking her there. Four years ago the Starks had helped me and my family clear the land for the cabin site. They were old country Catholics. I was afraid they would disapprove of me and my new bride. Diane smoldered. I took her there. I had reckoned not with the heart of gentle Veronica and Wladyslaw. She wrapped Diane in her arms, took her into the kitchen and did what farm-raised Polish ladies do best: she fed us and loved us.

Now in the midst of this record-high and longest flood, I suddenly had a chance to give some of this back to Veronica and Wladyslaw. She had not seen her brother Marion in thirty-two years. He was coming. Could I bring him the last mile of the way from Poland down Village Creek to their wooded island knoll?

Thirty-two years ago when the jackbooted Nazi army marched into Poland, one of the lesser tragedies, unnoticed by history, was the grief that eight-year-old Marion Pilip felt when he saw his beloved big sister Veronica marched away to the slave camps.

Three decades had smoothed the stones of history; the doors between nations began to open. Marion wrote to his sister of his dream of coming to visit her in America. Could she meet him in New York? More letters, explaining to Marion about the distances in America; Polish-speaking friends would meet him in Houston.

All this took three trips for Marion from his successful tobacco and fruit farm into Warsaw. Each trip to Warsaw required three days each of officialdom. At last he was boarding the plane, carrying two small, finely made Russian watches as gifts to his yet unseen niece and nephew in America. The watches set off the security alarms, Marion was grabbed, taken to a small room, stripped and put to the wall. "All these years of trying; now I have ruined it."

But after much delay, and his clothing picked to the very seams, Marion was on the way. But no, New York was socked in with fog; after circling for hours the big Polish Jet Liner was diverted to Boston only after declaring a low fuel emergency. Something about no agreement between U.S. and Communist governments for landings anywhere except in New York.

This time it was our side that kept the sick and weary planeload of humans locked up in the cabin overnight until the jet was refueled and could fly back to New York next day. They never set foot in the Colony of Massachusetts.

Their first night in the land of the free was spent as American prisoners in the plane.

In New York, Marion had just taken his first sigh of relief when the cold hands of U.S. officials halted him. There was no record of him being ticketed on into Houston, or anyone to meet him there. More delay while JFK Airport was searched to find someone who could speak Polish, the phone rang in the Stark home on Village Creek, New York authorities calling Veronica. Yes, she had indeed furnished a ticket, look again. The clerk at Delta looked in the last place, the top middle drawer of his desk. The ticket lay on top.

Marion was on his way again, but one more ocean separated him from his sister; Village Creek was flooded and so were the roads for miles around the bottomland. Over the phone Marion said never mind, he would wade in. His sister told him it was chest deep. He offered to swim. She told him he would be met by a newly married couple with a small boat at Huck Barry's at the creek, the high road by the bluff.

Marion was a handsome man, well dressed and in the very prime of life. Excitement was in his cheeks at being only a few more miles from seeing his sister at last. When he met Diane at the brim of the troubled creek, his greeting was profuse. A Bridal Blessing, or a traditional Polish greeting to the bride.

The words were foreign to us, but the meaning unmistakable. His hands drew altars and archways in the air about her head and he dressed them with flowers of words. Diane blushed at such honors. Ole Huck Barry, who with his brothers had found a home for Veronica and Wladyslaw on Village Creek back in the forties when they were displaced persons, had learned to speak some Polish from working with them at the sand dryer. He laughed and told Marion in Polish and us in English that we had it all wrong. That was no Bride's Blessing, that was a Polish rain dance to bring more water to the creek.

Still laughing we went down through the weeds, loaded in the suitcase and launched the little jon boat and watched in quick horror as it began to fill up and sink. Thieves had stolen my paddle, my shear pins and even taken the drain plug out of the back where the water spurted in. I had taken the motor with me.

In one quick flash of anger I understood why they used to hang horsethieves on the spot. To take a man's only means of getting there is serious. Marion seemed to say the Polish equivalent of, "Oh, no, not one more thing." But unlike the delays of the ponderous marchings of governments, here was something that the strength and skills of this farm man could deal with. He seemed almost relieved to be able to physically grasp a problem at last.

With powerful embracing arms he swooped down on the sinking boat, lifted it clean out of the water and shook it dry. He broke off a small willow limb, and with quick and practical hands he carved it to a tapered plug and launched the boat. It leaked badly around the plug. He indicated the need for a piece of cloth for a gasket. Diane understood at once, stepped aside and reappeared handing him a pair of nylon bikinis. Without so much as the flicker of an eye, Marion drove the plug through the folds to a watertight fit.

Later in the warm kitchen with his sister, sharing with us the sausage, honey and lightning-like Polish vodka, the story was told, as I am sure it will be retold to gales of laughter in the farmhouse in Poland, of how after all those troubles the last mile of the way was made on a pair of the bride's drawers.

But I wish you could have seen him on the way in. Sitting up so straight in the bow of the boat in his fine new Moscovite coat. Seen them in their reunion on Village Creek, as they met and embraced in tears and laughter at the water's edge.

Pearl

Suddenly in the midst of all this flooding we got a dry cat. She just came weaving out of the woods one day and said, "Hi. I'm the kitty."

Oh, she was shy. Arching and purring around the edge of the door, ready to dart away at the first sign that we were not the folks that needed a cat. Looking at her round and kittenful sides, I told Diane that apparently she had not always been so shy and swift. Diane picked her up, got that motherly look in her eyes. The cat looked at Diane and got that motherly look in her eyes. We voted. We got a cat by a two-to-one majority.

What's your name? we asked the poor, pregnant pearl-colored kitty. "Poor Pregnant Pearl," she sniffed. We all agreed that she would be an outside cat. Oh, yes, by all means, an outside cat. It was amazing and absolutely beautiful to see how quickly Pearl was able to train Diane to her neat little needs. From a humble pad outside by the door, to a comfy box on the porch, to being inside and owner of the rug, all in three days. And after only two tries she had taught Diane which brand of cat food she preferred.

The training of Diane went apace. One cold and wet day Diane told Pearl to go outside and use the bathroom. Now everyone knows that cats do not go outside and use the bathroom on cold and wet days. This standoff was resolved after Pearl improvised a convenience station in a far corner back under the bed that no one was using anyway. Diane cast Pearl out. The cat sat outside the French doors and glared at Diane in disbelief. Then she was gone two days. Diane was inconsolable.

Pearl came back. Marched in, laid down her hat and gloves and said in a low voice, "We are not going to let that happen again, are we?"

Tilley came by for coffee, saw Pearl airing around. We told him about the two terrible nights she must have spent out there in the floody woods. Tilley really got a kick out of that, and telling us he had seen Pearl lots of times about a mile down the road, hanging around ole man Giblin's house. "She lives there, left him lots of kittens."

So our Pearl, our Poor Pregnant Pearl was running two houses. Then Wladyslaw came over to bring us some fresh tomatoes. He was pulling his hay cart behind his tractor and his kids were having a good-time ride. They saw Pearl and cried out, "Hey, look, Daddy, there's Duchess!" "Yeah, that's Duchess all right, and if she ever comes back and has any more kittens with us I'm going to kill her." Pearl turned her coat collar up around her ears and kept moving.

So Pearl had three houses. And previous family commitments. And here we thought we had sheltered some poor pregnant teenager who had been taken advantage of. We all stared at Miss Pearl. She sort of grinned. A small-tooth grin, and fluttered her eyes. "Well, you never asked."

Wolf

A week after Pearl we got Wolf. The Lord in His infinite mercy looked down upon us in our Eden and He sent us a large shaggy dog.

Our first reaction to him was fear. He just materialized out of the shadows and bones of this place, a gray shape, running back and forth by the baygall, swinging his great head. What now? Crazed dog? I went out and stood a respectful social distance. He stopped, we stared into each other's eyes. I was telling my body to not let me smell like fear, if there is anything to that story.

The dog walked right up to me and sat down. "What's your name, fella?" In a low, throaty voice he said, "Wolf."

He was starving. A rack of bones. Crescents of white underfur showed along his sides where his coat was shrunken to his ribs. I touched him, stroked him. He felt rough enough to strike a match on.

Diane came out and knelt down with us. She touched him and he shivered all over. He looked at her, back at me; his eyes were pure liquid brown. We had a dog.

It was like we had expected him all along. Like the spirits knew we had a German shepherd in our hearts.

There was mothering, crooning, cradling his head. Diane was busying around, setting out plates of food. He was starving, but he had dignity. He would turn away from the food to thank Diane again and again. We had to go inside before he would eat. She put down an old quilt by the door. He curled up on it with a quivering sigh that trembled the leaves on the trees.

Who was he? Where did he come from? Why did he decide to leave there, what of the unknown journey through the wilderness? The only thing Wolf could tell us was that he was home now.

Wolf took out instant guardianship of all this land and management of the creek front. Folks who came to see us would stop at the barricade of long white teeth and hail us from their cars. One day Wolf announced the arrival of a pickup, and we looked out the window and there was ole Davis from the utility company trying to read the electric meter from where he was sitting on the top of the company truck. We went down and made the proper introductions and Wolf memorized his name. We never had to tell him twice.

But Wolf was not so smart about everything. After several sleepless nights and lying cursing in my bed, I finally convinced Wolf that the water well pump coming on automatically was not one of the things he had to bark at all night to save us from.

He also seemed to be bothered with hearing earthworms. He would cock his head, run in circles, leap up in the air and crash down jaws first and tear up great chunks of the yard. Same thing out on the creek front. His waterfront patrol keeps him terribly busy, especially the weekend fishing traffic. He has to be on duty to give all the boats a bark-a-long, then speeds back along the shoreline to skimmer bird dip the waves of the boat wake where they ripple ashore. At quiet times, when me and Di are sitting by the water's edge, he will be with us in his Noble Dog pose, then cock his head and suddenly go into a frenzy of pouncing into the sand, throwing up great gouts of sand and water and digging holes with his paws and jaws. We decided he hears clams too.

Wolf was the first to teach me that some dogs will swim for the fun of it, freezing weather or no, and along with his other marine custodial duties he has decided that it is unthinkable for any boat to put out from the shore without himself aboard. We have the pirogue, the canoe and the small outboard skiff, all tender-tipsy boats. From the shore Diane enjoys watching me, the captain, decide if I am going to invite Wolf aboard for every voyage, or will she enjoy seeing me get about five feet out and then try to cope with about 80 pounds of dog who has just taken a high running dive into the boat. The arms and legs waving, paddles flying, the crashing and frothing of white water and great sea curses being roared. The indignity of shallow-water capsizing and sinkings. Simple girl, easily amused. I may put her aside someday.

But there are two sides to the coin of the laughing dog. Like the time Diane took Wolf to the vet in the car. Wolf was not fattening up much. Tilley is a good dogman. He said a dog that eats dirt and stays thin probably has worms. That was the day I came home and there was Diane's car out in front, all the doors open, the seats out in the sun and her clothes hanging in the trees everywhere.

I was tired; it had been a long, ratsy day. I had been sighing to get home, and now this. Something told me that this day was not yet done. The story was that Wolf got carsick, looked at Diane with big sorrowful eyes and apologetically threw up in her lap. He holds about forty gallons. The vet was not in.

Next trip everything was under complete control. An appointment was made with the vet. Tilley would transport Diane and Wolf; he had snaffles in the bed of his truck for safe tie-down carrying of his deer dogs. I would keep a civil tongue in my head.

This time when I got home Diane was out in the yard with the water hose. She was hosing down Tilley and his truck, and Wolf was sitting to one side, looking pale and empty again.

Nobody wanted to talk about it very much. Yes, the vet was in, no, he did not see Wolf. It seems that just as they got there two bulls broke out of the pen and the rest of the story just rambles on from there, doesn't make any sense.

Tilley is a real East Texas dogman. Keeps a pack of the finest deer hounds you ever saw. Keeps them lean and mean, pacing the fenced-in run, lunging at their chains.

Now Wolf is the absolute D.I.C. (Dog in Charge) at our place, but in the soft evenings when we walk down the sand road to visit Tilley, it's another story. As we start out through the woods Wolf rides flanker patrol. Ranges far and wide out ahead of us, defending us from armadillos, rabbits, mice. But as we near Tilley's cabin and his dogs get scent of us and set up their deep baying and bone-marrow howls, Wolf is suddenly snuggled right up against us, on the offside from Tilley's dog pen. He seems to get smaller and smaller with his ears laid flat and no tail. Tilley's hounds lunge and jeer and call him all kinds of names. Time we get to Tilley's cabin door ole Wolf is so pale he is almost invisible. You can see the bushes right through him.

Once safely at Tilley's cabin door and past the hounds, Wolf would go into Noble Dog again and wait for us, but that was before he found about Delaney, Tilley's tomcat.

Now Delaney is a professional tomcat. He is midnight black, long of tail and short of ear. He was asleep on the warm hood of Tilley's truck, just the tip of his tail twitching from some dream memory he was having. Delaney woke up and realized that there was a dog. A big, stupid dog standing and yet alive right there on Tilley's doorstep.

I never saw anything like what happened next. You know how animals usually do a little bristling and growling and circling first? Not Delaney. I saw him coming up silently behind Wolf, pulling on his black leather gloves, loosening his guns in his holsters, pulling his hat brim low over his eyes. He didn't say "draw!" or nothing. He just walked up through the dust and gunned ole Wolf down. Last we saw of them Delaney was riding Wolf off into the woods, spurs dug in, quirting with one hand. Delaney came back, hopped up on the truck hood again and went back to sleep. He wasn't even breathing hard.

Since that time, when we go down to Tilley's, Wolf stops at some invisible turf line that only he knows and says, "If you folks don't mind, I believe I'll wait right here. It's cooler."

And if we go down to Tilley's by boat as we sometimes do just for the fun of it, Wolf knows Tilley's landing. It is the only time he is not ashore with the first liberty party. At Tilley's he just goes and sits in the back of the boat, way back there in international waters, and looks up at us and grins, "Y'all go on ashore. Believe I will just stay here and check over this old Evinrude. Hmmm, lemme see now . . ."

Wolf's sense of proprietorship about the boat is not limited to staying in it to save his hide from having Delaney tear along the dotted line. He once saved it for us during a flood.

We were gone on a weekender; the creek was high but stabilized. We did not expect a rise and I thought I had left the boat on high enough ground. When we got back the creek was up but the boat was safe on higher ground and had mysteriously tied itself to a tree by the cabin. The way I should have left it.

We puzzled over this a week or two until I met one of the sandy-headed kids from Willard's Lake, about a mile downstream. "We found your boat, drifting by our place, and brought it back." While thanking him, and telling him what a good kid he is, I asked him how he knew it was our boat. All Village Creek aluminum skiffs look about the same: green square enders, ratty, worn shiny on the bottom. "Aw, that was easy, that big ole dog of yours was settin' up in the middle of it barking his head off."

How could Wolf have known? The creek comes up very slowly, softly, The boat would have stirred only a little before starting its journey. Wolf would have had to step aboard right then because he can't climb the sides from swimming, although there are plenty of toenail marks where he has tried.

Wolf knew the boat does not make trips alone, so he elected to step into the unknown. Loudly barking, "Hey, look out here!" as he drifted in midstream past the first sign of habitation in the twilight. If they had not seen or heard him, a few days downstream and into the big river, and then a lonely, hungry figure in a drifting skiff, embarking into the Gulf of Mexico.

Wolf also counts any day a success if he gets invited to ride in the back of the pickup. He has overcome his mal de mer, rides behind the cab, my side, nose up and tongue flowing in the slipstream. That is all I can see from my side mirror, his tongue. Get the feeling I am flying a red flannel Bravo pennant.

He is jealous of his turf and is under the impression that his turf travels with him, whatever he can see from where he happens to be. Thus a fellow driver meeting me in narrow Silsbee traffic looks out the window, we "howdy," and an instant later he gets Wolf leaning out and barking. Kind of like having a howitzer fired point-blank into your window.

Much as Wolf loved the pickup, he seemed to be getting some strange weakness in his hind end or was pretending he couldn't jump into the truck bed. Hell, he could jump over the thing, or tow it.

Wolf has a great sense of ceremony of the rites of man too. He greets me in the predawn dark, yawning and scratching like me, probably for the same reasons. But he saves all the tail-wagging and thumping and boundings for the homecomings.

Diane is his goddess, and we were in gentle times. One of the most beautiful sights were the days when she would walk up the sand road to meet me and I would come round the bend and there they were, beneath a tall pine, Diane flushed and fragrant, Wolf trotting along, holding his noble silly head up high. I would get out laughing and hug them both. On days like that I took slow steps and deep breaths. Looked at everything and saw it sharply. Life so good, so sweet, that I tried to hold time still, when I would come home singing hillbilly songs to the roar of the truck and meet my bride and Noble Dog in the countryside.

Kittens

Things went gently for us inside the cabin, but outside, the creek was restless. Wet, muggy, our very souls began to mildew. And during a spell of high water Poor Pregnant Pearl disappeared again. We pictured her out there caught up in some treetop, stranded, her time come and her dropping kittens one by one into the swirling waters below. Better she should be having a litter of ducks.

Better yet we should have reckoned with the ways of Pearl. The creek was running a mile wide, we were coming in and out by boat, and Pearl appeared on the front porch, fluffy dry. Not even one paw wet.

And in the silence of the next day's dawn, Diane said, "Listen . . . kittens!"

We traced the faint mewings, under my desk; curled up on our brand-new carpet lay Pearl in cat ecstasy. She was purring like a rattly pie tin, making biscuits with her paws, watched proudly as we sorted out the dark, fuzzy, little rooters for the census. Four of them. Pearl spread her arms and looked at us with a half-eyed smile.

Thusly did Pearl introduce us to her biannual custom: kittens in the springtime, kittens in the fall. To be so socially active Pearl is a very private cat. She in no way deemed it proper to ever discuss with us whatever yearnings and burnings she may know in her heart.

There was none of the usual furor of courtship. We have never met any of her gentleman friends. None of this serenading of banjo-voiced tomcats by the pale moonlight. No big, furtive fellows darting around in the shadows downstairs, threeping. Threep is what a tomcat does when he backs up to a wall or a post to mark off his turf. His ears lie back, his tail stands straight up, quivering, and he goes "three-ep" on the wall. There was none of this tomcat courting. No dueling on the sandbar at dawn, with pistols for two and coffee for one and Pearl to the winner.

We presume she went to Miami, or perhaps Vegas. She would be gone for a few days, but like a high-class professional or business feme sole, Pearl found nothing in her relationship to us that included any need for a discussion of her personal life. She would just return home, place her little mandarin paws neatly together in front, blink at us sleepily and say to us, "Guess what?"

The only thing we were certain of was that the cabin would be plentifully supplied with kittens, a furry treasure that was going to quickly overrun the available number of friends and relatives.

Pearl is an ideal mother. She makes no more fuss over birthing and feeding her kits than she does over her immaculate conception. That the kittens will be born under my desk is a settled matter. I have adjusted to writing flaming copy of the 180-hp conversion of the old Piper twin-engined Apache while distantly feeling the nuzzling and the skitchy-skitch of little new claws climbing the summit of my toes and a warm, fuzzy belly being slowly dragged over my bare foot. I could, I suppose, learn to write with my shoes on.

She enjoys bringing them out at playtime and looks on warmly as Diane goes through all that kitten-to-the-cheek cuddling. If Diane intervenes and brings the kittens out before Pearl's scheduling, then Pearl stands around with her fists jammed down in the pockets of her smock. Doesn't say a word, but the moment Diane puts the kitten down, Pearl picks it up and makes a great scene of marching off airily with it. Won't make up for days. "Pink lady behavioral blackmail," Diane calls it.

Pearl, however, maintains her own independence, and sees to it that her civilian-born kittens do not grow up without being woods wise as herself. Early on she takes them out in a silent procession of little paws and teaches them the skills of overnighting in the woods without even a tote bag.

She begins these lessons by bringing in complete sets of frog works. That is the inner mechanism of a frog. If you had this, and an intact frog husk, you could build one. The kittens learn a taste for game cooking, with bowls of store-bought cat food sitting right there untouched. And we learn to be careful about where we step when crossing the porch barefooted in the dark. There is no way to describe the sensation of a cold set of used frog works squirting up between your toes.

Pearl also teaches climbing down a tree. Kittens are born with the natural instinct to go up a tree. Once aloft they tend to want to turn around and come down the same way they went up. That is when they find out that all their little fingernail hooks are turned the wrong way for this. I have never understood what Pearl teaches. If I did, I would franchise it to fire departments and be independently wealthy.

We found homes for all the kittens without having to resort to Stage III tactics. Stage III is to go into town with a shirt full of kittens, lurk around the shopping center looking for people with kind faces and little girls, slip a kitten into their shopping bags and melt into the crowd.

And we kept one. A little tortoise tom with a white vest. We named him Foots because that is the most of what he had. Foots grew in wisdom and in grace.

Chapter 9

River Rats

On a Wooden Island

This time it rained for forty days and forty nights. Man, I never saw so much water in all my life. I picked up the phone and water ran out of it. The catfish are up and running through the woods again, catching baby rabbits. The copperhead snakes have all moved out of my woodpile and taken to the trees and the owls are flying off with them. Sunday I saw two washed-out and starving spiders get together and weave a seine and start after minnows.

Tilley and Norma Jo came down and helped us move a lot of stuff upstairs, then we went down to their place. Their ridge is about four feet higher than ours and seldom floods, but their cabin is built flat on the ground. Fresh, clear, golden creek water was running about a foot deep across Norma Jo's clean waxed floors.

With sawhorses and boards we built scaffolds in the house and raised the bed and dresser and freezer. When we left they were sitting on the couch eating fresh roasted peanuts, feet propped up on the coffee table and watching the color TV. All of it on scaffolds and planks, life passing as before, with Village Creek running in and out the door.

We got support for the "hell, no, we won't go" from watching Tilley and Norma Jo. He's a machinist; she works downtown in the catalog department at Sears. They shove off at daybreak each morning, Norma Jo dressed to the nines with her yaller hair all piled up on top of her head, setting proud up in the bow of the boat, riding for the bridge.

The Tilleys will be back, even though their garden is scattered again and will be sprouting up all over the place if it ever dries out again. It's the chances you take for the beauty you get.

The flood got into Tilley's hog pen and we all went down to rescue Betty Lou. That's the hog. Tilley built her a crib in the back of his pickup. Claimed she was the only sow in town living in a mobile home. Then we got a call from ole man Giblin; he was sick and in the hospital. Said he had a vision last night that one of his cats was stranded out on the railing of the iron bridge and crying.

We got down there and the white water was crashing over the iron bridge just under the railings, but no cat. Then we heard a cat crying. She was up in a tree. We got her down and got to looking around; we could still hear crying. The trees were all full of cats.

Grumbling and swearing, Tilley waded over to the old Flying Red House Club to borrow some milk and a saucer from the Hookers. He was coming out with a bottle of milk in one hand and the saucer in the other and his britches legs all rolled up. He stepped off the porch and into the swift-moving sheet of water that was running across all the land; he took a quick chill and sneezed his teeth out. Saw them hit, and get swept away. Nobody dared laugh but Tilley's son. Junior said, "I'll catch me that big catfish someday."

"What catfish, Junior?"

"The one that will be wearing Daddy's big grin."

And we lost the old Woods Bus in that flood. Committed suicide, she did. The old VW had soul, had hauled every stick of wood in this place up here, and when she burned out engines they would just open the back hatch and rake out what was left like cleaning ashes out of a furnace.

I had hit a bad hole in the road coming in before the flood and the battery bounced up and landed on the engine and it burst into flames. I was on high, dry ground when she quit, and I stood back there with the engine hatch open and only one source of a stream of water. I was reviewing in my head any technical manuals I might have read about the backlash effects of peeing out an electrical fire. Considered for a time just walking off and letting her burn down. That's the sort of stuff Big Thicket legends are made of.

The Woods Bus made it back to the cabin, but the battery was never the same. Wouldn't start when the water started coming up. We tried towing her out, but the clay was too slick for a bird to stand up on, much less tow anything. So we figured she just died by her own hand. Water was over the steering wheel about a week. Once I opened the door and there was Jacques Cousteau shooting a movie about fish. "Shut ze door, monsieur, you are letting in ze alli-gators."

After the water went down I sold her to some hippies at Lamar University. When the tow truck came to get her all four wheels were frozen solid and she left long furrows, like a cat being dragged across the rug. A long silent scream.

"Flooded again?" cried my radio listeners. "All we hear about from you is floods. Why don't you move out?" Oh, no, man, let me tell you about all this beauty.

The solitude of the flooded forest all around us. Our wooden island, the cabin at night is like an old showboat, a palace of moving lights on the river. There is such a mighty power of God in a flood. Nothing man can do; drowsing off at night Diane and I are aware of the deep chords of it moving in our soul.

And in the days all is hushed in the dapple of sunlight on the waters. We move between the giant cypress trees in awed silence in the canoe and Diane whispers, "This must have been what it was like at the dawn of creation."

Then we find the secret mayhaw trees, berries red and ripe in the sun, and we fill the boat bottom with them. And big dumb Wolf goes roaring in his happiness, back and forth from end to end of the canoe, mashing our mayhaws to a bilge-water pulp. Move out of this for your cement town? Leave the tart taste of mayhaws from the trees and Diane standing wet and laughing in the sun with berries gathered in her shirt?

And each morning I buckle on my armor for the wild boat ride through the dark and cold and fog. To ride the river in the dark to the high ground where I left the truck is to have more adventures before sunrise than most men have in a summertime.

The first dark run on the creek was almost more than I could handle. That fourteen-footer and six-hp Evinrude sure did look little, tied in the dark, cold water down there, halfway up the front stair. I knew I was in trouble the minute I cast off. It took half throttle just to stay even, and a little more would flip it when the whorls grabbed us or I slammed against a dark, hidden log. Whole trees were just sighing and sloughing off into the current. And my marks were gone. The creek looks so different riding at treetop level. And the fog. That I really did not need. There was only fog on Village Creek, rising tendrils of it, enveloping cloud banks of it; my flashlight would flare back, blind 'em. I crept along, engine moaning, boat skittish, feeling for the bank, hoping to see the next tree in time to miss it. As I got farther out, the fog wrapped round my head and the light beam angled down and bounced up and there was vertigo, and a horror-movie sense of none of this is real. My Plan Two if we lost it was to roost in a treetop until somebody found me in daylight.

I gradually learned new marks on the river and the trips got easier. Only the first one had real terror in it. The water backed down off the county road enough for a truck to get into Stark's place and that cut my run down from forty minutes to the highway bridge to about four over to Dutch Lake. But a person can sure get to feeling different about something like an outboard motor when he is betting his life on it. I wanted to bring it up at night and put it by the bed where I could talk to it.

And as the flood wore on we lost some of the zing for it and Diane began to look a little rabbity around the corners of her eyes. She said it wasn't bothering her, but she took me up on it when I offered to make an extra run and bring her to high ground for a while. I took her to the All Night 76, told her she could have any kind of hamburger she wanted, and let her watch the truck drivers eat. She said I sure was good to her.

Now this crazy woman had a new complaint. Not so much the cabin fever, but a feeling of helplessness at being marooned on her wooden island. I was taking the boat out each morning, running the creek in the dark to Wladyslaw Stark's bluff where I had the truck parked. She wanted to learn how to operate the boat, take me to the landing, pick me up in the afternoons: "—so I will at least have the boat, an option, some choice in these matters."

Captain Envy, I decided. But kept it to myself. I explained to her how dangerous it was. The fog, the cold, the almost impossible sensing of which clump of willow tops led into the passage and the sloped bank where the truck was parked. The creek turns sharply there, goes boiling off to the right, it's a point of land on one side, and the broad waters of Dutch Lake lie off to the other side. The waters are confused, they swirl, and it is easy to get out of sight of the treetop line and get lost and swept downstream.

Furthermore that outboard motor is a faulty device at best. Like the toilet flush-tank mechanism, outboard motors have been with us for years but have never been perfected. If you enter the treetops too fast you can get crossed up and snagged and the current will swing you round and flip you. Coming in just right means to idle the motor down low, and that's the one thing it does not like to do. And if it dies you are at the mercy of the current, and if you turn around backward to restart it you shift too much weight to the back of the boat and the boat is small and tender and you can get to fooling around back there in the dark and roll right out of it, or dip a gunwale under before you are aware.

To all this professional advice on small boat handling in narrow waters, she replied, "Jealousy of art is the crippling division of the house of intellect. To say 'you cannot learn my art' is to betray your own insecurity."

We went out in the creek and took boat lessons. Crazy, pushy intellectual broad. She could probably talk that engine into behaving. The hell of it is that within an hour she had a quick grasp of the awkward back-reach intricacies of throttle down, shift, power up, and a generally good feel of small-boat handling in narrow waters. Sort of sense that I pride myself in from a lifetime of small-boat handling. She was gleeful. You should see her eyes at a time like this.

I soloed her, watched her make up-current and down-current

figure eights through the row of midstream willows. Then rode with
her through a daylight dummy run to the inlet, pointing out the tall
pines she would be able to see against the night skyline to know
where to turn. She nudged into the inlet, idling the motor, and kept
the prow against the bank with power while I stepped ashore. I told
her it would not be all peaches and cream like this in the fog and
dark. "Yeah, Ace, sure, sure."

Cocky, smart aleck female. She'd find out.

It was cold and dark next morning and there was plenty of spooky
fog swirling. But I said not a word. Just sat up there in the bow, let
her handle the light too. After all she would have to find her way
back alone.

She found the inlet first try, nosed in under perfect idling power.
We still argue about what happened next. I had taught her in the
drill that I would just step ashore, she would shift to idle reverse
and back out into the stream. No need to tie up. She interrupts
about here, accuses me of failing to take a line ashore and hold the
boat for her.

"Whatever," as my old friend Archie Bunker would say, she killed
the engine, and the current in the willows was starting to pluck her
out into the giant lost creek.

Unaware of this, I had stepped ashore, climbed the slope and was
feeling around in the trees for the truck. It was pitch-black. The
first I knew she was in trouble was when she shouted the word. She
had made the mistake of leaning far over and reaching out of the
boat to stop its drift. She rolled right out of it into ice water.

Men use the word in everyday expression and it does not sound
too bad. Women seem to hold this word in reserve and when they
use it, fire it single shot. You ain't never heard the word until you
have heard it from a mad, wet little Rivermouse standing chest deep
in ice water.

It flashed all around me. It hung in the trees. Started flocks of
crows. I hurried back through that billboard of the word, looked
and saw that she was ok. I laughed, told her, "Far worse things have
happened at sea," and began to instruct her on the error of her ways.

Man, she was furious. She rolled back in that boat, fired it up on one pull of the starter cord that would have dragged the crankshaft right out through the cylinder heads. She chewed her way through those springy willows, and disappeared back into the rolling mists full throttle with steam trailing up out of the orange collar of her life jacket.

I listened to her go, waiting to hear the crash, and thinking, Y'know, there's a lot of things about that girl I'm going to miss.

When ole Tilley heard this tale he laughed until the tears came. Said he was putting in for her River Rat papers, and been calling her River Rat ever since.

Me No KKK

In the interest of tasting all of the rich variety that life has to offer, Diane and I went to a Ku Klux Klan rally out in Vidor.

In a way it was sort of scary. When we stepped across the line into Klan Kountry we were greeted by uniformed, helmeted storm troopers armed with pistol and slung carbine. All during the rally, and into the twilight, there was a ghostly patrol of mounted men along a picket line back in the trees. In the dusk the sheeted horses looked like riders right out of the Apocalypse. But why a masked and hooded horse? An anonymous horse? We giggled, but softly.

Once inside we found a fairground midway mood about the place. Fair-haired children ran laughing among the sheeted and robed grown-ups. Friendly women were selling cakes in a booth. You could buy souvenirs, bumper stickers: "I'll give up my gun when they pry my cold dead hands off the barrel." And somewhere, just as the ring of masked men tossed their torches onto the pyre and the flames started licking up that thirty-foot-high cross, a Sno-Cone machine started up.

The one picture I wish I had was a Klansman, all fearsome and glittering in satin robes of green and gold, delicately holding up the tip of his hood to nibble at his Sno-Cone.

What got me in trouble out there was the cake auction, which took place before the singing, praying and cross burning. We got recognized, of course. The rules are, in the KKK, that you can tell anybody you want to if you belong, but nobody can ever tell if you belong. I often wonder where the Klansmen and their ladies hang their robes at home. Some of these outfits are quite fancy and look expensive. Do you reckon they hang 'em up in the front of the closet with their regular-life clothes, or hide them in the back and hope nobody finds them?

Anyway, we got recognized and during the cake auction there was some good ole boysmanship. A Klansman bought a cake and dedicated it to me. Well now in good ole boysmanship this calls for some response. You can either hang down your head and grin, or you can call his hand and raise him. I called and raised. I went up on that platform and told them they didn't know beans about how to run an auction and took over.". . . ahh whata I offered for a black cake at a white rally? . . . gotta five, gimme ten, ten, ten, gotta ten, gimme twenty . . ." I raised the price of cakes.

And that's when my buddy with the *Enterprise* snapped my picture and they ran it on page one. Hoh, boy. Everybody assumed I was in the Klan. One Jewish sponsor almost canceled his ads with me, my soul brothers called up crying, "Baby, say it ain't so. . . .!"

Man, you can't win. When I was in Atlanta at the funeral of Dr. King and marching along behind the coffin holding hands and singing, "We Shall Overcome," the Klan was going to burn a cross on my lawn. Now the brothers were going to come out and burn a watermelon on my lawn. Hell, I ain't even got a lawn. And I am not now, never will be, never have been, a member of the NAACP or the KKK.

But I can tell you a little about the Klan. They are white segregationists. Lots of folks are, but the Klan comes right out with it. They take a public stand against associating with blacks or Jews. The KKK sees itself today as an informative society bent on preserving an all-white, Christian-minority world. They are often denied the right of lawful and peaceful assembly and they seldom get a fair break in the press.

They also cling to some beliefs that are just crazy as hell. They think the press is controlled by Zionist Jews, that Jews invented

Communism, that Negroes are subhumans with bad blood and thick skulls and that the black man wants to mongrelize the white race.

But nobody in the Klan wants to remember that most of the light-tan blacks today came from some good ole white boys sporting around down in the quarters.

The Klan told me they won't burn down anybody's house anymore, unless they really have it coming, but in Vidor the sun really never sets on a black man. They also play a deadly little cat-and-mouse game with their calling card which reads:

> You have just been paid a friendly visit
> by the Ku Klux Klan.
> Would you like a real visit?

That scary little jewel reinforces my suspicion that a Klansman is still a vigilante at heart. He is your judge, jury and executioner.

The KKK is much like the Black Panthers in that they are extremist segregationists. I think both movements are slowly dying off because of a more enlightened and prosperous middle class. Full bellies and TV.

And so the Klan will go rumbling off into history, veering further right than Hitler ever did, wrapped in their robes, flags, the Bible and the Constitution. It's just too late in history for all that meanness.

Diane and I came away with an inner feeling of sadness for these folks. So nice in lots of ways, but narrowing down their lives and missing all the fun and chances of knowing someone not exactly like themselves.

Half a Wolf

During all the wet and cold Wolf began to limp, then began to run three-legged. Arthritis, we first thought, and they treated him for that. Then as the unused leg began to wither we got the more serious news that Wolf probably had hip dysplasia, a congenital defect in German shepherd pups. When this is found by show-dog breeders the affected pup is usually promptly destroyed.

Wolf looked at me with his soft brown eyes, the strength draining out of his hind end. Destroy Wolf? I swear if there is nothing they can do for him I am going to drill and tap him for quarter-inch bolts and mount a set of kiddie-bike training wheels on his old, broken-down rear end and let his front end drag it along.

But Wolf was going down, and it was breaking our hearts. He was thin as a rack and his eyes were full of pain. He had dug himself a hollow in the sandy ground by the big oak in front of the cabin and curled himself up in there and looked up at us like he knew he was going back to earth and could we please understand?

We took him to a vet and the vet went over again about how years of selective breeding to produce the classic show dog shepherd had narrowed the hips too much. The doc manipulated the faulty joint, showed us the withering leg and gave us his prognosis. The other hip joint was not good enough to carry him for long on three legs, Wolf would go down soon and we would lose him. Wolf just looked at us, listening.

Outside I asked Diane what we were going to do.

"Find another vet, that's what."

Billy Crenshaw was new. New Clinic, new wife, new baby coming. He has a warm open face, good hands. Once I saw an old couple come in there with a beagle they had to carry in their arms. He must have been a hundred and ten years old. Blind, deaf, gray-muzzled. They sat with tears open on their faces when Billy carried the dog back gently to put him to sleep. When Billy came out I swear his eyes were glistening too. That's pretty much of something for a man who has to put up with dogs and dog crap all day every day of his life.

Billy Crenshaw laid Wolf up on that big, shiny metal table, and Wolf was patient while he went through all that stuff again. Crenshaw looked up at us real steady and quietly said that he was going to build Wolf a new rear end.

He modified Wolf's hip joint, and Wolf got well fast. But he had gone limping too long. He wouldn't try out the new leg. Crenshaw countered by taping Wolf's foreleg on the opposite side up against his ribs.

We brought Wolf home and the first thing he tried was bicycling, that is, to attempt to stand up on one front leg and one back leg. He would get up again looking puzzled and say, "Aw, c'mon, now, what the hell?" Then, having no real choice, Wolf began to experiment with using his rebuilt hind end. He got it broke in fast and came to me one day and said it would be ok to unsling his front paw now.

That is the only time I ever felt Wolf's teeth. I was trying to be as gentle as I could, unwrapping his big body from all that adhesive tape, but when I got to the light upholstery on the bottom side, ole Wolf's head moved faster than I could see and I felt his long row of pointy ivories firmly enclosing my wrist. I read somewhere that a German shepherd can exert seven hundred pounds of pressure with his jaws.

I froze and we gazed into each other's eyes a minute. Wolf said, "You remember that article you read about how a German shepherd can exert seven hundred pounds pressure with his jaws?"

I said, "Uh-h, yeah."

And he said, "Then let's try something else about getting that tape off my belly."

I got some surgical scissors and went working on the light fuzz between his hide and the tape with about as much care as a philatelist removing that early airmail stamp where the Jenny airplane is printed upside down.

For all his barking and thundering and ground-shaking growling and stiff-legged, hair-bristling stance that Wolf can put on for intruders, the only other time I ever saw him threaten to bite somebody was when a kid kicked him while Wolf's legs were still weak and he was making a third try at jumping into my pickup over the tailgate.

The kid kicked Wolf up into the truck, laughing, the lout, and Wolf pivoted and in one motion bit about four pieces out of the air around that kid's frozen face. He could have had all of him he wanted, but Wolf is like John Wayne who will warn the baddies first by just blowing their hats off and shooting the gun out of their hands.

Wolf got well fast and he quit limiting his diet to stay at the light weight for running on three legs, and although he won't say much about it, he has one of the little pictures of Billy Crenshaw graduating from Texas A & M pasted up on the wall inside his den.

Diamonds on My Toes

I hate to tell you this, but Diane had been to a funeral and had come home in her best clothes and driven up in the clearing and found me down in the septic tank. She says I was drunk and singing.

There are extenuating circumstances. One of the few lasting contracts we had hammered out in this union was that of having too many animals in the house. Too many surprises. I was in favor of changing Foots's name to Carpenter. Because he was always doing odd jobs around the house. And Pearl was in a pink lady campaign with Diane about when the cat was going to be in, or when the cat was going to be out. She was blackmailing Diane with spite shitting. These were no ordinary accidents. Pearl does not have accidents.

I explained to Diane that in ordinary American civil matrimony the wife is expected to take care of small shit, the husband is in charge of large shit. Repairing the toilet, the septic tank, and so on. This was working like a charm until the day the thirty-two-ton county maintainer fell into the septic tank. A maintainer is sometimes called a road grader. It is a very large, long diesel-powered tractor with a big scraper blade for smoothing down roads.

I had conned the maintainer operator into making a pass down my flood-savaged sand road. He was trying to turn that rig around in the clearing when the front wheels went through the cement lid, shooting a column of its five-hundred-gallon contents high into the air. Then he backed down and dragged out one wall coming out, leaving the buried tank shattered and half full of broken chunks of the lid, tangled together with reinforcing iron wire.

This is what you call big shit. I fixed myself a few Ivan the

Terribles, and went out to do my duty. That is when she came from from the funeral and started the story going around that I was down in the septic tank drunk and singing. It only would seem that way to an outsider.

My wife left me. And my faithful dog Wolf left me too. So did Pearl, and that is real hypocrisy after some of the deeds she has done. And in the house and on purpose too.

Listen, y'all, it was terrible. I went down into that septic tank. My main goal in life became not to splash nothin'. I began to pretend it was trout. No, that's too real. So I pretended I was down in a diamond mine. It was all big diamonds and nuggets. Whaddya mean diamonds don't float? Mine did.

So I was down there knee deep in diamonds and nuggets, fishing around with the wire cutters trying to cut the tangles of reinforcing iron apart so I could throw up the big chunks of cement and trying not to throw up anything else.

Some things a man should never see. How they make sausage, how a Texas politician makes his bread, or this.

After I got the septic tank cleaned out, bailed out, scooped up, I had to go mix up a small batch of cement and try to jigsaw-puzzle the broken sides back together. For this I pretended I was a famous brain surgeon putting a skull back together. Only it was my own skull and I was doing it under a local, looking in a mirror. Climbed out now and then and had another shot of local.

It all came out pretty good. A little wopper-jawed maybe, like your skull might look if you had cemented it together yourself and in a hurry.

Then the cement wasn't coming out even. I mean I was finished and had cement left over. My ole pappy always told me that the secret of sopping was to make the bread and gravy come out even. So I climbed out and went wandering off in the woods with my cement bucket in my hand and diamonds on my toes. Gonna save the trees. Every time I came to a tree with skinned bark on it, left over from when Casey Jones was coming through here with those long trucks, I would slap a cement patch on the wound. Saved a lot of trees that day too.

But I could not close the septic tank. National Concrete said they could not have a new lid for me until the next day. Then they gave it to me free, in exchange for a promise to tell the whole story on the air.

I could have found my way back home with my eyes closed, with just my nose.

After we had quieted down again, and got back into the rhythm of Village Creek rising and falling, like our bloodstream, folks would come out from town.

They would walk all around, their shoes ringing hard on the floor, and they would say, "What do you folks do here . . .?" Why we had an intricate and involved social structure, same as folks do who live on higher ground.

Groveler

Tilley's kid named a pig after Diane. A little Yorkshire shoat that he got to raise as a high-school FFA project. "There is something about the way she raises up her snout when she's got both feet in the trough that reminds me of Diane," said the hulking youth with a sly grin.

She who had served the martinis, twinkling through the first-class cabin, Braniff International, DAL to JFK, had now achieved social distinction in Hardin County. A pink-nosed Silsbee High School pig named for her. A few nights later we found a way to return the honors.

We had just come out of the woods, pulled up onto the Lumberton Highway, inbound to the city to emcee a live studio TV show. Late as usual, and there in the sweep of the headlights, cringing down in the can-littered weeds of the median strip, was a scroungy little dog, wigwagging for help with his long hairy ears. "Help. Help," he signaled, a little clump of fuzzy life, flattened down between the roar and rush of lights between the lanes. In a minute he would dash a few feet either way and become another red smear on the road. Crow bait. I give driving directions to the turnoff by saying, "It's the second dead dog, or third dead armadillo, out of Lumberton."

"Stop, oh, please stop."

"We are late now."

"Please, he'll be hit."

"What can we do with him? We are going on the TV."

"Please."

Maybe we can give him away on the TV, I was thinking. Nice touch of pathos. It's a fund-raiser for Lamar University. I could auction him off. She was scooping the dumb, shivering mutt into the truck. Yecchh.

He was quivering down on the floor, a little mass of brown and white bristles, walling a white eye at me and showing a used-car dealer's grin. He was about the size of a roast. Had that same round heavy consistency, no fat. And those ears. "His ears saved him" she crooned. "He knew it was his only chance, those big radar ears."

I told her he looked disgusting. Probably had every disease known to dogdom. And look at him groveling there, trying to kiss her hand, and my ankle. Whiskerly and wetly. "That's it, we'll name him Grover for Tilley's kid."

"Yeah, and call him Groveler."

He padded briskly down the studio corridor at Diane's heels as though he were the anchorman with the six o'clock news well in hand. You've seen guys like that. Rescue them from the mob at your gates, invite them into the kitchen for some warm broth, and they stroll into the library with you, still in their tramp clothes, and have a brandy and help you go over your portfolio.

I have never seen such a change come over a guy when it was his turn to go on-camera. He sleeked back his hair, brushed the crumbs and straw off his tattered white vest, turned his head to the best side with a matinee-idol half smile and gazed into the lens with half-lowered lids. The camera picked them up on a medium shot, Diane standing there so demure, holding this wretched paw-dangling mutt up between her breasts. The camera zoomed in until you could count the fleas tearing along the farm to market roads across his sparse belly. The phones jumped off the wall.

We got twenty-four bids on Groveler, five for Diane.

Afterward I told this shameless pair it was time to call back the winning bidder and make arrangements to pick up that dog. "Forget that," said Diane. "He's our dog." And Groveler closed his long lashes and stretched out his whiskers in a smile.

This politician knew he was home. Back in the woods Wolf met us, sniffing the air. "What y'all doing with a dog in the truck?" Then Groveler leaped sturdily out. "Wolf, ole pal, I see you made it! Man, you've put on some weight, that suit really looks good on you. . . ." He was punching Wolf in the shoulder, Wolf was rolling him over on his back, scruffing him around in the sand. "Groveler, you ole pool shark. Wondered what happened to you, heard you had got hit out on the highway. C'mon in, boy, we'll put you up a few nights." Groveler was already in the bunkhouse, feeling for the best pillow and stretching out on the lower bunk, legs crossed and reading Wolf's copy of *Dog's Life*.

That night Groveler came bounding up on the creek front porch. The porch belongs to Miss Pearl. He came wagging up the steps, swinging his gold watch chain. Pearl slipped one hand inside her purse and around the pearl handle of her little Browning .25 automatic. She never raised a hair. She just whispered loud enough for Groveler to hear, "I smelled you when you got out of the truck. I see you ain't dead yet, but that is how they are going to find you if you start any of your fancy stuff with me or the kid here around this front porch."

Groveler was shivering pitifully, his eyes all walled back and his little bowlegs knocking at the knees. "Lawdy, Miss Pearl, you know I have always respected you. You is the smartest thing, Ma'am. . . ." And when he gestured toward Foots, the kitten, and Pearl glanced that way, Groveler took a box of French bonbons off her marble-topped table and trotted off down the porch with it. She never missed it.

The creek went down, uncovering the long white crescent of the sandbar, and Diane went strolling, looking for driftwood creek carvings, accompanied by Foots, the teenaged cat, and the fine-tuned Groveler. Pearl went along too, but stayed in the cover of the brush line, invisible. When Foots crossed the open white sand he cringed, looking acutely uncomfortable. Diane wondered why the cats avoided the open spaces. I explained it was Pearl's training. Keep under cover, avoid the contrast of a dark kitty on the white sandbar, lest some giant kitty hawk swoop down out of the trees and carry you off in his talons.

Diane was out ahead, approaching a long, irregular chunk of driftwood that seemed to be half buried at the water's edge. As she came up to it, Groveler's whiskers grew stiff and weird. Diane started to kick the driftwood loose with a tentative foot when suddenly it raised up and gave a long hiss and looked her in the eye. She had found our first alligator, basking in the sun.

The little group stood astonished as the woke-up alligator glided off the sandbar and into the cool depths of Village Creek, but not before he looked at Groveler and gave him a long-toothed grin that seemed to say, "You know how much us alligators love dog meat. I'll be back." And he was gone, leaving a long vee wake and Diane to come running to tell me about finding alligators sleeping in her front yard. I gave her consolation, told her that's what keeps down the water moccasins.

All this was before Wolf had gotten his hind end fixed and he was still running on three legs. Diane pointed out to me that Wolf was Groveler's model and his hero, and that Groveler had adopted Wolf's gait and was skipping along on three legs too.

I told her that was nonsense. "What we got here is one good-headed dog with no legs, and a runt dog with four good legs and no head. That bowlegged, bewhiskered cull ain't never gonna grow up and be like Wolf, no matter what he thinks."

Diane was indignant. "Would you destroy a lad's belief in his country? Let Groveler go on dreaming that someday he will grow up and be just like Wolf. This is still America, ain't it?"

Only in America can a con man, a bushy-eyed feist like Groveler, run free and unhanged.

You've all known guys like him. Too light to go out for the team, yet always dating the cheerleaders. Comes from the wrong side of town, yet mothers trust him out with their daughters that real guys couldn't get near. Invite him into the kitchen, pat him on the head, he gets tears in his eyes, shuffles all around, says, "Aw, shucks, ma'am, don't do nothing special for me," taking the piece of pie and all the time figuring out how he's going to sneak back in and steal the rest of it.

Diane would let him stay in the house if the weather was bad and cold; he'd just fall down on the floor and go all to pieces with helpless gratitude. Not looking me in the eye. I knew that before we were a mile down the road Groveler would be sitting up in my chair, smoking my good cigars, sipping brandy and reading *Esquire*.

Really, one time we were going upstream with both the dogs in the boat and we put in at a strange landing and had to cut across the yard of some folks we didn't know real good. We were all walking polite, like decent trespassers do, ducked under the clothesline where the wash was hanging out. When we got out on the road there was Groveler with a pair of socks in his mouth. And I had never let him out of my sight.

There is a place about two miles upstream from us, by the mailboxes where the blacktop ends, we call it the tavern. They got a pool table and some tame beer drinking, and they keep their own yard dogs. Some good-looking shepherds and a black Doberman that looks like a sketch by Dali. When my dogs walk with me to the mailbox the tavern gang comes down, it's their turf. Everybody circles and is real polite, then as we are leaving, Groveler will make a suicidal rush at the pack, disappear in a wild tangle, and then come streaking out just ahead of death. Then with the most delicate timing and control, he'll skid to a stop, lift a leg and pee on the last tree at their turf line.

I think this is the kind of stuff that got him when he was missing a couple of days. When he dragged himself home whatever had got him was big enough to get the back half of Groveler into his mouth. Nearly bit him in two. His goatee was all messed up, both elbows gone out of his sweater. We took him to the vet thinking maybe alligator.

The doc sewed him up and repackaged him and as soon as Groveler could walk he was gone again. Wolf went out and got him and brought him home, both of them looking over their shoulders with awful tales to tell. Back to the vet, who braided him together this time with steel wire.

Along about here I was starting to consider what all this was costing me as compared to what Groveler is worth. We don't have Dog Cross Insurance yet, you know. Diane staying up nights, bringing him hot soup, mooning over him while I had cold suppers. I had about decided that if whatever was getting the little sneak didn't finish him off the next time, I would. And just tell God and Diane that he had died serving a grateful nation.

Same thing next time. Soon as Groveler could move again he was over the hill and gone again. The lady who runs the tavern called about midnight. "You got a little, brown, bushy-eyed feist with a white vest and his behind in a sling? You better come get him."

That big, black, razor-totin' pinscher grinned at me and rolled his eye. Anybody who'd fool around on that man's turf deserves to get laid open.

Groveler didn't go back. She came down to see him. She was a living doll. A small lady shepherd, big long lashes, lipstick, fur coat, silk stockings and a cigarette holder. She stood up twice as tall as Groveler. Don't ask me how he did it.

Wolf came out and took one look at her and nearly fainted. All the lady dogs he'd ever seen up to now wore poke bonnets and sat around shelling peas. And Diane was furious. "If I'd known you were getting your behind tore off fooling around I'd have let you die the first time!"

Wolf was the only one who was never taken in by Groveler. On a cold night he'd drag him up close and use him for a foot warmer. And if they heard something awful sneak up on us out of the Holy Ghost Thicket, Wolf would nudge Groveler in the ribs and say, "Run out there in the woods, boy, and find out what that is. If you can't handle it, call me."

That's how we came to recognize what we call a "One Dog Alarm" or a "Two Dog Alarm." But the night that something got the tomcat Foots we didn't hear anything at all.

Fleetwood Keats

Foots, the cat, son of Pearl, had never seen a paved road or more than six people at one time. He was a woods cat. We took him with us to the post office in downtown Lumberton one time and he just crawled under the truck seat and lay there trembling the whole time with his paws covering his eyes.

From the day he was born we taught him that it was ok to love and to trust. Diane would wear him draped around her neck on our woods walks in the long light and Foots would just lie there, purring and looking swimmy-eyed.

Foots did not seem to know that he was a tomcat, or what was expected of him. He would sit at the table with us on Sunday mornings, have his coffee, read the paper. He was a hiking cat. Went down the sandy road with us under the trees, traveling along with the dogs. He never seemed to realize that cats are not supposed to get dusty, but are supposed to sit at home on the carpet soaking up the air conditioning.

One day he went all the way down to Tilley's with us. Nobody had warned him about Delaney. The dogs hung back at the invisible Delaney Turf Line; Foots walked right on up to the door with us.

Tilley came to the door and we all watched Delaney. Instead of going for his guns, Delaney just smelled Foots all over, head to tail.

"They gonna fight?" I asked.

"Not now," said Tilley, "Delaney is just measuring him to see how big a hole he'll fill."

After Foots got his complete set of jangles on him he sort of halfheartedly took up his career as a professional tomcat. I think he really wanted to be a musician.

He never returned from his second war patrol.

Thus it always was in the forest deep. I tried to tell Diane, but she grieved, sometimes whispered his name across the waters. Me too. Sometimes going out of the woods before daybreak I would believe that the headlights caught a glimpse of his elegant tuxedo shirt front and white spats. Far down the road, by the old Dean place.

I don't think Delaney got him. Delaney would have sent something home as a message to the others. The truth is that Foots just vanished into the mists and the mysteries of the Holy Ghost Thicket.

One of the few times that Miss Pearl ever made a deal with Diane was after Foots vanished. She looked with calm and compassionate eyes and promised her at least one tortoiseshell, high-legged tomcat in the next production schedule.

Pearl was really pregnant. She was twenty-one inches around the middle and looked like she was going to carry for nine months. Diane thought maybe she was going to have a puma. I said she had probably opened up a sack of cat food and made a glutton of herself and was not really pregnant at all.

Diane said, stroking Pearl, "Well, something just kicked my hand."

"Pantry weevils maybe?" I offered.

Pearl reached up and got me by the hand and said, "C'mon, we are going to have those kittens now."

I said, "Whaddya mean, We? You have kittens. I need a drink. I do not have anything to do with having kittens."

Pearl insisted. "Come on, I got to have you, and I am going to honor you with having them right under your desk like I always do."

"Pearl, don't be ridiculous. You have had at least forty kittens by yourself. You have had kittens in every house in the Big Thicket, and up in the trees during floods. You go on in there and have those kittens. You got a nice new carpet and air-conditioned place, you go on, and come show us when you are through."

Diane said to me, "Your hamburger is ready."

Pearl said, "The kittens are ready."

I said to Pearl, "Go on, cat, I am having my supper."

Pearl got me by the hand and carried me off, tail high, to our desk. She arranged me lying on the carpet with my head up under the desk, rubbing her stomach for her and counting labor. "C'mon,

Pearl, that's a nice one. Co-ome on, one more, bear down now. Push, Pearl."

Pearl was smiling up into my eyes dreamily, holding my wrist with both paws and purring. Imagine me, midwifery? Midkittery? Diane thought it was hilarious.

The main thing to remember at a time like this is which hand you got the hamburger in.

Soon the furry four were at the Let's Discover the World stage. They tottered out the front door under Diane's guidance to see for the first time the great things out there such as sunlight, leaves, and find out about down, i.e.: fall off the steps. They walked right out the front door in a herd and right under Noble Dog Wolf who was on duty standing guard there.

The kittens did not know that they were walking around in the shade of a giant German shepherd. They thought they were in the forest made up of big, hairy tree trunks. Then one of them decided to look up. Up, up, his little button eyes went until at last they came to the big cloud of dog at the top.

"Omigod!" he screamed. "Run for your life!" And four little straight-up cat tails disappeared under the couch all at once. Z-zip! Like snapping an umbrella shut. And Wolf yawned and grinned at us. "Ho-hum, kittens again."

And one of those kittens, true to Pearl's promise to Diane, was her very own special-order tomcat. He was the legendary, smooth, ball-bearing and discriminating Fleetwood Keats.

From the time he was a fluff ball of a kitten Diane taught him that it was not uncatlike to be cradled belly up, in arms, and be whispered to. He grew up somewhat pampered by the women in his life. Diane's cuddles and fixing him crunchies and milk, Pearl going out into the woods and bringing him a fresh lizard.

It was the lizard part that I objected to. Everybody got mad. The lizard is mad because his brand-new suit of fine genuine lizard skin is all punched full of holes and leaking.

The cats got mad because I rescued the lizard and set free the ones who had not yet had their main spring broken. Everybody would stalk around on their high keys for a while.

But Keats never wasted life by being uncool for long. He would stroll slowly by in front of the mirror in his turtleneck sweater, or spend hours tending to his karate suit which is oversize and luxurious. He sits, smoothing down his lapels.

One day I was watching Keats pouring himself across the carpet, rippling with silent power, looking around to see if anyone needed any good strokes. He was fluid-driving along, hugging the road, fender skirts sweeping low, and I cried out, "Diane. I know who this cat is . . . look at him, he is Fleetwood Keats, the Houston Cadillac dealer." There is no other creature on earth so elegant.

Fleetwood Keats will live long. He shuns risky war patrols, feeling no need to prove anything. He keeps in shape at the spa, weight lifting. Attends social functions at the Sugar Creek Country Club as needed, but never to the excess of fawning. He works by appointment only, window sticker, list price. He descends upon his clients as a great, warm, furry cloud sent from above. The Very Standard of the World.

Chapter 10

Pit Stop and Crisis Center

One of my sponsors came by the studio. "There's a woman I want you to meet. She and her husband are good friends of ours, she has listened to you since she was a little girl, she mentioned one time that if there was a spare moment when you could drop by . . . But, Gordon, let me go with you. She's a wheelchair rider. Had triple polio when she was about nine. She's just a little bitty thing. . . ." He seemed to be having a hard time finding the words he wanted to use. "But after you have talked to Betty an hour or so . . . you won't notice . . . I mean you'll actually forget that she's . . . well, it would mean a lot to her if I could take you over there."

An invitation like this happens now and then. I really don't want to go. Meet some bent-up human being, looking up with big eyes. My imagination runs too swift. I stand there in my good body and my long running legs and I become them. I become their everyday struggle to just stroll over to the icebox and get a drink of cool water. I become them, waiting for someone to lift me into the car and then fold and lift the glittery, shiny wheelchair and tuck it somewhere, time after time, until its passage has worn a special place in the upholstery. Forever. Sitting in a public place wondering if my bladder will last, or will the door to the booth be too narrow, or will it be one of those that nobody flushed for a week and the only way I can get on it will be to put my hands all over it.

One time I broke my foot skydiving. I knew I would break something if I landed with the chute swinging, but I had drifted over a canal and I got a horror about how nylon will cling and smother you in the water. In skydiving you take the best of bad choices. I slipped past the canal, and hit oscillating in a speeded-up descent.

My leg was in a cast only a few weeks. The orthopedic doc muttering as he swathed it, "The jumpers. I get all the jumpers." And me answering him, "Doc, you ever notice that all the guys who wear jump suits are the ones who never jump at nothing?" It was all a very good time. But within a week or so I was a horror over that cast. That heavy stinking plaster that had taken part of my body away from me. Denied me my own foot, my own nimble little ankle. That cast became a personal enemy and a nightmare in the dark. I did a lot of imaginings of how to escape secretly. To saw my way out with a jeweler's saw and visit and croon to my leg at night. To fondle my leg, to get it back again.

When I see a person who will sit in a wheelchair for a life, I run out of the limits of imagining that much courage. Of that much endurance. I picture me captured like that in the spokes, and because it is beyond all my limits of how much bravado I think I may have, I tend to look at a cheerful cripple in a concealed panic.

Betty Em met us at the door, rolled her chair back by way of bidding welcome in. Just as I thought. The biggest, most beautiful eyes, her flawless complexion, that of nuns and house people. Her short-cut hair. Oh, she was radiant with happiness. She looked like a little just-feathered bird, bobbing at the nest edge, the short-feathered, lovely little fledglings that if they fall the cat eats them alive. I wanted to fall to my knees and embrace her little shoulders and wheelchair and all and sob out, "Oh, my God, Betty, I'm sorry." And part of me was recoiling, thinking, Lordy, I hope she don't want to touch me. Suppose it rubs off?

Betty Em was watching me working through all this. From whatever solid, broad, concrete ramp she had built in her mind over the years, Betty was sitting at eye level with me, watching and waiting for me to work my way through. With different people it's different ways. The sugary. The backslapping. (A back slap would wreck her like tinkertoys), the insy, chance-taking humor. (Don't get up, Betty, I'll go to the door.) The folk-liberal (Hi, I'd like you to meet me friend, Betty Em, the cripple.) Some get arrested along here at different stages. Some few make it all the way through and have to look back on the times they thought of Betty Em in the Wheelchair. She was about thirty then.

We sat down and got intensely interested in her middle name actually being Em, and yes she knew that was a printer's term, taken from the space of the old square *M* type, and that an em pica is one-sixteenth of an inch, and no, she couldn't remember why her mamma named her like that. Our talking ranged wide. It got to be intense, and it got to be fun, and it lasted long after the guy who introduced us was squirming and ready to go. And it lasted.

All the good things you can hope for did happen. When she met Diane they became the yin and yang of friendships that sometimes bond between women. When I met her Bernard he seemed to be watching as I twirled my rotating hangers of personalities to see which one to slip into for him. He admired the performance with the softest laughing brown eyes I have ever seen into and said, "It's ok, they all look good on you."

And there was no pairing off. The friendship, then the love, was like a four-seeded pod. It just grew that way.

Diane has always had the capacity for an intimate friend. In her airline days in Dallas there had been Charlie Brown. Her apartment was the one upstairs right over Diane's. Her apartment looked like Diane's. When we drove off in the U-'all truck from Dallas the day we moved Diane's stuff to Village Creek, I looked back at Charlie Brown standing there alone in the wasted boxes. I told Diane then, I bet you Charlie Brown sorts it out with Bill and marries him within the year. She did too. Within a year or so of when Diane and Betty Em took up, Betty had asked Diane to come over and do the walls in her living room like she had done ours.

Telling it in examples like that is shallow, but I have no ladle deep enough to dip in and serve up a taster of what all is in there. That would be like walking into Betty Em's kitchen when Bernard's mamma has filled the house with the aroma of her cooking some weekend and asking Mrs. Giarratano to tell you in words what's in that pot.

I learned some new dimensions about love from Betty Em and Bernard Giarratano that I didn't even know existed. Bernardo is one of the best-looking Sicilian men I have ever seen, and they all got that something about them. Like Dean Martin, the older he gets, the better looking. So I am looking at Bernardo and little bent-up Betty Em and I am wondering, What the hell? She was nine when the polio hit. He never saw her any other way. All right, he is a dropout from the seminary. They first met when he was a grocery boy delivering groceries from the family store. You want to try to put it together like that? The rescuer and the broken bird? I'm sorry, but that's no good. He has his master's in social work. Bernardo is a professional family counselor. They married for love. They took the awful chance of adopting five-day-old Scott for love. All the great songs and books and plays and movies are about love, and there is a great big gaping hole in the middle of all that, waiting for Betty Em's story about love. No house of brides has yet to make a wedding-cake-top figurine with little sparkling spokes under the bride.

But the background music has got to be straight. If you fade into too many violins you've lost it. The music has got to be the same as any four-legged wedding. The same piccolos, oboes, chase music and cannons. If you don't do it that way, you've lost it.

Betty Em wanted to go flying with me. I took her up in the little Cessna 150, a little high-wing, two-seater grasshopper. A 150 will do you no harm. She fairly sang with the beauty of flight. And after a time she said, "See, we are just alike now. Seated, strapped in, yet free. Totally free in every direction." We went low and did graceful sweeping S turns over the streams of traffic going down Highway 90. Them confined by the yellow line, the center stripe and the ditches and fields. We swept it all on wings, like hunting hawks.

In the later years, after I was grounded when I lost my medical qualifications, I came to Betty to pour it all out.

"I know what flying has always meant to you, Gordon, so what now? What will you do?"

"I don't know. I'll write about it as long as that lasts. I had over twenty years of flying, most men have none. I'll keep that in my heart. Then there's the canoe on the creek, that is motion and beauty and movement in fluid, minus only one dimension. . . ."

And she told me I would make a pretty good handicapped person.

I was able to give Betty and Bernardo some things too. One night we were invited to be guests of the owners of the Circa 100, Beaumont's only attempt at a dinner theater. Opening night. The dinner was bad. The theater was worse. They tried for *The Fourposter*. The ingenue was over forty, dyed red hair, weighed two hundred stone. Her swain groaned audibly, and we heard his knees and back snapping as he manfully pressed her upward for the bed scene. I looked at the program to see how many acts there were yet to endure. Decided I was going to escape. "But you can't," they hissed, "we are guests of the house."

"One of my rules is, you don't have to stay," I said, getting up.

"Not without us you don't," they scrambled.

We tried to make it with grace, at intermission. Betty Em ran a wheel over a lady's foot. The lady had her legs crossed and one open-toed sandal out in the aisle. She yelped, her other foot jerked up and got tangled up in the spokes. They went "thrang-g-g-g."

There is no way to slink out of a room in a wheelchair. In the narrow stairway down, carrying Betty Em, we encountered the owner, our host. He refused to give ground. "But why? Why are you leaving?" I searched my mind. We could have used Betty Em for the alibi. She calls this "playing wheelchair." It works good going in. Seats up front, always. But I reached out and clasped the man's arm and said with compassion, but right into his eyes, "It's bad. Bad, and we are leaving. But, thank you."

Bernardo never forgot that. He calls it the "Circa 100 Rule"; i.e.: "You don't have to stay." He says that's valid.

The Giarratano home in Beaumont became our way station. Anything having to do with a trip from the creek into town and back has to be measured in terms of an hour. The complexities of "I'll meet you in town," or "I can't be sure for an hour," or "Leave the car off for service," all began to hinge out of what we came to call "The Giarratano Pit Stop and Crisis Center." We flew to Bernardo too, when we were trying to discover the mystery of why being adversaries to each other seemed to be the easiest thing we knew how to do. But when we did that we made appointments and met at the office. Well, mostly. Sometimes I think we let some of these scenes go on and develop in his living room with the hope that he could study the preignition circuitry and have a great aha of discovery and prescribe a cure to us.

He did remind us that anything you have been doing for over six months which works to ensure your continuing misery is described by Dr. Eric Byrne as "racketing."

Our blowup came during a midnight rambling, on the creek. Me and Diane sitting across the kitchen table from each other again, going on and on.

She said, "This is probably the wrong thing to do, but here goes. I am really hurt. I'm scared. Time is passing quickly and my whole body aches to conceive. I see the pleasure your children bring you. I'll probably never know this, I know this is turning you off.

"My position is so shaky. I live in a house built for another family which belongs to you. Not my house. Not my children . . . and so many women have gone before. And they stand here in the shadows, waiting for my mistake.

"I have a shaky claim on a man that I turn off by my aggressiveness and my need for a conditional claim for a home. A choice between the need of the love of my man and the need to give birth.

"I am sad, and hurt, and scared. Not angry. I'm not going to cause another scene, or go crazy. I am a survivor. I will work this out.

"For God's sake don't appease me by saying things you don't mean. False hope is cruel. I would rather confront the real you, the truth, and work through it, however difficult, than build dream castles on a fault line."

I only heard fragments of what she was saying. Flash words got through; her total meaning was lost to me. I heard, "—my whole body aches to conceive . . . not my house . . . scared . . . a shaky claim . . ." The rest of her words spilled across a set of books already closed. Marked "Beautiful women are usually half crazy," much of it written for me years ago by Pappy, much of it written by me as "easy answers to some problems you can never solve."

The baby problem I had decided to leave conditionally open. Part of that is God's business anyhow. We had done nothing to prevent a baby. Our loving was as intense as our quarreling and the cycles were short and bewildering to me. One night I would hold her in our cabin so safe and full of the most intense human rapport here on the crescent white sandbar of Sweet Sister Creek and I would brim over with the knowing of how total this was, and how rare. I could lay my head upon her and feel the magnetic lines of force in my brain go into orderly patterns and told her that I was certain I had discovered the Center of the Universe.

Then some unknown word or deed would shatter this fragile polarization. Fragment us, and the next night I would be thinking what in God's name will me and this intense little woman do with each other? Shackled together here in this hut of mud and boards, cut off, alone, the mad ones, staring at each other with eyes getting rounder and rounder.

"Not my house . . . a shaky claim . . ." The words rang. I had gone to the lawyers and had given her title to half of everything I owned on the creek. I reminded her. Oh, vile remindings of one's own largess. Words to stick in your throat.

She stopped short. Her eyes and mouth popped open. She leaned across and started tapping me on the chest with each word. "Not land. Not titles. You know that all means nothing to me. It's you. The commitment I want is in here," tapping my chest. "I am talking about you making some real commitment to yourself and me."

The last clear thing I remember before the wall of red rage swept down on me was, "Why that ungrateful wretch."

This house. This land. This lifetime of work for all of that. This breaking up of the family circle. "Now you are going to blame me for that too?" she cried.

Axes and knives. Away all boarders. We swung round and round, things broke. I was upon her, bore her down, brutally pinning this soft flesh that I had blown the tenderest breath across.

She writhed. She stormed back. More furious at being overpowered than hit. I straddled her. Physically subdued her. Panting. I looked into her eyes.

I had lost.

Violent man, you are all alone in the silence again. How do you manage to do this?

The window at the foot of the bed looks north. I lay there cold, but still feeling the satisfaction of the slap. Madman.

I stayed carefully away from her pillow. No note, no warm panties under there this time. She had left with the dignity of walking away from an animal cage. Now I lay alone, remembering unbidden scraps and fragments of her.

Once we had waked up here at 2:00 A.M. to the smell of green cat shit in the house and she had said, "Look. How bright the stars." What woman's mind could work like that?

Anything after Diane is going to be seconds. And what are the choices? Go home to Mamma? That's how it ends in all my old movies. Or go back to rutting again? Just keep the traffic moving, thin bodies, fat bodies, black bodies, more-than-one bodies. That reminded me of what Jan had said.

Jan had passed through some years ago, playing my game but better than me. She had left me unhorsed. A really bad time to get over. By way of farewell, and not without kindness, Jan had said, "You really don't know anything about love. You will get older, and lonelier, and go for younger and younger chicks, and end up paying for it."

I shuddered. I have an image of the main nerve line in my body. It's about two inches thick and runs direct from my brain to my gonads.

"All right, Ace, what do you miss most about Diane, right this minute?"

"I miss her mind." (He could look you straight in the eye and say that.)

"Her what? That's the only part of Diane you can't get along with."

"Maybe we ought to try to quit thinking of her as parts."

"Ace, you may be having a sane moment."

"I will try to cherish it."

"What you might better be doing is sober up and start trying to think of what you are going to say to Diane. I don't think the penitent boy and feeling her up is going to be much good this time."

"Yeah. That's what I'm worrying about."

She was at the Pit Stop and Crisis Center, her face still swollen from the crying. Huddled up like a wet bird under the eaves. Defiant.

"Diane, all I know is that I don't know the right way to treat you. Nor you, me. But I do know that after you, the rest of my life will be downhill. Will you come home? Let's try again."

She was putting her stuff into her little airline tote bag, but she was staying out of my arms. She told me that my touch was still the memory of the violence. To reverse the roles, think if I lived with a stronger person and the uncertainty of not knowing when I would be hurt again. I had never thought of it like that. "I can't live with you or love you if there's ever any more violence," she said.

There was nothing to say, nothing needing to be said, to Betty Em or Bernardo. And yet I felt the need. Alone in the kitchen with Bernard, I turned to him, working for the words. Turned to Bernard, the Professional, in my guilt and shame. So Bernard, the Professional, answered me as the friend. With mock seriousness he took my arm, "Remember, into each and every life a little bad-ass must fall."

We were laughing, Bernardo poured the wine. Diane came and stood close; I could see into her eyes again.

But sometimes I think they gang up on me at Bernardo's. They are all liberals. Sweet pansy liberals. When we sit and talk politics the clock hands seem to jump ahead hours far into the night. They claim you would have to step off the world to get to the right of me. I try to explain to them that the fundamental flaw in liberal thinking is the concept of, "We owe these people something."

"Look at the wilderness we live in," I patiently explain to these group thinkers. "Each creature is born alone and naked in the jungle.

It's not something you have to fret about; that's why there are no short, weak oak trees. No slow rabbits. The natural way of selectivity. God's plan. How do you think Eddie Rickenbacker survived that life raft? Do you think Lindbergh could have ever got off the ground if he'd had to clear it with Occupational Safety and Health Administration?"

"How about Richthofen?" said Diane. "You left out the bloody red baron."

Badgering me, they were all laughing.

"Well, he was effective at his trade. He just happened to meet one too many Englishmen."

"Name your favorite President," said Betty Em.

"Kennedy, and, ah, Roosevelt, I guess. FDR."

"Aren't those the guys who socialized America?" said Betty. "I would have thought you would have gone for Teddy; he sure knew how to handle all those gooks in Cuba and the Philippines."

So I sang her a little of the Spanish-American War song, "—underneath a starry flag, we'll civilize 'em with a Krag . . ." Then in the most condescending manner I could get together, I explained that the song was meaningless to antifirearms people who would not know that the Krag was the rifle, U.S., M-1898. This did not get the heat off; they had me at bay.

"You ever read Thoreau?" asked Bernardo.

"My building my own cabin in harmony with the woods IS Thoreau," I snapped.

"Thoreau is one of the great liberal thinkers of our time."

"Aw, c'mon, Bernardo."

"The trouble with you, Gordon, is you are a fake conservative."

"A closet liberal," added Betty Em. "We ought to turn you in to the KKK and have them tear up your card."

"You ever read Fromm?" asked Diane, softly.

I shook my head. "I gave you a copy of his *Art of Loving* when we first met. You told me then you had read it."

"I would have told you anything then. Whatever I thought would work, to get you to relax and lay down."

This frosted her over. I needed to lighten this whole thing up, quick. "Do you know that all dogs are Democrats, and all cats are Republicans?"

"What do you mean?"

"Well, just look at how dogs operate. Tail-wagging, grinning, licking your hand so they can keep living off of you free. You never hear of a cat on welfare. Cats never run in packs, baying mindlessly behind some leader who doesn't know what he is howling about either. Cats never get lost. But get a dog separated from his group protection and he'll just stand out on the freeway until something hits him. You seldom see a dead cat on the freeway."

"And if you do," she said, "you can bet your Nixon-Agnew button that he was probably cut down in the hot pursuit of something illegal or immoral."

"Just look at cats," Diane continued. "Dry-mouthed, aloof, sly, secretive. The minute you turn your back on cats they take over and try to run things."

"Sounds more like Presbyterians," I said.

"Same thing."

Then we all got to laughing again, remembering the time Diane and I had given the Giarratanos two of Pearl's prize tomcat kittens, and they had named them Tilley and Fritz, and then went down to the vet and had them both fixed.

In mock outrage I heckled Betty Em about this on the air, and she had answered me in her newspaper column. A letter written by her cats.

Dear Uncle G.:

You will find that this is a family of causes. Interested in national and international events and local politics. We call it being involved.

When the family discussion was held, and the decision was made to have us neutered, we took it like gentlemen, naturally, after having lived in this enlightened environment. We agreed that unwanted kittens are not desirable, and that we could sacrifice fatherhood for the greater good of society.

It wasn't really all that much as compared to your goings-on over the radio. We had a little soreness; now we are home, frisky, and have joined in with saving the world. Election day is soon, the whole family will be out campaigning the neighborhood again.

Sincerely,

Tilley & Fritz

I had Keats, our genuine ball-bearing mousetrap write the reply:

Dear Ms. Cats:

I am sure sorry to hear how things turned out for you guys. So what are you now, throw pillows? They might as well have taken you to a taxidermist and had you filled with kapok. Then you'd be soft and fluffy all year round and they would always know where you are at night. Looks like they might have taken just one from each of you. That way they could have gotten a complete set, and you'd still be able to vote.

Course I understand how those whimp liberal minds work; they feel like they are responsible for all the cat problems in the world. But there will always be cat problems in the world. I can't help but think that when the vet got out his nippers and hung up your gloves, forever out of the ring, you surely must have thought, Why ME?

Now you know why I always keep my legs crossed when I am around liberals.

Got to go now; its springtime and we are going out acaroling tonight. Sorry we can't invite you, but we don't need no sopranos.

So long—

Fleetwood Keats
Full-time, Professional Tomcat

Diane and I could leave the Giarrantanos still laughing, each with each other. She and Betty Em would have traded some new book "—that you just got to read . . ." and we would drive home, slowing when we got off the gaseous zoom of Eastex Freeway, and rolling the windows down in our hidden woods road to smell all the fresh new air of the night leaf making. We would drive slow, edging around the new rain puddles in the twisting sand road, beneath the arbors where trees and vines met overhead. At daybreak there is a fresh melon smell to the creek. Every leaf and flower pours itself forth and a thousand bright birds sing like there will be no tomorrow.

Tilley knew, somehow, when we had been fighting. He would find some excuse to come down to our place, bringing a covered pan of Norma Jo's cooking. Tilley can kid us about it. "You know, Gordon, the skinny little tires on that thing she drives ain't but about that wide," holding thumb and fingers spread, "but when she's taking off out of here, sore at you, she can go through a mud puddle twenty feet long and leave it bone dry." Diane can laugh at this from Tilley. "If you ever run her off for good, boy, don't come hangin' round me no more."

One of the things we love about Tilley is that we never have to listen to him while guessing what he's really got on his mind. Diane says he is a man without guile. "He knows who he is," she says simply.

Tilley is Tilley, deer hunting in the woods, running a union negotiation with top brass from Goodrich-Gulf, or in his solitude on the creek, tending his hand lines. Of the stuff I've written about him, Tilley says, "if anything ever happened to me you'd starve."

Tilley is pure Eastex except that he doesn't use tobacco. In a country where the whited ring of the snuff can worn into denims is a badge, and where working in the explosive petrochemical plants has bred a second generation of tobacco chewers, Tilley has no use for tobacco.

Beechnut

I am convinced that smoking is a filthy habit, that it's going to carry me away someday, that I am hopelessly addicted to nicotine and that such people are depraved and utterly lacking of character as we go hacking along, smelling up the earth, an abomination in the sight of man and God. That the wily Red Indian recognized Christopher Columbus when he saw him, and knew deep in his primitive heart that this was the beginning of the end, and his cunning act of total revenge for a lost nation was to give the white man the leaf of the tobacco shrub.

Some mornings when I first wake up and paw blindly for the makings to raise the nicotine level of my blood, I can hear the ghostly laughter of Chief Black Hawk coming through the walls. I got his land, he's got my soul.

All right. Ken Ryan came by the station other day and he said, "Whancha-chaw?" That's tobacco-chew talk for, "Why don't you chew it?" I told him, sunk in sin that I am, and having smoked and lit anything that was combustible, that I had never got so low as to eat the stuff.

I've known him since he was a kid, always thought he had a facial deformity or a speech impediment for years before I realized he had a permanent chaw in his jaw.

He laid a pack of Beechnut down in front of me and he drawed the line. Told me if I was a real redneck, drove a pickup, lived in the backwoods, drank muddy water and slept in a holler log, then I'd have to chaw. In my heart I knew he was right. We call them Hardin County Racing Stripes, those long, streamlined stains down the side of a pickup.

He told me he bet Willie Nelson chewed tobacco, and the editors of *Texas Monthly*, and truck drivers. Everything that I hold dear. He said that a tobacco chewer made the Marlboro Man look like a sissy. I said it would ruin my love life.

He had brought his wife with him. Now I have known these folks since they was just children, and I want you to know that Barbara could walk across any street in the world and the traffic would stop for her. And she was standing right there by his side, like she always is, and she just sort of snuggled up against his arm and got a funny light in her eyes and said, "Tell Diane it'll give her marriage a whole new flavor. You might be surprised."

I decided then and there that either they were a couple of the worse "preverts" I ever saw or I was missing something. I reached for the Beechnut.

Dear hearts, I learned a whole bunch of new things in the next hour or so.

I had always wondered what goes on in there, but you can't just walk up to a guy and ask him anything that personal. Do you actually chew it? Or just let it soak? Does it satisfy the tobacco lust?

When do you know when to spit? That's an awful word. Spit is a dirty. Spittoon is a clean. They advertise cute brass spittoons in Junior League catalogs, and that's cutesy, but I bet you ain't going to be around long spitting in one, not on that Jr. League pale blue carpet.

Well, I'm going to try to tell this story without excessive use of the word spit, and I tried to make it through the morning show neat, and the chaw was good, and rich and delicious and satisfying. Not like snuff, which is like getting shot in the nose with a .22 bullet. This stuff made me think of Mamma and home. But I know now why the tobacco chewer is the strong, silent type; he's got to give a lot of consideration to time and distance before he opens his mouth.

Tobacco chewing is never going to be big with radio announcers.

Right away it changed the tone of the morning show. The commercials got shorter, there was a genuine Kirbyville sound to it. In Kirbyville, among chewers, that's pronounced "Curb-ville." That way you don't get any on you or the folks in front of you.

I got self-conscious about spitting in front of Linda Joyce, the newsgirl. I didn't see any real harm in swallowing a little. Even learned to bypass coffee. In about an hour I was pale green and going down fast.

Well, that's about it. If they ever solve the spit problem, chewing tobacco is going to be the real answer to satisfaction without chest X rays. I tried it one more time going home in my pickup. Learned a lot about airflow dynamics. The first shot circled the truck and I ran through it.

When I got home that day Diane asked me two questions: "What's that in your jaw?" and "Where were you planning to sleep tonight?"

Water Bed

Where I planned to sleep that night was curled up against her warm buns in our water bed. The water bed was part of my dowry. Diane claims she had it because of the great relief it gave her back. Yes. The water bed will also relieve your front. But don't let me get into that heh heh heh stuff about the water bed. That happens enough when townies visit. "Ho? A water bed. Heh heh heh." "Go on, and lie down on it," says Diane. "It will make your back feel so good." They all want to, but few are free enough, not in front of people. Kids love it, but they are just thinking of it as a water bed. Some guys will lie across it, but it shows in their faces. And sometimes their ladies, the bold ones, will lie back across the water bed. In their foundation garments and with their shoes uprooted, they look like a tumped-over outhouse. You can almost see their minds working: There must be *something* in the Bible against this. . . .

The water bed is squared by a handsome and strong wood frame, but it needed accommodations for on-board commodities, small stores, emergency equipment and consumables. With the heavy, dark, two-inch-thick lumber left over from house beams, I built a headboard. Solid and high enough for pillow propping and reading, yet open so that a groping hand could find the magazines, cigarettes, pipe, tobacco, jelly sandwiches, revolver.

I wired it for the phone jack, electrical outlets, twin reading lamps with dimmer switches that turn them down to golden candlelight. Recesses cut for ice water, soda pop, ashtrays, whiskey. All of it stressed for nine Gs and rated fully aerobatic. Nothing fancy, just the necessities for the average couple on an ordinary night.

Of course there is no really good scheme without a few flaws. You cannot get a warm place in a water bed. The water tends to assume the same temperature as the setting on the air conditioner. You wake up next morning tired. What has happened is your natural body mechanism has spent the whole night trying to heat up twelve hundred gallons of cold water. You can't even do it sleeping with a Norwegian.

I finally looked pitiful enough to carry the idea of a water-bed heater. A little rubber place mat, with a thermostat control on the wall. The mat, under the center of the water mattress, will, in a few days, give you a bed that is always warm. Then you can relax. That is if you can forget about all that electricity running around underneath all that water you are lying on.

And of course the second thing people think of when they see a water bed is, "What if it busts?"

The water bed busted on Christmas Eve. I was at the Christmas office party and was drunk already. She said to hurry, twelve hundred gallons of water upstairs, new carpet, and a seam splitting in the water bed.

You ever try to buy a water bed on Christmas Eve? They don't sell water beds in bed stores. They sell them in head shops. I had to find somebody under thirty to tell me where the local head shop is. The mojo in the head shop saw me coming in out of the rain. Me, an old, wet, drunk dude, wearing salty jeans but carrying a brief-case. He decided that if I was a narc, but wearing a disguise that bad, he might as well give me some play. He sold me a good water bed, showed me some nice hash pipes and offered genuine Indian jewelry. He was nice, but could not compute me.

I came sliding home in the mud to save the day. Diane had let the dogs into the house because she feels sorry for them when it is cold and wet. I try to tell her that each dog is issued one genuine water-proof dog suit for life, and that it is covered all over with warm dog hair, but she cares. She lets them in.

Wolf was curled up under the Christmas tree, grinning in his sinful sleep. He sprang up joyously at his master's footsteps, stuck his big brisk tail up into the tree and wagged down a bushel of ornaments. He left, blushing, wearing a string of flashing lights.

Diane gasped that we had twenty people coming for dinner and that the oven was freaking on and off and it looked like they were going to get cold turkey, but never mind that now, fix the water bed!

I fixed a hose to it and siphoned the old, leaking water bed out the bedroom window. Then, with a knife, I slashed the top out of the old water bed, where the leak had been, and left its good sides and bottom as a safety liner to install the new water bed in. Good thinking for a drunk.

I got the new water bed all spread out in position, hooked the siphon hose up to the garden faucet downstairs and started filling the new one. I laid my twirling head down on the cool merging plastic, soothed by the gurgles coming in. Some claim I went to sleep.

I was awakened by a shout. It was the shout most dreaded in

water bedsmanship or in any hospital room: "Come quick! The hose has slipped out."

I leaped up; cool water had been happily running across the top of the partly filled new water bed, through my shirt pocket, and spreading into the topless casing of the old water bed below. What we now had was two water beds. Each half full, one floating inside of the other. And another cold turkey in the oven. And twenty people coming closer and closer.

I am afraid I may have said some things that are inappropriate for the eve of the Lord's birthday. With towels, sponges and fury, I sopped out the water bed. Then slapped the oven.

Diane withdrew, taking this as the start of another scene of violence. I had to explain to her my theory called "Justifiable Equipment Slapping."

From a lifetime of working amongst faulty electrical devices in the radio station control room, I had learned that a balky turntable, or a control board that has just shorted us off the air, can be cured by slapping. Now this must not be the heavy blow of an angry man. One must pause a moment and pick up on what electrical genies inside there are no longer dancing hand in hand. The slap, always delivered curtly and with the flat of the hand, must never be of more force than required to repair the apparatus. It surprises me that the serious scientific paper on this is yet to be written.

Diane listened to all this as a mother would listen to a child. I pointed to the little red light in the oven, cheerfully glowing, cooking turkey.

The guests came, the evening was a success. Many of them touring the house admired the water bed. As usual, some asked, "What if it busts?"

Listen, you know all those books and pamphlets about how to put the excitement back into your marriage? With a water bed, you got it.

Actually I would settle for just one unexciting, ordinary day in our marriage. Diane was standing with her hands on her hips, out on the big, gracious, screened-in gallery that runs the full width of the house up under the treetops. I had built it there for the rows of bunks and the crowds of grandkids who never came.

She was silent, head tipped to one side, a dangerous sign.

"You know I was thinking of what a beautiful room this would be . . . glassed in, carpeted, looking down over the creek, this long side shaded and green high up in those big trees . . ."

I stood beside her, patient, understanding, with my arm about her shoulder. "That sure would be a great idea someday." Then I pointed out the major plumbing and wiring upheavals and finding some other place for the washer and dryer to live. And that floor-to-ceiling panels of glass on four-foot centers would have to be quarter-inch commercial-grade plate, and did she have any idea of how much all that would cost for a twelve-by-thirty-foot room? "But it sure would be a great idea someday. . . . We could call it the 'Glass Room.' "

The Catfight

I was high up on a ladder, greased with sweat and plenty of paint, preparing the frames where the glass would go. Diane had been working below, and laughing at Keats. The tomcat was giving himself a course in All About Tall Ladders. He had worked his way up with the usual mixture of cat caution and adventure, estimating ranges, considering death-defying leaps into nearby trees. At last he was at the top, sharing an aluminum rung with me and a gallon of smeared paint. Sensing the intrusion and bad manners, Keats extended a baggy leg downward, groping for the lower rungs. Diane was starting to snicker.

Keats, not willing to risk extending enough cat, gathered himself back up on the top rung and, with proper humiliation, looked into my eyes, nose to nose, and said, "Me dow-wn?" I made the trip down the ladder with cat, spent five minutes more at the bottom getting him unhooked from my clothes and skin. More girlish laughter from Diane.

Fleetwood Keats, the Houston Cadillac dealer tomcat, had got his full weight on him and a fine ruff and had developed an oily-smooth, ball-bearing lurk and a fairly respectable pounce, but he was only less than a year old. He spent his time good-guying it around the house or out rippling in the winter sun playing with dried blowing leaves. He was not yet aware of the true purpose of why his fine self was created; he neither smoked nor drank.

Now Delaney is something else. That's Tilley's tomcat from up the creek a quarter mile. Delaney dresses in tight-fitting solid black. A little string tie, silver sequins up the pant leg and buckles of solid Mexican silver, worn smooth. Delaney wears both guns low and loose, string tied to his thighs, and flat, Santa Fe crowned broad hat pulled low over his eyes. Delaney has seen things in his life that cause him to never again smile. He will glance at you with pale yellow eyes with little black gunsight slits in the middle. He smokes long, thin cigarillos, takes them slow from the lip, never dripping an ash. Delaney will gun you down just to see you jump and fall. In his game there are no second-place winners. His daddy was Hipshot Percussion; his mamma was a puma.

That's why I was so surprised to find Delaney in the house. I had heard the low snarling and thought perhaps an electric motor was burning out and surprised Delaney by the low Grandpa chair. He whirled, one hand on leather, then saw it was me and out of the side of his mouth curtly ordered me to git out, that this was none of mine.

Then I saw the gray tip of Pearl under the chair. Bent and looked, saw her laid flat in pure silent wrath, and realized what had happened. Delaney had come calling on Pearl, a purely business, professional and social call and right in her own home.

Pearl's wrath was partly from her own delicate sense of propriety and partly from betrayal of the fine balance she maintains between herself and my wife Diane. There are, after all, some things ladies never speak of in the social relationships, much less ever get caught at, clothing disarrayed, in a tawdry scene such as this.

It was while we were standing aghast at this social dilemma, this frozen tableau, that Fleetwood Keats sauntered in. He had been out with the Little Leagues, still had his ball and glove tossing casually. "Hi, Mom—"

I'm sure that's the last thing he remembers. To this very day he has never uttered that phrase again.

I certainly cannot give you a clear picture of what happened next, although I was standing right there, and from the tire tracks and skid marks we measured later it must have passed right over me at least twice.

They conducted classroom experiments at Columbia University on experiences such as this to test the credibility of eyewitness accounts. Had six, rough-looking men burst into an unsuspecting classroom and dash about, shouting and shoving and firing their revolvers into the ceiling. Of course that was some years ago. It happens every day at Columbia now and no one thinks anything of it. But back when it was a novel social experiment they found that no two eyewitnesses ever see or remember the same things.

I do recall seeing something that looked like those brawl scenes in the funny papers. A swift-moving dust cloud which was obscure, with "pow!" "biff!" "bang!" appearing in bold type above the rolling cloud and a hand or a foot sticking out here and there clutching a knife or a gun.

It rolled yowling and screaming out of the living room, down the length of the sun porch, mounted a tall cabinet and then flew back in the kitchen window over the sink and crashed like a flaming meteorite into a sink full of dishwater.

Jacques Cousteau nor none of his man-eating sharks or even a German U-boat could have lived long in there. They beat up a high, quivering head of foaming suds, someone screamed, "Torpedo!" There were thuds, gurgles, watery groans, then it was all over. They streaked out in all directions; at a glimpse they looked much smaller, slicker. They left watery suds trails, all out different doors, and Diane standing there clutching the kitchen cabinet in a puddle of her own giggles.

All but Keats. We could not locate Keats. We trolled for him in the sink. Drained it and viewed its toenail-scarred but empty sides. Looked under all the beds and dark cat places, but no Keats.

I returned to my typewriter, to my corner desk, and there in a gap in a row of books sat Keats, like one of a pair of wet-owl bookends.

Unmoving, unblinking, he stared out past us. You remember those old World War Two pictures of the British Tommies they got off the beach at Dunkirk after the panzers had them? That oil-smeared, flatted, blank, thousand-yard stare? Keats was like that. For days.

Pearl came back that evening. Had on her hat and gloves, marched in, mouth all set prim. We never mentioned it, of course, and Keats did not say, "Hi, Mom." Not then or since.

Keats had gotten in touch with the real world. He was still affectionate and loving to us, but there was a slight personality change. He became more reserved. Sometimes in the evenings he would just sit down by the water's edge and look beautiful. Often coming home at night my headlights would swing through the forest as I turned in to the house and pick him out, barely visible, sitting out in the woods. Always in the same area. We came to call it "Keats's Place."

He survived Delaney's plan to come down and finish him off. We never heard those night ambushes, but Keats would calmly saunter in to breakfast with another chunk gone out of the magnificent ruff around his neck. Diane would baby him, and doctor him and say, "I think Delaney is planning to take his head off. He's worked his way nearly all the way around the dotted line."

We didn't get any reports on what Delaney looked like, but he must have given it up as a low-yield enterprise. After a while he left Keats to his forest musing. I was never really worried that Keats would vanish of Holy Ghost Thicket natural causes as Foots had done. What worried me was his big, bushy, elegant tail, carried curled aloft. In squirrel season the townies come out and tramp all over this place, shooting at anything that moves. I wish Keats didn't look so much like a giant squirrel.

The Night of the Outlaw

We dread the opening of squirrel season. It sounds like D day in our peaceful woods. Sometimes spent shot falls, rattling on our roof. I have two shot holes in the front windows. I went out on my road and nailed up No Hunting signs on the few places you can get

it. Next day I found them riddled with shot. Hardin County men-
tality. The right of a good ole boy to carry shotguns in the back
window of his pickup. I would go down and shoo them off but only
with the utmost tribal manners and caution. Lots of "howdy" and
foot shuffling and chewing on a straw. The only reason that made
any sense to them was letting them think we were saving the game
for ourselves. True. I just don't kill anything for the fun of it. I
guess I would kill a deer, but only in self-defense. If one came up
and bit me on the elbow.

Now ole Tilley is a deer hunter. Hunts deer with dogs, an old
East Texas tradition, a kind of a moonlight opera in the woods.
"Listen, that's ole Blue . . ." "Yeah, and there's ole Tater, hear that
music? Boy, he's hot trailing." The hunt is a ritual with Tilley. The
preparation at daybreak, the hounds jumping and excited. Tilley
lives for the music of the chase. Winter evenings around the glow of
his red-hot cast-iron stove, Tilley will retell a hunt, he barks and
bays and brings it all back to life in the warm room. Tilley is more
alive when he is telling the voice of each hound than at any other
time.

The dogs scatter all to hell and gone. Most of them aren't found
for days, or weeks. There is a strong tradition in East Texas about
returning a tagged deer dog. Men have been killed over deer dogs,
and if you can get a local jury, they turn you loose.

Tilley hunts and fishes for the table. "I'd be a hard man to starve."
Many times we've been invited down to Tilley's cabin, to the long
tables set out under the trees, loaded with fragrant barbecued venison. I even ate coon there once. Had to keep shoving down the idea
that Keats or Delaney would look much the same.

For all his love of the hunt, Tilley told Diane that he would never
run deer on our peninsular bend of the creek. Diane nearly held her
breath. "He really means that, doesn't he?" We had seen deer jumping, some nights coming home on the country road.

Then Wladyslaw came to visit and told us that he had seen both
a buck and a doe, living between his place and ours. Diane's eyes
grew soft, talking about it later. "Just think, if a family of deer could
get started right here in our woods. . . . Could you go ask the

men . . . ? No, I suppose not. That would only tell the ones who don't know about it yet." And so she added one more quiet hope. A transference, you might say, of the hope of a family springing up here.

There is another family that lives far back from the creek, on high ground in a little mobile home shack. We had to keep telling ourselves that it was in all innocence and in keeping with the values they grew up with, when the two boys went around showing off the fawn they had just slaughtered.

Sickened of killings, yet I love guns, keep guns. I am an antiquer, a life member of the National Rifle Association and I get their magazine, *American Rifleman.* "Gutslammer," Diane calls it.

I like guns, but not the shooting. I do restorations; each old gun opened up a window into history for me. I am fascinated by the craftsmanship of early gunmakers, learned to run a little lathe and gas welding rig, to copy their work in restoring missing parts. Liking old guns was my redeeming grace with the rednecks. "Ole Bax, he don't hunt none, but he knows guns. You can take him an old one and he can tell you when it was made and what it's worth."

We do keep loaded guns in the house. "House guns" is what you call it, when the nearest police protection is at least a half hour away. And we are both good shots. But I had to explain to Diane that there is one thing I will kill, kill with lust and satisfaction: roaches.

We get bull roaches. Arrogant roaches. Big shiny ones that swim the river from the Louisiana side and stroll through the woods and take up with us. They will come right out and walk up the wall when you got company, making whiskers at them.

I shoot roaches off the wall. My wall, shoot roaches off of it if I want to. I told Diane about this before we were married, when I told her about all the other bad stuff: being vain, bad temper, cursing, farting, getting drunk and playing Willie Nelson too loud. Gave her every chance to back out if she wanted to.

On this particular day I had been drinking, didn't have my glasses on, and this bull roach was boldly making his way up the wall. I drew down on him, pistol wavering badly. Diane cautioned me about not hitting any of her paintings. The roach had gotten himself into a narrow place on the window facing, right next to a painting. A difficult shot, especially in my condition. The bullet grazed his liver, entered the end grain of the wooden window facing, was turned, and deflected out through the living room window.

I tried to explain to her that bullet holes in a picture window give a house "character." How many women did she know who could claim such? And that it would mean a lot when the grandkids visit. "My grandpa lives way back in the woods and shoots roaches off the wall with a pistol. What does your grandpa do?" Part of me becoming a legend in my own time.

Diane observed that "—mosquitoes are flying in the house again through the hole in your legend."

I told her that I may be getting too old and unsteady for shooting roaches off the wall with a revolver. That from now on I would use the .22 rifle. You would have thought that would mean more to her than it did.

It was during this time that we made the cat hook for the door. We were getting an excess of cat traffic in the middle of the night. Keats would come, lean over my ear and say, "Me out, me-e o-uut" until I woke up and opened the door for this gentleman. The cat hook solved all that. It kept the front door propped open three and a half inches. Easy access for the slippery cats, no way in for the dogs, each of whom contained about one-half gallon of loose sand in their hides.

The dogs would stand outside, looking like their feelings were hurt, and I would explain, "Cats are in because cats are neat. They are better than you, understand? This is discrimination. The plain, old-fashioned kind that you can't hardly get anymore. And you being dirty dogs is only part of if. Groveler there is pushy, a social climber. He forgets his place. The cat hook is for cats. Cats are polite."

Two things we failed to take into account here are that Wolf is afraid of thunder and gun-shy. Loud sounds send this great dog cringing. We are thankful for this during hunting season when the woods are full of idiots firing away at anything that moves. To get a shot at Wolf they would have to lay on their bellies and fire up under the truck.

But Wolf is equally convinced that thunder is out to get him. A thunderstorm lashing over Village Creek is a magnificent sight. When we first moved here and fought a lot, I had convinced Diane that the only and proper time to go sweeping and sluicing the leaves off the roof of the cabin was during a thunderstorm. It was really kind of wild and exhilarating up there with the treetops whipping and torrents of rain roaring on the rooftop, frothing away our sweepings. She quit doing it after she decided I was using her for lightning bait.

Today the first crash of thunder is followed by the second crash of Wolf flinging himself prone against the French doors. He lies there, trembling, loaded with sand and water, trying to outpitiful Diane.

We found out about the flaw in the cat hook on the first thunderstorm after it was installed. Diane cried, "Come quick, you won't believe this!"

In walleyed desperation Wolf was coming through a slot three and a half inches wide. You ever see an eighty-pound German shepherd trying to make himself three and a half inches wide? It makes for a very tall, thin, foolish-looking dog. He turned his jaws sideways and got them in. He shrugged his massive shoulders and got his chest through. When we caught him in the act, he was trying to shrug his hips. You ever try to shrug your hips? You can't do it. Go on, try. What he looked like was the old Red Skelton classic comedy routine of the lady putting on the rubber panty girdle.

With much shamefaced grinning he made it in and composed himself considerately near the door for easy sweep-out of the accompanying sand pile. He saw me coming, looking authoritative, and he desperately grabbed a pen and note pad off the top of Diane's desk and in a first-grader's scrawl began to painfully write, "You wouldn't send a dog out . . ." "All right," I cried, "enough. You can stay, but we are contributing to your psychosis." Diane pointed out that Wolf had done as much for me, often enough, pretending that my every homecoming was a hero's return.

Wolf settled down, safe. There was peace in the cabin. One of

Pearl's current crop of kittens came out to explore Wolf's paw which was extended out in front. What was this thing that smelled so bad, stood tall as a new kitten and looked so easy to climb? Wolf held still, the kitten climbed him, started at his wrist and began working his way up to the elbow, skitchy-skitch, little claws digging in. Wolf looked up at us, down at the kitten, trying to hold still and not giggle or sneeze. You ever see a great noble beast like that holding his breath, with his brow actually furrowed?

Wolf finally let out a long sigh which rippled the kitten's fur all the way down his back. The kitten looked up, tracing the wind-storm, saw all those jaws and big, liquid-brown eyes, turned himself into a little gray bottle brush and blew away, flat-faced and side-ways.

Diane was still watching all this, laughing, and missed the big brass bull roach on the wall and me bringing up the rifle. I got him. Right through the chitterlings. Wolf screamed, decided there was thunder in the house too. And that's how the front French doors got tore off and what happened to the idea of the cat hook.

Diane and Wolf exchanged lots of ugly comments on the trials of living with a gun nut and how some persons are utterly without consideration for the feelings of others, but the events of the next day and night bore home the truth of why guns belong on the frontier. We were glad we had them.

When the helicopter came beat beating over the cabin at 9:00 A.M., I knew something was wrong. It was such a beautiful Sunday morning. I had whistled up the dogs and made the early morning run for the paper, a mile through the cool birdsong woods. And we had enjoyed our Sunday-morning luxury squirm of hot coffee and the paper in bed, and reading parts of it to each other and knowing we didn't have to be anywhere. There was lots of purring going on inside, cardinals and squirrels were dipping and dodging outside. The words were upon me to write. I could hardly wait to get to the typewriter. It was all of a good day you could ask for.

The helicopter came back. Beat beat beating so low that the downwash of its blades fluttered the papers on my desk. Beating a growing feeling of unease into my chest. What the hell is going on out there anyhow?

I held the outside idea that maybe Dan Green had conned somebody out of a helicopter and was giving us a buzz job, or maybe about to set it down on the sandbar for a high-style visit. Such things are within the realm of being friends with Dan Green, the legendary lover, fighter, and master of the helicopter and the eleven string guitar.

I heard it coming again and went out on the sandbar. No way to even get two thoughts lined up end to end and do any writing with all that going on. And I knew what I was looking for. It was going to be that little blue sharpy that belongs to the DPS. It was. Banking off over the woods again, low and serious.

I already had it put together in my head when I went in and called the Department of Public Safety. Story in this morning's paper about some guy blowing another guy's guts out with a shotgun; they were hunting him in the woods. The lady at the highway patrol was real nice, that's what it was all right. I asked her if there was anything we needed to know. Nope. Told her if we found him I would stretch him out on the ground and give them a call. No hurry. She said not to do anything heroic.

That's not heroic. That's the facts of life back here in the deep woods. It would take the law a half hour to get here for anything if we needed them real bad. Long time ago we made arrangements, including target practice for Diane, so that they could just send out the coroner. No hurry for the coroner.

I got a private theory that is why there are so few burglaries in Vidor and Lumberton. There is a gun in every house and in every pickup, and folks just itching to use it. That would not be burglary. That would be suicide. And the burglars know it.

That helicopter beat the morning into pizza slices of noise for nearly five hours. It brought up memories of lingering terror in Vietnam. The only thing worse than riding in one is to be in your hole somewhere and hear its constant thudding. It can only mean one thing: somebody is willing to spend a lot of money and man-hours to get a little of somebody else's blood. They are oppressive.

We might could have won the war by just letting them beat all night over Ho Chi Minh's house for a few nights. Both sides shot at them. I found myself considering going out and shooting at this one.

And there ain't no way you can see a man in the jungle from a helicopter. We live in a jungle. A double-canopied rain forest. I got a shiny tin roof that is fifteen hundred square feet. I have flown low over it, looking for it, and can't see it. I pictured the Outlaw standing under a tree somewhere, holding his shotgun, laughing his sides out. I considered putting on my badman's hat and taking the rifle and going out and skulking up and down the open white sandbar just to give them a thrill.

Then the boats started going by. Boat roar and helicopter beatings blended for a while. The birds sat and looked stupefied.

There is always a lot of boat traffic on Village Creek on Sundays, but it was easy to tell which ones were laws. They wore big hats, sat up very straight, being careful not to be having any fun.

The Outlaw hunt went on all day. We kidded and snorted about it. Then it got dark.

I went around locking the doors, chambering live rounds, showing Diane how the safeties worked on the ones she doesn't handle much. It got very dark. Fort Baxter.

Groveler went out and started a steady barking at something off in the woods. We reminded ourselves that Groveler will sometimes spend half the night barking at a frog. Then Wolf went out and joined with his big-jawed hollow sound back there in the woods. A Two Dog Alarm. I turned out all the lights in the house and sat around fingering safeties, letting my eyes get used to lining up the sights in the dark. I heard Diane coming out of the bathroom; she stopped around the corner of the door: "Hey. It's me."

We sat around and talked about it and agreed this was spooky and scary as hell. They write books about and tell legends of Outlaws in the Big Thicket. And by God this is for real. "Grizzly Adams" is out there skulking around somewhere and here in Fort Baxter I am taking comfort from the solid weight of good wood and gunmetal. Them fanciful outlaw stories are a lot different when you are in one.

I carefully stepped over the rifle and went to bed, my mind working on the newspaper description of Grizzly Adams, and working on the moral aspects of what to do really? Just get off a kill shot and hope and pray that was him? Cripple him with a knee shot, maybe? Then if it was somebody else we could go down and apologize and hope he gets well real soon. I don't have much belief in the "freeze!" command à la *Hawaii Five-0*. I don't think ole Grizzly would freeze. Better I should freeze him. But what if he got a haircut and shaved off his beard? It would have been a most inappropriate time for either Dan Green or Alan Rayne to have showed up. Red beards were "go" in the Big Thicket this night.

We lay there in the darky dark. Diane got to giggling.

"What's with you?"

"Oh, I was just thinking. Hair-triggered and heavy-caliber armed as you are right now, if one of those cats knocked a food bowl off the top of that porch table it would take five hundred dollars worth of lumber and glass to cover up all the holes."

I reached over and gathered her up. The protective gesture of the husband during the long night of the Outlaw. What I was hoping she couldn't figure out was that as much as anything else, I was just holding on.

Sheriff Billy Paine's men on horseback with hounds got Grizzly Adams next day. He had spent the night hiding in the woods about a mile from here.

Distant Diesels

I kept hearing the distant diesels, late into the evenings, sometimes it seemed like on the weekends. I decided it might be a distant drilling rig spudding in. They wildcat up here in the Big Thicket sometimes, and in the winter when the trees are bare the sound will carry a long, long ways. I wouldn't let myself think I was hearing clear cutting. But the sound was getting closer.

Then last week I came around the bend on the county road and met a log truck loaded with fresh pine, and at the next bend I came up on the dozers clear cutting.

I've seen what clear cutting the Big Thicket does from an airplane. The dozer leaves long swaths of grayed-up earth and the hardwoods and brush are shoved up in windrows and burned. And a couple of years later flying over the same acreage you see the orderly rows of little green pines. The plantation pines. Good timber crop. Nothing else can live there, but they come up pulpwood size in a few short years and being it's rows, it's cheap labor to go and harvest them. Good timber management. Death to everything else that ever lived in the woods.

I've been watching clear-cutting dozers destroying the Big Thicket for years as I flew over it, but nothing ever prepared me for what I saw here. I guess that's why Big Timber never lets you civilians see it going on. They always leave what they call a "screen" of the natural beauty of the forest between what they are doing and the road. But here they were turning the tractors around in the county road, tore hell out of that too. And left it.

I stopped and watched in a sort of sick horror like you might not be able to tear your eyes away at the sight of a gang of depraved hoodlums dismembering a dying dog. The dozer would lock one tread and spin about, leaving churned earth, and go straight in toward the tree that was marked with the cancer-blue splotch of death. The driver shoved over all the chinky pin oaks and little magnolias and shoved the bright green holly into the earth and churned over it. He was clearing a swath wide enough for the log truck or the skinner to get in there. It's a machine big as the dozer with a big shiney claw on it. After the mature tree is brought to death it goes in there and drags out the corpse, destroying whatever ferns, flowers, eggs, nests, and hopes and dreams that the cat tractor might have missed.

I've seen places that looked like that before. In Vietnam after a good fire fight. There ain't nothing left alive. Nothing, just splinters, stumps, churned-up gray ground.

"You fellers ain't leaving much of the forest," I said to the cat driver as he paused for my pickup to get by.

"Nope, shore ain't," he grinned good-naturedly around his chaw.

I compared this worthy to the forester that this same timber company has on its big billboard spotted along the highways through the Thicket. Picture of a handsome young man in a white hard hat, he's bending over tenderly holding a pine seedling in the palm of his hand like it was his own baby. The billboard reads, To be a forester, you've got to love the forest.

I drove on through the remains of how much these guys love the forest. The once-shady, mile-long road to where the private property begins was now a gaping, bombed-out, still silently screaming scene of waste and horror. Well, hell, I reasoned with me, it's their woods, they can do what they want to with it. Like everywhere else, time is money. Rape is quicker than persuasion. I just never had seen a motorized timber crew at work. It's a sickening sight. I thought of my place on down the road. My road was crooked as a tromped-on snake because I didn't have the heart to take out not one single mature tree. I got new pines about eight feet tall that I saw start up as seedlings when we first came here in '68. I got little oaks about two feet tall that we are careful to step around because we remember the year of the great bounty in acorn fall and we've watched them come up. I'm what they call some kind of a nut.

I keep thinking that there used to be 3.5 million acres of Big Thicket and only one-tenth of it's left, and supposed to be protected by law. Haw, haw. The big ole Holy Ghost Thicket, where seven major ecological systems overlap, where we got 350 species of wild birds, 1000 species of flower plants, all 4 major brands of poisonous snakes, and deer and fox and coons and cats and wild orchids grow within fifty feet of cactus at my place. And people walk into this and down to the tall cypress in the hush of the ferned baygall and you can almost touch God's toes. Nuts. I must be some kind of a nut.

Big Timber got to make a living. They make all them paper sacks you use once and throw out, and all those paper cups, and plywood and 2 X 4 studs. Man we can't live without that. It's wood. It comes out of the trees. You like steak? Don't visit a slaughterhouse.

But still I'm sore about it. I can't reason me down. Sore because Big Timber is using the Big Lie. Just like Hitler and the oil companies did. If you tell a lie often enough and big enough you can get anybody to believe it. They tell you they use up all the tree but the shadow. Buelle Chitte. Go back in there and look at the thirty-foot tops they left smothering out the mayhaws. They tell you they plant so many trees for every man, woman and child in Texas. Go back in that charnel house they left and count how many seedling to ten-year-old trees they wasted. They come on the TV and in the papers with all that good-guy varnish about their game preserve and how they are looking after them little foxes. What they don't tell you is that all them trees they are planting are pines, in rows, and nothing grows. It takes acres of real woodsy woods to support that family of brilliantly beautiful wood ducks that still survive behind my place. I guess I wouldn't be hating Big Timber so bad right this minute, with a deep, smoldering hatred of hopelessness, if they were not grinning and lying at me at the same time they are laying waste to the land. The gallows joke in their own excellent and well paid PR office is, "There's a stump in your future."

I don't feel right about ranting and raving and not coming up with some constructive answers. I don't have any. But I tell you what they are doing out there in the woods is wrong. We are consumers, wastrels, gobblers, stripping our own little planet bare. Maybe at the Tricentennial some student will present this yellowed clipping to his class and read it and they will say, "Good Lord, did we really act like that back then?" Or they may ask, "What was a forest?"

Chapter 11

So Long, Kid

House wrens are good luck. They will only nest in a house where there is love. But, like in all affairs of love and nesting, terrible chances must be taken. Those involved will get put out of shape.

Last year wrens nested in the seat of my favorite cutoffs which I had laid over the porch railing to dry. You ever wait for eggs to hatch to put your pants back on? Or wear a pair that had a recent bird nest in the seat? All this in exchange for the song of the wren at daybreak.

Now they are building in a hanging planter which swings on the front porch. Their front porch. Step outside and they flutter up into the tree, about two feet, and glare and shake their fists at you.

Fleetwood Keats, Houston Cadillac dealer and Junior Tomcat, absolutely cannot believe his good fortune. That wrens are nesting right there, right above his place in the sun. He just sits there fascinated, watching them come and go with bits and twigs in their beaks. I can see inside Keats's head. He is dreaming of Southern Fried Wren, Wren in a Basket, Wren au gratin, Wren Roccaforte, Wren on the half shell, Wren & giblets.

Pearl is watching too. Pearl has her own inner thoughts: she is bulging and poking with kitten elbows again. Diane is watching. She is longing to be carrying bits and twigs in her beak, to be bulging and poking with elbows. She softly says to me, "Every hollow in my body wants your baby."

A man who attempts to raise baby birds and cats on the same front porch has his work cut out for him. You ever try to change a cat's mind? Or a woman's?

I am not sure what having a baby will do to us. I am sure of what denying a baby will do to us.

That's not much, but it's logical. And a man who seeks logic in love deserves whatever he gets for supper.

There was a change in our lovemaking. No longer was the bark of the fox heard sharply over Village Creek. Now she held me, the crooning began with me, thinking baby. She lay soft and still long afterward. "No. Don't move. Hold me." At first I attributed this to perhaps my great technique. Or our newfound friendship and closeness. What she was doing was marinating.

Her intensity employed her total mind, which in turn reached out and used up books and every other shred of information available through science, folklore or witchcraft. She wanted to siphon dry the mind of her OB doctor. She came home in a fury the day he gave her the herd-through-the-chute treatment and patted her on the head and said, "There, there, little lady." She condemned him and all his progeny to the darkest pit and got another doctor. One who would sit down with her after he had stripped off the glove and debrief the mission in clinical detail.

M.I.T. would have paid a ransom just to have her come in and read thermometers. At a tenth of a degree fluctuation I would be summoned. Not even a kiss on the cheek. "Hey, you! Here," patting the bed. In reply to my mild complaint she said, "Now you know how the harem girl must feel. Get on, Ace, or are you only going to stand around there and talk about it all day?"

She counted down her lunar month in hours, not days. "We are fifty-six hours late now. My breasts are tender; do they look swollen?" And I would count the days back in my mind, yes, that could have been the time. I remember actually praying at the instant, "Dear God, give us a baby, now that we are ready." And that night I was awakened by her coming back from the bathroom, curling up little and cold against me, and hot tears splashing on my chest. Rejected again. And I remember holding her and praying, "Aw, c'mon, God, surely . . ."

And then there came a long lunar time. Stretching out still longer, silent goings-on in there, measured by the hard round thumpings of a heart beating beneath a swollen breast. We guarded our emotions. Did not order confetti or champagne. Both of us fully aware that the intensity of her mental powers was capable of creating almost real events in her physical process. But this time went on. And on. Could she simulate morning sickness? Normally she is never late. You could regulate the tides by her body. We decided to risk the pregnancy test. It came back negative. They got it wrong.

At what we figured five weeks we did the test again. Still negative. Nonsense. Something has got her. Her whole body is changing. We began to be careful, so as not to disturb the little fellow clinging to the wall in there. At six weeks medical science caught up with a mother's heart. Confirmed what she already knew. We called her family and mine.

Daughter Molly, at the prospects of having a little sister more than thirty years younger than her: "You are going to have an interesting old age." Son Roney: "Where your head was twenty years ago made us pretty interesting guys. I can't wait to see what kind of a kid you and Diane will have from where your head is now."

She began to sign our tuckaway notes "me & the kid." She took on a protective and supportive role to tide me through this difficult time, that is, my pregnancy.

"For encouragement and concern and tender love, I thank you. The Kid may not be so bad—he might be president of the U.S., or a jet pilot—after all, he is your kid." And this: "Imagine that! A little being 47 days old. Half you and half me. It is going to be interesting and smart and sexy too—just like us."

I was scheduled for a flight to do a story for the magazine. The doc said, "No, don't risk it." She said, "I'm sorry." And I told her

I could make it alone, but most of all not to ever say, "I'm sorry" again for anything having to do with being pregnant. "The new being in your body is about one-quarter inch long now. That's not much, but it is the first time he has changed some events on earth. Changed our lives. There will be many more. Not sorry, be proud . . . for the rest of our lives."

I returned through perilous skies; the storm had felled a giant oak across our road. Power lines down. No light, no water at the cabin. Diane was at the Giarratanos. Feet up, pale. Cramping and spotting. She comforted me. "If we lose it, it's God's rejection of an imperfect fetus. At least we know we can conceive." Strong, she is strong in the real crunches. We had been given three days from knowing we were going to have a baby to knowing we were going to lose it.

Next day I cleaned house. She made rude remarks about what if my ole pappy could see me now, doing "woman's work"? I told her I still don't do windows. Betty Em and Bernard came out that night and laid on a great Italian supper. We had the red-checkered table-cloth, the candlelight and the wine. Diane was good. She only chafed a little about "—not knowing what's going on in there. Give me enough knowledge and I can handle anything."

Next day, getting ready to go, she said, "I feel seedy." Getting packed up to go to the hospital and lose her baby, and she was worried about how her hair looked. I shampooed her, and we sat out on the porch awhile, drying and watching the light change over the creek until she was soft and bright as a kitten in the sun.

On the ride into town she began to hurt, to twist in pain. But she never said, "Poor me," or "Why me?" She cried a little while, but by the time I was checking her in, the tears had stopped and her face cleared in strength. But I was running. I was talking to me inside my heart. Why are you running, old man? Running because all you touch turns to pain? The brightest flower swells, and blooms in beauty, then bursts and lies open in corruption, even as you too must in your grave someday.

Who do you run from, ole man? You touched them, they loved you, then drove you out, then want you back. Nothing ever helps, eh? Go on, pass in the night, showboat, but do not stop to corrupt.

Then she was in the sterile steel room. That is no place for love's sweat to cool. And the little Dacron priestess who guards the door had put me out in the corridors among the peasants. "Look, Junior, that is the man you see on the TV. See him cry?" And then there was an officer at my heels saying I must come and move my car. Everything has its place here. Where is your place, ole man? You must ever move among them, but never touch their lives in your living fantasy.

Crouch now among the peasants, wounded out here in this corridor. You are not of the peasants nor of the kings, but you are a thinking machine, aren't you? What would you give to be able to shut your mind off right this minute? The one that told her, "This is God's business, this borning, this dying. It's always God's business." Bravo. I wonder who it is in there who is not ever going to get here.

The kid didn't make it. Had his birthday and his funeral all in one day in a room they call Blue 7, then went out with the garbage. Bummer.

Heard her bark like a fox twice in there. No screamer she. The Lord giveth, the Lord taketh away. A pile of bloody rags. Amazing grace. Why am I crying? Why can't I stop? "Blighted ovum," he said. Blighter it was. Why do I keep crying so hard? She is relieved. She is bucking me up. We had a short funeral, like we do table grace, holding hands. Only the table is cleaned up now. Little blighty is gone.

The kid didn't make it.

So long, kid.

We had to go back, of course, for the D & C. Pearl had kittens. I had to be in Jasper as parade marshal for the rodeo. They rolled Diane back to her bed. She came swimming to the surface. "Water. Just wet my lips, please. Cigarette. Just a drag. . . . Pearl is not ever going to speak to me again. . . she's got brand-new babies . . . and I'm whisking everybody away . . . do you really think I am pretty? . . . Oh, I hurt."

I brought her back to Village Creek. The critters gathered round her, moon-eyed, waiting for her touch on their heads. She held up a handful of kittens. "I might as well have kept the bloody rags. That's all the baby I will ever have. . . ."

Drove sixty miles to the Jasper Rodeo. Rode in a big black Cadillac with my name on it. Out in front of the high-school band and the cowboys and cowgirls and clowns and gunfighters. All I had to do was wave and grin. Didn't even have to throw out the first horse turd at the rodeo like they do at baseball. Went to the country club, played millionaire, got drunk.

Came roaring in, slamming doors. Diane wide awake, wanted to tell me about all her bright new plans for next time, for redoing the bedroom for a nursery. Watching her hands move through my whiskey eyes, moving like winging Canadian geese headed south. They keep coming. Some of them always get here.

Village Creek Will Heal You

The waters of Village Creek will heal you. Not surprising that little has been said of this in the scientific community. What do they know of the tangle tongue elm that will cure toothache? Or why ole Archer wears a red rag on his shoulder when he's got bursitis? Or why does a dog roll in dung, or about snow snakes, or revelation among the frogs?

The waters of Village Creek will heal you. Aches and wounds get better right away. I taught Diane this when she first came here, to wade the creek and make the awful red welts of mosquito bites go away. Mosquitoes do not bite me. They circle and sing, but never sting. I have a natural immunity. Diane says it is the awful load of tobacco and whiskey fumes I carry in my bloodstream. That, plus my natural venom.

We went out on the creek after we lost the kid. Took the canoe and just drifted in silence, looked and listened, trying to find some answer to, "Why, God?"

Everything in the Holy Ghost Thicket is God's work. Man cannot create nature, he can only change things. When we look out our windows we see only the works of God, and in His works we find His word.

In the dark baygall the tall cypress is blasted by lightning. She grieves, then the stump heals and sends forth tender shoots to fight for life and to be whole again. In the stillness of the night before a thunderstorm, we hear a forest giant crash. We go there next day and look upon the thrashings of that death. What we see are new seedlings sprouting. New life to be nourished from the body of the parent who is returning to earth.

If the bright hot days are too constant, then wait. God is sending an infinite variety of wind and cloud and rain. If all the familiar stars in the sky are shifting in a bewildering pattern of summer and winter, then look, there is Polaris, always constant.

And all of the creatures of the forest live and die in the same delicate balance of the wheeling of the stars of the universe. Did God make the delicate organs of the lunar moth any less intricate than those of the fox? Or less wondrous than the motions of the stars? All things set in balance and in a harmony of life. Life springs out of death in the fecund forest floor. The young sapling trees bend before whatever forces confound them, but reach ever upward toward the light.

In the long twilight Diane and I walked in silence down by the water's edge. There was dead calm, not a ripple of wind. The tall pines stood at the reflected painting of themselves.

We waded in the shallows, seeing our bare feet on the clear white sand bottom, standing naked. The full summer moon rose into the pine tops like pale music. With infinite care I leaned her head back, washing her hair. It flowed dark from her trusting face.

We stayed until the Eastern star rose bright over our sand-floored cathedral. And the other day a fellow asked me if we went to church. . . .

Gimpy

Pearl had littered again and cast a bad one. This is not to speak poorly of Pearl who for the past five years has brought purring into this cold world a fine and high grade of woods cats at the rate of two litters per year, five cats per borning, or a total of about fifty pussycats whose fame and reputation have become widely known. But Pearl cast a bad one, odds on that someday she would. A little black kitten with only a flipper for a right rear leg.

Tradition is long established back in the deep woods about what you do if you get a bad one in the litter. The man of the house waits until the womenfolk have gone on ohing and ahing about how cute the little darlings are, and ain't it a shame about that one, then he picks up that one and goes off and closes his mind to it and quickly does what he has to do.

I knew what I had to do, and that we would never speak of it later. I decided first thing in the morning. One more day would not make any difference; little thing did not have its eyes open yet anyhow. Days dragged by. We did not speak of the matter. I was waiting for a time when Diane would not be there. Gradually I began to notice that she was always there.

The little broken kitten began to emerge as a somebody. Shiny black she was, and just as good as her brothers and sisters at rooting in Pearl's soft belly for a place at the lunch counter. Her eyes opened. She would curl up in the palm of my hand and gaze at me with bright, round button eyes, her little head bobbing, trusting. Gradually I began to know that we were stuck with a three-quarter cat. And that I did not mind. We called her Gimpy, naturally enough.

I will never understand how there could be such a force of personality in such a tiny grotesque creature. Skittering, quartering, across the floor like a blown leaf. She held her tail out to the southwest, stiffly, balancing. No problem to Gimpy; she never knew anything about being a four-legged cat in her life. She takes good care of Gimpy, but seems to be the most affectionate of the lot. She comes wide-eyed and open, looking for laps, looking to see if anyone needs a warm place, some purrs.

Young Doc Crenshaw fell for Gimpy. The two of them did all sorts of experiments with bone grafting and metal pins. Gimpy seemed to be able to work it out with Diane. "You mean we are going back to that place again where they hurt my leg and I wake up with such an awful headache and some new kind of a cast to drag around? Well, ok, I trust you."

There was repeated surgery, the tiny kitten hippety-hopping around, always in a good humor in your lap. "Please excuse my cast, I know it looks awful, but I think they are getting my foot turned around like it ought to be. You want some good neck-arching purrs? I got a strong neck."

And if you asked her about it, Gimpy would repeat in a childlike voice, but with surprisingly well-ordered thoughts, the technical details of her case as she had heard it discussed in his office. "He said he had neither heard nor read of a congenital bone deformity like mine. He said it was really an interesting case." And Billy Crenshaw, who sees all sorts of busted-up valuable animals all day, including thoroughbred racehorses, always asks if Gimpy is putting her foot down yet. And I think he undercharged us too.

Crenshaw and Diane then got into a discussion over the prolific Pearl. The prognosis: "She will wear herself out having kittens." The diagnosis, to meddle with the law of the jungle again. He explained that The Pill is now available for cats.

Diane elected The Pill over surgery because of the bleakness of a future with no Pearl cats at all. She also feared that Pearl's voice might change and she would grow a mustache if she were disconnected. Pearl was not consulted. Too bad.

Cats, of course, are never unaware of what is going on in your mind, and Pearl warned Diane. There was a standoff and a lot of wary eyeing of the two ladies stalking each other around the house. Diane persisted, even after Pearl went into the other bedroom and got up under Grandma's bed into the most remote and inaccessible corner, committed an unspeakable act of great revenge. Either that or a puma got into the house.

Diane wailed, "What do you think she is trying to tell me?" I said, "Why don't you go read it like tea leaves." Pearl resolved the contest by exercising her total independence. This time she left us a note. Written in a looping backhand on her personal pink stationery, it said, "Freedom and independence are states of being without which no one can ever hope for individual rights."

She left her car keys hanging on a nail, and we later learned she had her phone disconnected and canceled *Family Circle*. We had lost Pearl.

All through that cold and freezing winter to come, Diane would pause, forget what she was doing at the moment and gaze out the warm cabin windows into the dark rainy night, wondering if her little gray velvet friend was warm and dry somewhere.

I tried to give consolation. "A cat is never lost. A cat always knows where she is at. People get lost, cats don't."

I heard that she had crossed the Sabine and got a job in a bar in Louisiana. Someone else said she was working for an attorney in Shreveport.

Keats knew. He began to give himself airs at the food bowl. Took to sunning himself in Pearl's places, not even bothering with the antimacassar.

Pearl was gone. Our original woods creature. To have faulted Diane for this would have been needless and cruel.

Rape

There was enough cruelty already, blowing across Texas, a high, thin, poisoned wind. We got a call from Diane's friends in Dallas: "Come quick, Lea has been raped. Beaten and raped . . . she needs you. . . ."

Diane's friend Lea is a gentle, almost dreamy person. Never married, twenty-five, and with that special beauty in her face that chubby girls always seem to have. Lea has always been attracted to the medical profession, dreamed of being a doctor when she was a little girl, but Lea does not have the edge in her for that. She reads fine books, leaves them opened, facedown on the floor where she fell asleep. Her house is bright with art, posters, she never puts a lid back on a jar. She will loan you her old VW anytime, and empty soda pop bottles will fall out of it for five minutes after you open the door and then you'll find out it hasn't had any brakes for years, the lights don't work and the horn peeps every time you turn a corner. Lea wears yesterday's clothes, and will sit up all night with you talking and laughing about how the world ought to be tomorrow. She is a rescuer. Her hospital jobs are nearly always taking care of aged men whose lights are slowly flickering out, or with drawn-back little children in their institutions. She'll bring the worst one home for Christmas, the little boy no one can reach. In her personal life Lea is not exactly what you'd call a swingin' single.

Ponytail stalked her.

First the obscene phone calls. Then threatening notes pinned to her door. Then the hate in him seethed over. He hit her at the curb. There was a surprised scuffle for the purse, then she saw the knife arcing at her. Lea threw up a defending hand; it took eighteen stitches to close up the slash. As he ran he yelled, "Now I got your purse. . . . I know all about you. . . . I'm not finished with you yet. . . ."

To the Dallas police it was just a part of that night's dredgings of assault. The family huddled, Lea's Daddy gave her his shotgun to put under her bed and nailed windows shut. Ponytail kept up his campaign of terror ever so lightly. Just enough.

It was 2:30 A.M. when he slit the back-door screen and reached in to silently unlock the door. When she woke up the knife was at her throat. He left a little skin cut there too.

"He kept beating me with his fists. He would beat me unconscious and I would wake up and he would start hammering at my face again. I was expecting to be dead, that would get it over with, but I could still feel the pain of his chewing. Not just biting, he chewed me. The sharp pain is going away now, but not the things he was saying. Talking to himself about killing me . . . and the hate."

He cut the phone lines and left her unconscious.

Lea's next beating came from the police and the doctor at Parkland Hospital. "They all wanted to look. I stood around like a side of beef. There were forms to fill out."

Well, let's be reasonable. Dallas is a big city. How were they to know that this was not just another lovers' quarrel? The lab work was done. "There was too much blood flow from where you got chewed for us to get a specimen. I'm afraid you'll just have to file assault charges, ma'am."

Lea said the rest of the interrogation was just like you read about it in Rape Crisis Center pamphlets. The questions led up to, but never quite said, "Did you provoke him? Did you fight hard enough? Did you enjoy it . . . just a little . . . heh heh heh." And Lea began to carry part of the guilt.

"There was no one to advise me. No one to tell me what I was supposed to do next." So nothing was done.

Ponytail came back. First by phone, then leaving chicken guts and blood smeared on her door. The police took the "complaint calls." Lea moved in with her parents. Ponytail had that phone number too.

Lea's dad and I talked about it now that his house was a fortress. "Go public with it," I told him. "Write a letter to the *Dallas Morning News*. They'd love it, and it would heat up the cops. Make it as important to them as if it had been the mayor's daughter." That worked.

But time had passed. When they called Lea down to view the lineup, she said, "That was probably him, but how could I point an accusing finger at one man's life? Suppose I was mistaken?" They turned them all loose.

Lea's dad had been a South Pacific Marine. He is a sort of a quiet and deliberate man. He kept the loaded Colt .45 within reach for a long, long time, but mostly he would sit in silence with a whetstone whispering over the edge of his machete. "I don't want it to be too quick for him."

Lea stayed awhile with us on the creek. Village Creek will heal you. Diane and Lea squandered the nights, laughter came back. They played "spoon," the silliest game you can imagine. A little girl game. Lea healed. Went back home, found another hospital job. Nothing will ever heal Ponytail.

Pearl's Back

I would have gladly shared that awful winter with Diane, but duty called me elsewhere. I explained to her before my departure who to call for a chain saw in case a frozen tree fell across the road and trapped her. I instructed her on shutdown procedures for the pump and other exposed plumbing which was never designed for extreme cold. Warned her that if the well head and lines were not drained down their freezing could burst the expensive cast-iron casings. Provided for her with every detail of thoughtfulness and consideration before I was forced to take our private plane and fly away for a week in the Bahamas. A must assignment from the magazine.

Oh, I begged her to go. She was eaten up with the What Ifs. "What if I am pregnant? What if Pearl comes back? What if you fly that damn thing all day and it falls in the ocean?" And so with great reluctance I left her alone in the winter woods, guarded by our faithful friends, Wolf, Groveler, Keats and a three-legged cat.

And I vow to you now that each evening when we came up from diving off the reef at Lost Hope Bay Lodge, and sunset painted the clear warm ocean in purples and gold, and the drums began to beat and the rum to flow and the limbo contest began and the barefoot dancing in the sand under the palms, that all I sought was some good companion to listen to my story of that brave lonely maiden back there in the woods held in winter's grip and how I love her.

And that brave and lonely maiden was even then up on a stepladder with winter's grip on a Crescent wrench, teetering and pulling at the frozen threads of a rusty drain cock on the cast-iron pump of the well head. She was strong. Good muscle tone built up from carrying four buckets of water across the sandbar and up a flight of stairs each time she needed to flush the toilet. She was warm, although the night was cold and blowing a freezing wind, for she was carrying an armload of blankets to swaddle the pump with, and she later said, each time she thought of me it warmed her.

Suddenly she sensed that she was not alone. Something had emerged from the woods and was approaching the foot of the ladder. She tried to look, but just then the petcock opened and a stream of refreshing water, flaky with ice, spurted up her mackinaw sleeve, into her armpit and trickled down her sides.

"Meow."

That small-mouthed little voice. My God, it could only be Pearl. She swung the flashlight beam down; the water began to run down now and off the end of the light. "Pearl! Oh, I am so glad to see you. Home, you're home. Wait, honey, just one minute, Mommy's in a kind of an awful fix just now, I'll be right there. Soon as I get that stupid old pump fixed, and if this ladder doesn't shift again and kill us all, and we will go in the house and celebrate. Hot soup, peaches. Oh, Pearl, I'm so glad you came back."

Pearl raised up her tail until there was just a tiny little hook, right in the tip of it, snugged her fur jacket up under her chin, and sauntered off into the dark around the edge of the house, saying something under her breath about, "If you are all that glad to see me you would quit monkeying around up there and leaving me standing out here in the wind; anyway, you are sprinkling stuff on my coat."

And Pearl was gone. Again.

Tilley came down next day and helped Diane sort out the pump. None of the plumbing was lost, but she couldn't get it reprimed and Bellinger, our well man, wouldn't fool with her and she was still carrying up buckets of water to the toilet when I got in from the Bahamas two days later. Boy, I had some great flying stories to tell her. And Pearl came back same day I did. And both of us spent the next three days sitting and staring at each other, playing, "Guess what's the matter with Diane?"

You would think she would have been glad to see us. Or at least talk to us.

The Jelly Tree

Springtime started with a tiny budding, urging outside winter's gray window. The very most fragile folding of infant leaves, bidden to come at stark branch endings.

Springtime skipped into the high elder trees and showered down jasmine. We came over pathways carpeted with perfect yellow trumpet blossoms.

Springtime suddenly swept the cold dark woods and left it shimmering dots of new green dancing in sunlight against the somber shadows.

Such a sudden silent bursting of life, calling us to come out of winter's cave. We could almost feel the earth heave with it as we walked the baygall to this bidding song.

And this our first year here in the Holy Ghost Thicket to not be flooded under icy water at springtime. The dry winter kept Sister Creek low, showed the savaged scalloping of what's left of once full-breasted white sandbars. The curse of man's management, of the United States Corps of Engineers and their dams. Ah-h, well, no time for bitterness. Let it be upon their heads.

So we walked the new ground where once there was water moving among the trees. Our footsteps crunched September's leaves down into dry hollows where the ancient creek once flowed. To that special place of things that grow where they know the waters will return, the shaded cool places of cypress trees and cypress knees and water trees.

And here we discovered our hidden mayhaws.

Now the mayhaw is a scraggly little tree. A shrubby, scrubby, little gauntling of no distinguishing characteristics to mark such a glorious creature that grows the most delicious jelly in the known world.

A shy tree that hides her head in the lower reaches of this double-canopied rain forest. She seeks out the hidden and hard-to-get-at places. The places of dank and dark and misery of the bones and she only raises her voice twice each year. Once in February when she is first down the cotillion in her white lace dress of a million bee-buzzing blossoms, and again in April when I guess each blossom rounds itself into a juicy red berry and she becomes the jelly tree of the innermost heart of the snake-crawling, turtle-splashing, crow-cawing Holy Ghost Thicket.

So we found her, and her sisters, and we marked the places in the secret map of our minds. And now I am already dreaming of this as the lever for a glorious reunion with nasty ole Archer, stooped and nose dripping over his steaming kitchen caldrons of mayhaw jelly making.

I will bring mayhaws to Archer, white-eyed and grinning I will come before him and compromise him into enjoying his seventy-third springtime. And I will hem Diane up in the kitchen with him to study his slightest move and to read the mumbling incantations of his lips so that she may capture the secret of the jelly tree which will make a jar of pale jelly that will curl up your toes on the chair rungs and make your eyes water and your nose run and you will know that there is indeed a God in heaven in all His mystery.

Archer owes me about four-hundred jars of mayhaw jelly. Not collected when I wrote for the cast-iron editions of the flatbed press *Kountze News*. He paid me for thirteen years of learning how to write on his cut-sheet pages in mayhaw jelly and gourds, but I didn't collect. I was too caught up in worldly affairs then to see that the wounded world was actually looking for Archer and the truth that came out of this crazy old man who walked like a bear.

You know Archer Fullingim was famous for his mayhaw jelly before he and Senator Ralph Yarborough saved the Big Thicket, and Arch got discovered and featured in *National Geographic*, or even before he went on the NBC *Tomorrow Show*. We watched him on that thing. I could tell he was going to sleep. Went to sleep, nodded off right there on the whole network, live, with all that prattle going on. The MC woke him up.

"What did you go to sleep for?" He was a little hurt.

"Got bored, I guess." Actually it was way past Archer's bedtime, but he'd never go out of his way to keep the wind in a feller's sails.

But Archer was famous in a way before all that. He had met Lyndon Johnson when LBJ was hand pumping across Texas for the Senate. Archer always used to say, "I'm a brass-collar Democrat. I'd vote for a blue-nose mule if that was the only Democrat on the ticket." He and Lyndon hit it off right away.

Arch sent Lyndon mayhaw jelly during all the years in the Senate, and then it was another one of the things the White House staff had to learn about the new president from Texas. But he and LBJ got crossed up over some policy the president announced, and Archer blessed him out in the *Kountze News* and cut him off. No more mayhaw jelly to the White House.

Little bits of sincere meanness like that will make a man a beloved figure in Hardin County. Even Arch, who was cordially hated by most of his subscribers.

Another living legend of the tart little berry is Big Mamma Mayhaw.

Big Mamma has a beautiful Indian face and a voice like lutes and she weighs two hundred and twenty stone. She goes out into the baygall before daybreak with her giant-size bib overalls tucked into rubber boots to keep the water moccasins from crawling up her pants leg and she gathers mayhaws and sells them on the roadside by the Pine Island Bayou bridge on the way to Silsbee, beside her old purple Mercury.

Last year was a poor year for mayhaws and Big Mamma. She only got seven hundred gallons. Got $2.25 for the early ones, $2.50 for the late ones. She says the early mayhaws are squatty.

Big Mamma says the government takes most of her mayhaw money. And that her belly is too big for her to bend over and pick up the berries, so she goes crawling into the bushes on all fours with her dark hair hanging beside her face. Goes back to where the thorns and vines are too thick, then she lies down and pulls herself along. If you could see where Big Mamma went in for mayhaws, it would look like there had been a hog fight there.

Big Mamma is a protected species in my mind. I think of her as the tender springtime bud of the American system of free enterprise. She is the factory, distribution and retailing. I give her free advertising. One radio station was aghast when she asked them for that. They said not on your life we won't. She put a curse on them.

And I wish Big Mamma could be tax exempted, like a schoolhouse or a church. An eleemosynary institution, maybe? Or if not, I would relish the idea of an agent of the Internal Revenue Service in his natty suit and white shirt and careful tie accompanying Big Mamma on her rounds. Back into the baygall with her before daybreak, maybe on a day when she has to range up as far as Kirbyville to find berries, and waller through the mud and chiggers and wonder if a moccasin is going to crawl up his pants leg.

And then stand out beside the Eastex Freeway with her all the rest of the day in the traffic zoom and the purple Mercury and rows of rusty cans of bright berries heaping. Let him smell the hot copper of her pennies and count out his share of the first wadded bills when the night hawks come swooping. Or let a member of the Senate Appropriations Committee do that. I bet that money would seem like real money to them then.

Sometimes I wonder if money is real anyhow. We bought an airplane, and that's a big chunk of our money, but I couldn't ever tell any of it was gone. I never had owned an airplane, never would have bought one, but that was not because of money. That was because I didn't think I deserved one.

Airplanes have been almost mythical in my life, becoming a pilot over twenty years ago was like entering holy orders. To me, all of flying still has a halo around it, but renting planes, bumming planes, fitted my station in life.

Diane understood all this, but viewed it from standing outside the spell. "Why not? We can afford it, you earn part of your living flying. Airplanes have always been so much a part of your life . . . go on, free yourself up, Ace."

I think part of this came from trips she had shared in rented airplanes. The cockpits of rented airplanes always smell like burned oil and full ashtrays. Most had a gaping hole in the panel where some instrument had burned out. The door would pop open in flight on a few of them.

We found a ten-year-old Mooney. A Mooney is what Sammy Davis, Jr., would have been had he been born an airplane. Flying that swift little song-and-dance airplane and thinking of it as mine, to use anytime, was to raise the beauty of flight to a plateau I never knew existed.

There is no way I can think of its song of beauty as something I had exchanged money for. Actually I never saw any money changing hands. I just signed some paper in the bank, the owner handed me the keys. I fled before they realized that all they had was some dry paper and I had that whole round little airplane.

Tankers Is Tankers

I had only sneaked out to the Grass Airport to see if maybe my airplane was lonesome for me, and the place was swarming with TV newsmen. They were really hyper, burdened like camels, nickering and shoving at each other. I asked airport manager Pappy Sheffield what was up. Air Force One going to make a try for our four-thousand-foot runway or something?

"Naw, there's another Liberian tanker aground out in the Gulf of Mexico, and all my planes are out, and these guys are all eaten up with wanting a plane and pilot to fly the cameramen out over the scene."

In less time than it takes to say "oil spill," I had a handsome TV newsy strapped into my Mooney and the only instructions above the roar were, "One hundred and eighty degrees and twenty-five miles off Sabine Pass."

I told this turkey beside me that he could plan to start filming in exactly 12.5 minutes, but as the coastline faded, that old feeling of "this sure is a lot of water out here" rose up in my chest and I privately called Beaumont Approach and advised them of where they should start looking, and whom to call for the distribution of my personal effects.

And as the little Lycoming went to "over water rough," I got to thinking that there sure are a lot of boats out here in this oil field, and if the engine quits I hope I can bounce in close to one, and the water sure looks cold. Other than that, I kept my lean, Pappy Boyington profile to the sun. Inspiring confidence.

Sure enough, right on course, right on time, we came upon a huge rusty tanker, lying dead in the water, listing to the starboard slightly as though she were shouldered up on the mudbank. She had one anchor down, and barges alongside, and another tug coming with more. Combining my nautical background and flying skill, I told the boy that they were trying to pump her out into barges and float her off before the weather made up and the seas could break her up.

Then I dived on the ship and did a screaming low turn over the bridge. A shot right down the tonsils of that dying tanker skipper, who seemed to be standing out on the bridge shouting something.

Boy, it was exciting! I went to quarter flaps and down-on-the-deck passes, gave him up-angle shots of the skipper who now seemed to be leaning over the rail shaking his fist. We drew a crowd of lesser aircraft who had not been so skilled at bringing their cameramen straight to the scene. There was a helicopter and a little yellow Stinson now circling with us. I had the speed advantage over both, and my P-51, gun-ship passes delicately cut them out of the pattern. My camera turkey got into the spirit of all this and started filming the air show too. Quick shots of the rag-wing Stinson ducking away, the chopper doing pop-ups. Man, oh, man, was I every going to enjoy the six o'clock news tonight!

There was only one thing spoiling all this instinctive savagery for me. The camera guy kept trying to convince me that the tanker was Japanese. Only because she flew the flag of the rising sun, had Japanese Lines in letters fifteen feet tall down both sides, and on the under-the-stern passes we could read Tokyo. I calmed the kid's fears. Told him it was all part of an international plot. Liberian tanker hysteria. Nineteen Liberian tankers have run aground, sunk or blown up, spilling a quarter million tons of oil. How long do you think they will keep admitting to being from Liberia? And anyway, here comes the Coast Guard.

I could tell by her tubby lines and the forward cargo of sea buoys that she was the local buoy-net tender, but he couldn't. And she did have the clipper bow and the bright red sash painted down her hull and was making lots of foam. And when you are hungry for film, you can make yourself believe. I set up the pass at the Coast Guard so he could get a camera angle, but the binoculars on the bridge would miss my N numbers. A lot of the fun in this was being replaced by feeling furtive.

Going home, the car radio carried a Houston reporter's live report from another plane off down the coast somewhere. He was over a stuck Liberian tanker. Sunken, I called the news director at the TV station. "Steve, about that tanker . . ."

"We already know."

"How's the film footage?"

"Magnificent."

"What you gone do with it?"

"Run it. Just the long shots. Tankers is tankers."

Well, why not? Who ever heard of Liberia? Could you reach right out to a map and put your finger on it? You ever meet a Liber? And I got to thinking about the captain of that Japanese tanker when he got home and his wife came to meet him. "Hello, honorable captain-husband. Have a good trip?"

"Mamma-san, sit down. You would not believe this. Tell me, do I look Liberian? Or was that crazy Confederate Air Force doing Tora Tora again twenty-five miles off Sabine Pass?"

Lady with No Name

It was a dog day in the radio station anyway. Not just finding the wrong tanker, I just couldn't seem to get anything started, not even a good fight. Oh, I was getting a few calls from the same little old ladies. You'd be surprised how quickly you come to recognize their voices. In my mind's eye I could just see them; they got the radio, the Ex-Lax and the telephone all lined up on the shelf with the clock. Regularity. They call me regularly.

Bax, that is ungracious. Thirty years ago those were your teeny-boppers. They came in your studio in their saddle oxfords and twirled around to sit down and you craved them, sniffing the air.

It was just a wrong time, a wrong day, when this one called. She started out. When we get old all of us start out. We don't make statements, we are all storytellers. She started out, "Bax, I want you to play me a real pretty record. . . ." And I clipped her right there. Got her before the story. Said, "I sure will," and punched her right off the button.

I was still feeling how sassy and nasty that was when she called back. They never get mad. They just say, "Now you listen here . . ." and talk to me like I was family. So I settled back, sighed and listened. Eleven minutes to go on the show, two spots left, traveling light. Be nice.

Then I started hearing her. ". . . back from the hospital . . . lung cancer . . . three months left to live . . . no one to turn to . . . all alone now . . . mustn't tell my name, don't want Granmaw to know . . . Oh, Gordon, I don't want to go . . . I am younger than you are . . . so much I never got to do . . . I'm really not ready to die . . . I'm scared . . . don't want to go. . . ."

I had been playing Kristofferson's "The Fighter" off his Easter Island album. Only good cut on it. Now my scalp was crawling and the horror of this was coming up inside me. I can usually handle an off-air call and do the show too, but one of the two gets skimped. Right now everything was getting scrambled. I had part of her voice on the air sometimes; I kept setting the needle back and replaying "The Fighter." Somehow it seemed appropriate. I was leaving the listeners to fend for themselves, hoping they were picking up enough of this to know what was going on. But most of all I was trying to reach out to her. Looking for words, for an idea, anything to hold her, to cradle her.

She was going on and on. Sometimes she wept in the most bitter grief of seeing all that is herself gone from here before autumn. Then she would abruptly stop her crying voice and there was force in her. Anger. Injustice. No fair. And there we hung. Two people connected by a telephone, one looking at the certainty of her own death, the other feeling the awful inadequacy of how do you talk about death to the dying?

". . . nobody knows me . . . nobody cares or loves me . . . and now I will be dead . . . gone . . . it isn't fair! Oh, please help me. . . ."

She said she wanted three things. She wanted to hear Don Hebert read the 23rd Psalm to her on his Sunday-morning show, she wanted Don Jacobs to write "her story," she wanted someone to know, to miss her.

I told her the only thing I could think of. I told her we care. We do care. Then she was off the phone and I sat there in the longest on-the-air silence, part just thinking, part giving her our rarest gift, silence on the air. Then Don Hebert came in the studio.

Came carefully, slowly, the nearly blind. I had not seen him in over ten years. This lady had called his name, now here he was. We decided to see if we could find a Bible and read her the 23rd Psalm then and there. We both knew there wouldn't be a Bible in that radio station. We asked our newshen, who is really a straight kid. She said, "Whaddya trying to do, spoil my image?" And blushed. Then it was six o'clock and the show was over.

But I still have you with me, Lady with No Name. And now I have given you into the care of thousands of others. Through big iron printing presses you have risen up and into so many hearts. And you keep this clipping, for it is your story. No longer unknown, no longer alone. Some of us will pray. Some of us will do the shocking thing of thinking ourselves into your shoes and try to guess how we would behave. And some of us, quite unknowing, will be dead long before you are scheduled to be.

I think perhaps the cruelest thing to you is being given ninety days to live. And how would each of us live with that? Or would you want the doctor to be honest with you?

This is so terribly inept. Telling your story. An infant loved, cuddled. A young girl, and all those first days of school. Of romance, when you were happily young to still believe and be romanced.

Dying is so unfair. But don't withdraw as you walk among the living. Think, him too, and him, and her. The hand that writes this, the good doc who told you, each and every person who struggles through reading this. All of us too. But for right now, and most of all, we care. Think of yourself surrounded by the warm, rising, invisible column of all of us around you. In faith, and love, we care. You are not alone.

Israel

Somehow Diane and I got netted in with a group of thirty-one "distinguished Southwesterners" who were invited to a "fact-finding tour" of Israel by the Israeli Government. I knew they wouldn't spend the money except to do a job on my head, and I was ready for it.

What we were not ready for was falling in love with that besieged little pea patch of a nation that has stuck so badly in the gullet of history. That just happened. Not so much in the auditorium presentations, which were brilliant, but in wandering around in the ancient cities, shopping for a pipe, talking to people in little shops. Or out in the countryside, talking to young pioneer farmers, who were trying to coax a crop up out of rocky brittle ground that looked like San Antonio. Or a night of good wine and music as a guest in the apartment of a broadcaster and his family.

For months Diane and I had vivid dreams about Israel, both of us in vivid dreams of trying to find some way to help save her. And yet, today, here on Village Creek, where fresh water sometimes runs three feet deep and four miles wide through the downstairs of our house, I still reach out quickly and turn the water faucet off, thinking, Wouldn't that desert farmer love to have that water?

We got back from Israel and I couldn't move it out of my mind. It was in my radio show, in my newspaper columns. I got back on the civic-club luncheon and rubber-chicken circuit again, which I swore I would never do, but we would refuse no one to go talk about Israel. We got a warning from the KKK in my mailbox, got invited here and there as speakers for the United Jewish Appeal. There is some appeal, if only in the humor of it, of having a couple of green-eyed goys standing up there in the temple raising money.

Here is what we told them.

We have just returned from Israel and I am full of it.

Israel today is what America must have been like during the frontier days, the winning of the West.

It is a nation of young people, come from all over the world. Strong and beautiful, they tend their crops in the tiny communal farms under the brow of the Golan Heights, plow in one hand, rifle in the other, their babies laughing in the warm sun, playing by the nursery outside the bomb shelter.

Along the borders into the Arab states there are minefields on one side of the barbed wire; the Israelis have planted apples on their side. Tanks growl on the one side of the border, cows graze on the other.

I was surprised to find the Israeli borders open, for this new nation has been at war or in a state of war since it was founded more than thirty years ago. They leave the border open to the Arab cousin, invite him in to visit, be friends, on the thin hope that if people come to know people they are less likely to be whipped into war again. That's why the Israeli Government invited us, one on one, people to people: "Come, get to know us." "Yeah," said one cynic, "they should, they couldn't live without America's support. The fifty-first state, that's Israel."

True, with one important exception. America has spent its treasure and blood of its youth saving Europe twice, a couple of attempts in Asia, we rebuilt Germany and Japan, we helped Russia, India, Egypt and Africa, and the emerging Arab states.

With the exception of tiny Finland, Israel is the only nation that ever paid the bill or said thanks. Israel is paying back every U.S. dollar, with interest, and wants no U.S. troops. She has held off invasions in 1947, 1956, 1967, 1973. All with her own young men. There are a majority of lovely young women in Israel, and that is her tragedy. The men they might have married sleep beneath the sand. Israel pays her own way.

Israel looms large in history, but is surprisingly small. She would fit into East Texas and not crowd Austin. From the West Bank of the Jordan to the Mediterranean Sea her waistline is about as far as Beaumont to Houston. You could drive a tank from the Gaza desert up to the Golan Heights in a hard day's push. Lots of people have tried it. Nobody has made it.

Israel has no fortifications, she does not even have legal fixed borders, just truce lines. But every young man, and most young women, are trained soldiers. You see them off duty, hand in hand, him with a black M-16 slung on his shoulder. Time is so short that there is no time for a barracks call to muster. When they come again, and they will, the young Israeli seems ready to hold the square foot of ground he is standing on.

So what is this, a nation of warriors? Not if left alone. It is a nation of builders. There is a boomtown breeze blowing all across Israel. New construction, new farms, new universities, and new people pouring in. Mostly youth, looking for some commitment in life. Israel is the land of the bare, brawny back, cement pouring, high-rise coming up, sprawling industry. Nothing is wasted. Not one inch of precious ground. They build rock terraces and farm crescent strips of scraggy topsoil on mountainsides that would make a goat faint. They dole out precious water to make the desert bloom. I talked to a farmer, young guy, nice home in the trees and flowers, field crops, brooder houses full of turkeys and hens, greenhouses full of exportable roses. He owns a tractor, a pickup, the family sedan. He's got a total of nine acres! Many of us in Texas waste that much land between the house and the mailbox.

The Israelis have a lot of desert. The country ranges from what looks like the Kerrville-Bandera hill country on down to blistering bare rock and sand. For over six thousand years the Negev Desert served mankind no better purpose than an invasion route as ancient nations fought back and forth through the Mideast. The Israeli sits on that hot dry rock and figures out a way to make it live again. It once did, a millenium ago.

He has built a new university at the ancient city of Beersheba. There he is studying ways for man to live in the desert. They have discovered that most desert cap rocks are over deep salty lakes. So they have found a way to irrigate with salt water! They have taken men's most common slime, algae, and are finding ways to make the sun turn it into cattle feed. They look at the withering Dead Sea, loaded with the ages of precious mineral. They plan to mine the minerals, and save the Dead Sea by digging a tunnel through the mountains of the Judean Wilderness and let the Mediterranean drop twelve hundred feet down into the Dead Sea.

From right under the mountain where God gave Moses the Ten Commandments they will extract free power, and they are offering Jordan, across the sea, to lay down her guns and plug in on the power and light up the tent of darkness before time runs out for us all.

First she was legally given her land, then she fought for and held it three times. Any other nation in history always got to keep whatever land it was strong enough to hold. Israel is still having to explain and argue that the land is theirs.

There are conquered, proud, Arabic people in the land that is now Israel. In history most conquered people became slaves or were driven out. It happened lots of times to the Israeli in his four-thousand-year history. Maybe that's why he is as gentle as he can be and calls it "Administered Territory." And the Arabs within are free to stay or go, do business, attend school, become citizens, have freedom of religion.

Always in the past whoever conquered the Holy Land destroyed the temple and exterminated the people. The Israeli holds equal religious freedoms for Jew, Moslem, Christian. His democratic government is open to whoever can get elected. There are seats in the Knesset for Jews, Christians, Arabs and Communists, and in-betweens you never heard of.

Israel is a tiny nation of 3.5 million people, surrounded on all sides by ten Arabic nations whose landmass is equal to that of the United States. There are 125 million Arabs who would like to see them dead and gone.

Israel's nightmare is that time will run out on them from the extortion of Arab oil. The United States is now dependent on Arab oil, and Israel is dependent on the United States. In the 1973 invasion our airlift saved the country. Tanks backed out of the C-130s and came out shooting. It was that close.

Now what if the Arab decides to extinguish the light in Israel with another oil embargo? Would you give up your Oldsmobile to save that little kid down in the bunker under the Golan Heights while his dad holds the wall and his mom passes the ammunition? Would you turn out your lights to leave the light in Jerusalem? Would you? That's what the Israeli asked me.

Israel, Lighter Side

Thirty-One Distinguished Americans, landing back in the U.S.A. after a two-week fact-finding tour as guests of the Israeli Government, crowded into the nearest restaurant and ordered ham, bacon, sausage, pork chops, chitterlings, sow snouts and pickled pigs' feet. Asked if Israel was as dangerous as it was kosher, one

Texan, just back from the borders of Syria and Lebanon, replied, "The most dangerous part of the trip was crossing New York City from JFK to LaGuardia."

The streets of Israel are safe at night. But a New York cabby, looking at the Lower East Side address the Texan was going to, said, "Let's leave your bags at the hotel. I don't mind stopping my cab there, but if we got out and started unloading those bags from the trunk we'd never make it."

And just before we left for Israel, a local leading clothier called me and said, "I know you always dress like a bum. Before you go to my country and meet officials, if I gave you a new suit would you wear it?"

Who could turn down such a deal? I carried that going-to-Jerusalem suit halfway around the world. It stayed packed. Israel is too busy for coats and ties. From cabinet-level ministers, to foreign service diplomats and university presidents, the uniform in Israel was open-collar sport shirts.

I have a private theory that the viability of the "Movement" in any emerging nation can be judged by the clothes worn. So long as Castro still wears fatigues, the revolution is still on in Cuba. Until an American union leader buys his first tuxedo, he still is part of his background as a workingman. Nixon's first sign of decay was wanting to dress the White House police like the Queen of England's Buckingham Palace guard.

But all of us brought suits, so our hosts in Israel gave us a "dress-up party." It was held in a three-thousand-year-old camel caravaner's cave, just outside the walls of Jerusalem. The national folk singers and dancers appeared in native costume and did the ancient handclapping circle dances. Then the beautiful Israeli maidens beckoned into the crowd for volunteers among us. I was first on the stage, and oh, how the crowd roared and laughed as this old man cavorted through the high-kicking steps. Later, back at my table I said to my wife, "They really enjoyed my dancing, eh?" "No," she sweetly said, "you still got the tags on the back of your new suit."

We had with us one Beautiful American. He's the one who interrupted the minister of education and culture by loudly blowing his nose. The one who came out of the mind-shocking display of the "Holocaust," a memorial in photos of six million humans on their way to death in the gas chambers, and as we stood there blinking tears in the sunlight outside he said, "When we gonna go back to the hotel? I wanna ice-cream cone."

He overloaded and passed out in the camel caravan cave and me and a member of the Israeli diplomatic service carried him out on his shield. His comment next day: "You mean that place was three thousand years old? Oldest saloon I ever been carried out of."

And at Tel Aviv, where they greeted our hot, tired busload with a table of orange juice in the lobby, crystal set on white linen, he got into a hassle with a lady at the desk. She didn't understand that he was part of our group, then she said, "Oh, you're part of the group with the juice . . ." And he said, "Yeah, we got plenty of those."

Ari, our guide on the bus, was an old soldier, a scholar, a philosopher. We passed a shot-out Russian-Arab tank beside the road coming down from the Golan Heights and he stopped the bus so we could take each other's picture on the grim reminder. "You know that's the second tank we've had here? You Americans wore out the first one taking pictures of it and we had to ask the Russians to send another."

We had two New Testament Christians who sat in the front of the bus, King James Bible open on their knee, leaning forward during the whole time, trying to convert Ari. Once they tried to get him to judge the actions of the Arabs. Ari would not be drawn into this.

Preacher: "Then you believe anything goes?"

Ari: "No, I believe everything goes. It's human. I don't confuse judgment with religion."

The same preacher, a Presbyterian, made fun of Ari's accent one morning. Ari had pointed out a snake crossing the road the day before, crying out, "Look! A wiper!" meaning viper. Next day the preacher pointed to two small scratches on his ankle and said, "Ari, I got bit by your wiper." Ari looked, with great solemn manners, then smiled the Presbyterian straight in the eye and softly said, "It was predestined."

Later he grinned. "I'm not smarter than you, but remember, I read the Bible in the same language that Jesus spoke."

The poet philosopher David Hartman spoke to us last. "We are here because we never left. For eighteen hundred years Jews all over the world prayed in February that the fruit trees would blossom. Prayed in summer that the farmer would have a heavy dew. He prayed for The Land in his heart, when in his head he knew there weren't any farmers in Israel then."

"Sadat says it will be twenty-five years before he will even talk to us. We still believe that men of goodwill can live together. The hope for peace is deep in our throats. Men will love God when men love men. God becomes love through you. Two thousand years of killing and suffering in the name of God. Stop it. Cut it out. I do not want one Arab to suffer. Judaism and Islam must listen to each other. But if he says he don't want me here, that we are not friends yet, then let us have fifty years of soccer instead of bombs. Don't force me to hit.

"Many of us in the younger generation cannot understand the Holocaust. How could six million Jews be led away and killed like that? We have come back to David, the earth strength of the Biblical man. Our model is a people who will fight for their culture, not beg for their culture.

"We are the people of the Bible. We have discovered reality with all its pain and uncertainty.

"We don't go cheap anymore."

All of this was taking place before Sadat took the awful chance of making his Nobel Peace Prize visit to Begin, and long before the Carter–Camp David talks. At this point in history the United States was pulling back its military support and asking Israel to "—trust in the conscience of the West." I enlarged on a *Newsweek* opinion written by George F. Will and wrote a slam-bam column called "Don't Do It, Begin." I pointed to Munich, Yalta, Cuba as the cemeteries of free people who depended on "the conscience of the West." The story got a wide reprint circulation. On November 30, 1977, I got an ordinary-looking personal envelope from Jerusalem. No hurry to open it; we were still writing back and forth to many friends there.

When I finally read it, it was a nice thank-you note. It was signed by Menachem Begin.

Chapter 12

Jenny

Barefoot and Pregnant

January '76 came cold, wet and ascraggly to the woods. Cold and scraggly in my heart too. Me and Diane circled each other like two sullen clouds full of lightning.

"We sure spent a lot on Christmas."

"I was only trying to please you."

"That's not what I meant; I mean we gave stuff to people we hardly know."

"Well, they are all your family."

"Yeah, but my ex-daughter-in-law's kid by her new husband?"

"Would you give one child a present and not the other?"

"Ok, Ok, you're right. That was a good thing to do; let's be friends."

"Not while you're trying to be nicer to me than you can be."

She had nailed it. What I was really thinking as she began to "get mad at me," was that somewhere at about forty-five I had decided to reject my role of growing old, and to identify with the kids, and had married one.

What she was really thinking was that her life would never be fulfilled until she had a baby of her own, and she had married a man so infantile in his own demands for attention that a baby in her marriage would be too threatening to him to even mention it.

When she talked about babies I knew the emptiness she must feel, but I wondered how much of that was to prove something. Mary had borne eight, you know, pop pop, just like that. And one of the set pieces of derision in my memory was of the high-strung, pushy women I had known who calved one precious time late in life. When we were boys we could pick out such a kid in the crowd. They had a milky translucence to their skin and their eyes were open too wide. Still I had done nothing to prevent my being a father again. She had cried out, "That wouldn't be fair . . ." True, but what more kept the option open was my fear of having anybody fooling round down there with even a little bitty sharp knife. And also I cannot imagine getting into a crowded elevator without being able to glance around and think that at least somebody in there could be in danger of getting pregnant by me.

She knew that, and classed it right along with an earlier conversation about us having a baby in which I had said, "What, and mess up my playhouse? Goddammit, woman, don't you know that's how I lost my first wife, that row of babies between us?" Long up-to-here with first wife, and no champion of that cause, Diane still flinched at that and thought, Wonder how he'd describe me next time he's running free with his hand in his fly.

She sat up in bed, in her characteristic manner of holding her back straight and a forearm keeping the sheet above her breasts. "I am almost sure I am pregnant." And she looked at me steadily, waiting.

My first thought was, Dear God, that a woman should be married to such a man that she comes to announce new life within her in the same manner as if she were telling him she had just wrecked the car.

I did and said all the right things, of course. Us Southern Gentlemen know how to do and say all the right things when the little girl is sitting there so forlorn on her rock in the swift river, holding the sheet up over her breasts. I cradled her face in my hands, and looked deep into her eyes. And while saying all that good stuff, was thinking that this might not be so bad, having a kid when I'm fifty-four years old, and wonder what they will think about *that*. And don't you know a kid out of me and Diane is bound to be really something? And I wonder if the making love cutoff date is going to be now or later? Hell, this might not be so bad, and I really am glad for her sake.

It was one of those times when I could not see into her eyes, but when I tried to gather her up in my arms, her back was still held straight. And the making love cutoff point was now. She was pregnant, the tests came back soon, but she was precariously so.

Spotting, hurting, she lay for days with her feet up like they told her to. Dear God, isn't anything ever going to be just ordinary and easy for us? The orderly household around us began to disintegrate surprisingly fast. Like an army base when a crack infantry outfit suddenly moves out, and newspapers begin to blow across the parade grounds and drift up against the barracks. I had been bringing her things; now without talking about it, I began to do housework. I guess that was the first long step toward Us and Our Baby.

But she grew worse, remembering this was how it began when we lost the last baby. I was taking care of her because I really cared, but she wouldn't let herself believe all of that.

I cradled her head in my arms. She said, "I'm sorry."

I said, "No matter how this turns out, quit saying you are sorry. I will do floors, windows too, but don't ever say you are sorry again for new life within us."

She nodded, her head snuggled close, and I prayed, "Dear God, please let us carry this one."

Her OB clinic, one of those four-doctor, baby-processing plants, was treating her like she was sick. Feet up, stay in bed, don't move. She lay there getting pale and paler. Put anybody to bed a week and you can make a sick person out of him or her. We decided to get another opinion.

Cliff is an old friend, one of the last of the GP family doctors. He had one great medical advantage; he knew us, both as friends and as patients. At first he said, "Diane, you know I don't do mommies anymore."

"Cliff, just think of me as a friend, asking for help."

"Then go back to living. No lifting, and keep the stud over on his side of the pasture for a while, but you will know what's best for you. And, Diane . . . you will either carry, or you won't."

Diane got up and got better. Winter dragged on, and I was into another crisis at the radio station. L.A.-style hard-formula radio finally got to Beaumont. They hired a consultant, and the first thing a new guru has to do is get rid of the old guru. I was making it easy for him. I not only refused to play his flip-flop, top-jock, Top 40 play list, I made fun of him on the air on his own station. I explained that the essence of radio was not how tightly you cued up the records, or which joke service you subscribed to, radio is whether or not you have anything to say. A man with nothing to say to those listening should go home. I offered to string out a hundred yards of mike cable and meet him in an open barren field and see which of us could keep an audience. He offered to meet me outside the control room.

A supple youth, shoulder-length blond bob and motorcycle-cop mirrored glasses. I thought, Well, he's going to beat the hell out of me, and it's been a long time, and I sure do hate all this. So I got my weight in line, and let him see all the other beatings in my face, but all he said was, "Oh, man, lay off me. You go around here like you are God. Omnipotent. We hate you."

That's a beating.

I came home from my dragons in town to the bare and freezing woods and Diane, her face gray and scared. Sometimes I came home drunk. Sliding through the woods in the pickup, stomping time to Willie Nelson.

Then one day Diane met me at the door. Standing up, smiling, "I'm cried out. I asked myself, What would Nancy Drew do at a time like this? She never lied, she never quit, she faced the odds squarely. Virtue always won out."

Miss Pearl schooled around our legs as we stood hugging. "Look at Pearl. She's kitten full again. Maybe by this time next year our kitten will be playing with Pearl's kitten." But Diane held back. She wasn't ready to risk that much yet.

I knew she was better when she started buying books again. "Look, this is an eight-week-old fetus." In the color picture he was sitting up like a transparent little pope, a hand poised in the blessing: "—see our baby has fingers already."

I believe she bought a book for every week that she was pregnant. And through books she brought me in and shared her womb. I would look at her budding belly when she was dressing and mentally superimpose the kid in there, neatly curled, about the size of a Big Mac, his large head bowed forward slightly, the thin little cage of ribs already housing a beating heart.

The cramping and bleeding stopped, but now Diane was saying, as she woke up from several naps a day, "Look at me, not getting a thing done. Why am I so tired?"

I knelt in front of her, and in my fairy-tales-for-children voice, I told her of what I had read. "You must be still. They are putting the little fingernails on today. They come sealed in sets of ten, marked R and L. What they are doing is peeling off the back paper and sticking them all in place. That's why your body is asking you to please be still awhile. So they won't get them on crooked. According to the book he only weighs a quarter pound, but they are already doing eyelashes too. Can you imagine how fine those stitches must be? Lay still."

I was captured, drawn in. Already involved with our baby in her womb. She knew it, and things were easy between us for a while. But she became more and more centered into herself. Her breasts became more magnificent than my wildest teenage imaginings, but she shielded them with her arms. I bought copies of *Hustler*, and once looked back to the prenatal books to see if there was anything in there about hair starting to grow in the palm of the husband's hand. None of the books had anything to say to husbands at all.

At the radio station I found two accounts logged for my show that belonged more in the penitentiary than on the air. One was later charged with felony theft from a customer. I knew them, struck them from the log and initialed it. In the showdown with the sales manager and owners I knew I would lose.

"Are you making moral value judgments on our accounts?"

"Yes, I am."

"Do you think you are running your own show?"

"I've got to. And I always have."

"As soon as we can afford it, we are going to fire you."

I drank more at the end of the day, me and Willie drove the pickup through the woods more wildly than before. Let it roar. Slide the tires and let it roar. It's only about a mile stretch, the road belongs to me. I can graze the trees if I want to. It was the only stretch between here and there where I didn't have to hold in, be careful of others, I could let it all hang out. I felt like I was suspended between layers. I ruined the return anyway when I slammed in the house and said, "I wish *I* was somebody's baby."

That started another circle. "I'm sorry, Diane, I know what you are going through and how you feel, and that was rotten and childish—"

"It's all right, Gordon, I know there is a lot of tension at the studio right now, and you know how supportive I am of you."

We bowed and circled, like the Japanese ambassador in the White House on December the sixth. If only one of us could yell something we really meant, that would be far out enough that the other would just crack up laughing, like:

"You hopeless jackass!"

"Well, you married me, and you had every pilot in Dallas to choose from."

"Yes, and I'd do it again. I still think you're trainable."

But we couldn't do that. She went out and joined the foreign legion of all those other pushy broads, the Lamaze method of motherhood. Lamaze, Leboyer, Les Books, Les Meetings, Le Witch Doctors, Le Breathing, all for Le Baby. No La Pussy, no Le Whiskey, no Le Farting or Le Cursing. Ho, boy, are we ever going to have a baby. This is going to be worse than I thought. Whatever happened to those good old days when we just circled the wagons and the women just went off behind the bushes for a little while?

Throughout the known and the unknown world, at this very instant, somewhere a woman is hunkering down to have a baby. Thus it has always been. Now Diane is talking about me going to baby-having classes, about buying carpet and furniture and redoing a whole room, and going off to Houston for some science-medic journey into sonic photos via ultrasound and something else about amniocentesis. Jesus! Come to think of it, Jesus didn't even get fresh hay. Of course He may have had help from the Home Office.

One kid, born of an intellectual, late in life. I kept remembering that one we knew when we were boys. Blue veins showing at the back of his knees, and on any good adventure he was the only one who got a rusty nail through his foot, and his mamma all over us like a sea gull.

Diane simply withdrew at that outburst. Pulled back into her books and made a lonely decision by herself.

"May I talk to you about something?" I felt like she held back on the "sir" to avoid setting us off again. She had the percentages, the odds if you wish, on the chances of a woman over thirty-five delivering a child with a serious birth defect. Open spine, Mongoloid or other catastrophic malformation. The odds are an astonishing 200 to 1.

The procedure for prenatal detection is almost simple in its mechanics. A long hollow needle is inserted into the sack of fluids beside the fetus; a cell culture from the sample is accurate. Many OB doctors still consider any invasion of the baby's natural protection more risky than it's worth. Diane had gotten those odds too, and had changed doctors.

Now she was standing before me. "I want to go through all of these tests, but it's your baby too. . . ."

All my life I have looked curiously at courage. Wondered if I had any real guts, like when me and Jimmy used to shoot at each other with .22 rifles to see if we had the guts to go to war. Like the chasing hurricanes and riots and going into real shooting in Vietnam when I was past forty. I labeled it and said it out loud before somebody else did. Before anybody caught me at it. "If you ain't got much talent, then take chances. Haw haw haw."

But now I was looking at Diane, her face flattened with real courage that she was not even aware of. Courage is doing something you are really afraid to do and no one may ever know how much courage it took you to do it.

She was standing there with her arm across her belly, protecting all that was dearest to her as life itself. The doctor had said in the interview, "You know that in all these procedures we are only looking for bad news."

She nodded.

"And if we find it, you know what comes next. If you do not understand and agree to that, then there is no point in going beyond here."

She nodded again. Courage is to do something you fear but believe in, even though there may be public disapproval. Later she was to tell me, "I was never sure. Oh, dear God, I was never sure."

I had always wondered why, when a deed of solitary courage is found out, some people so recoil from being treated as heroes. Diane did not see her decision as heroic.

Sharing all this on my radio show too, I got few on-air calls from indignant right to lifers. Listening to their strident slogans, how could I answer back? In my mind I could see Diane's soft face and her eyes looking into some infinity beyond me. So all I said was, "Any woman should have the right to decide what goes on inside her own body."

We traveled to Houston for the sonogram. The doctor who did it is a lady from India, so skilled that there was always a gallery of interns learning from her. She anointed Diane's belly with sound-conducting jelly, leaning over Diane, a long sheen of her blue-black hair hiding her handsome face. She crooned to Diane and to the baby as she moved her pinpoint conductor and mike, seeking the ventricle of a heart no bigger than a button. The shower of harmless sonic waves showered into the womb and those bouncing off our baby painted his tiny white outline on the green screen of the scope. "—see, there is the curve of the little spine, the two white dots here are kneecaps . . . look . . . look . . . oh, what a fine-shaped head. . . ."

Kid, it was only early March, and you were not due here until the leaves redden along the creek bank, but I was seeing first baby pictures of you.

Then the lady from India was moving her little mike, hunting for your heart. "—got it . . . ah-h . . . moved again didn't you? . . ."

Our kid, rolling around in there in her luxury, perhaps smiling. "Ah! That's it." The room had been undertoned with the steady whoosh-whoosh of your mother's blood pumping past you; suddenly I heard your heart. Clear, distinct, like running-child foot pats.

"Ah!" said the woman from ancient India, rising and turning all around, almost laughing. "Such a strong heart. Such a good heart." She held the sound of your pattering, entwined with the deep strumming of your mother's heart, until you flipped neatly over to the other side again. Kid, I think I was yours from that time.

The amniocentesis procedure was two weeks later, on March 14. A somber business. The six inches of long, shiny, hollow steel needle was plunged into the red smear target place on her belly. Her grip on my hand was the only pain I could share. One of the advantages of being a "Lamaze couple" was it banished the American Puritan hospital code that the husband may not see the wife undraped in the presence of others. It was natural to be with her. The doctor was conversational.

"How do you know where you are in there?" I was thinking of the baby getting stuck in the eye.

"Experience." He was swishing the needle around in little circles, pulling up on the syringe, trying to get the 20 ccs of clear fluid. "We are getting pretty good at this. It is possible to locate a vein and give the fetus a blood transfusion."

He was pulling, but nothing was coming up. Diane, not able to tip her head down far enough to see well: "What's going on down there?" Diane smokes a lot; she was unable to keep her promise not to smoke during pregnancy. I said, "He's hit the ashtray, the needle is stuck in a filter-tip butt and plugged up." Diane clenched out something about whose belly she wished the needle was in.

The doctor, continuing in his original line of thought: "Sometimes babies are born with needle marks, but that is the least of the dangers in this." He withdrew the needle, bore-cleaned it with a little steel rod, inserted it again. Diane's leg muscles were rigid. The doctor: "What we are getting here now is a random sampling of the fluids. Sometimes the cells will not grow in a culture, or we may get a contamination of the mother's blood. We have to do it over. About one in ten."

He had his sample, the nurse was going off down the hall with it. "Don't drop it," I called. Nobody laughed. "We will call you in about ten days," said the doctor.

We went home, waiting for the deadly cramping or bleeding that would signal our folly. Nothing happened. I asked Diane how she felt. "Good, just my legs are sore."

"Your legs?"

"Yeah, when I saw him coming at me with the needle my legs said, "Let's get up and run," and they are sore from fighting with the rest of me to get them to just lay still on that table."

We settled down to wait, boy, girl or nobody? One of the things they know from the cells is the sex of the child. They give you the option of withholding that information. A funny time for us to get so old-fashioned, but we agreed that if God had wanted us to know He would have found an easier way. Like leaving a little pink or a blue bootee on the doorstep, or something.

We waited, and the listeners waited. Just like being tuned to your favorite soap opera, except this is real and happening to people whom you know. Only they never found out. Three days later the station owners had completed negotiations to hire my strongest competitor for the morning drive time on radio and they fired me.

It was all very polite and gentlemanly, came at the end of an ordinary Thursday on St. Pat's Day. I already had my stuff in boxes. We shook hands, the blade dropped on eight years there, and the peak of my radio career.

There was a brief flurry. The newspaper headlined it, "Bax Axed." Channel 12 did a stand-up interview for the evening news. "What happened, Bax?"

"Well, it's the second time that the boss's son has grown up in a station where I have worked a long time, and come in and fired me."

"What are your plans?"

"I'm gonna go lay back in the woods and wait until I get a job offer from some guy who's had a vasectomy."

Then I called Diane and she fixed a steak and champagne supper.

The Texaco refinery blew up before I got home, eight dead, an inferno. There was light rain and fog, nobody would fly a camera crew into it. I took the Mooney and flew it lower, faster, harder than anybody would have. That night on the Channel 12 news the film showed my squared, orange wing tip in and out of the black smoke billows and between smokestacks. That helped, being Ole Ace again when my real world was going to hell.

There is an old saying: "If you want to find out how badly you would be missed, stick your finger into a glass of water, withdraw it and examine the hole." There was a satisfying outcry when the public finally realized I was gone. No formal announcement was made that I know of. It is broadcast tradition that once you get the rascal out, you never again mention his name. But I took much comfort from the letters they forwarded saying I was a part of their lives. And I'm equally sure that the owners of the radio station took as much satisfaction in what was probably an equal load of mail congratulating them for cleaning up the town.

What really surprised me was the shock to my own system. I woke up next day at the usual 4:30 and my body said, "Up, up, you slugabed, you got a show to do." And my mind said, "No we don't, we is free. Free at last." Half of me was being a rational human being, looking forward to getting organized, to establishing new patterns, to getting on with serious writing. The other half of me was baying like a hound.

I went out and walked the woods, thinking, Free. You are really free. Thirty-two years of deadlines and you are free. Every step was another link off the chains on my leg. Me and the dogs walked the green, green woods. I watched them stop to sniff and enjoy. Dogs don't know nothing about death or wages. A light rain came up, shaking the new leaves, bringing down showers of yellow jasmine. I started to pull up my collar, Wolf threw his head back and tried to taste the raindrops. We walked the woods and I took "Free" lessons from the pups.

But in the twilights I would think, The morning hour will come, and my body will answer, but there will be no call for me. Harden

me, oh, Lord, that the sun will rise without me being on the radio."
And the sane part of my mind would just fall up against the wall
laughing, Oh, you silly, sanctimonious old jackass! And Diane held
me through some of this. Held my head to her breast like a baby.
More than me, she knew that I was never as contemptuous of radio
as I had always pretended.

A letter came from Molly and Alan, the eldest of the kids. Alan
and I had done two-man morning radio for years. Probably as good
as it could be done. He wrote:

Dear Pop,

I see by the dispatches you have had an unexpected opportunity for a
mid-life career change. Perhaps you will recall a phrase from an earlier
conversation, "At some point in his life each man stands at the open door of
his gilded cage. Most turn on a heel and go back in."

There were some other excesses. Coming back from town I picked
up a jug of tequila rojo and was belting it warm, straight and raw,
right out of the brown paper sack, sick of Willie Nelson, and singing
"Jack o' Diamonds". . .

> "I'll eat when I'm hungry,
> I'll drink when I'm dry.
> If a tree don't fall on me
> I'll live 'til I die."

All of my whole life was roaring in me to the music and playing
that five-speed transmission of that truck. Broadsiding down that
mud road in the rain. Good-lookin' women, fast cars, rainy nights,
fistfights, roping and riding hurricanes, flying thunderstorms in
lightning, chain-looping that old Stearman biplane with the propel-
ler blast over the cockpit. Hot damn, it's all been so good! Then I
hit a glass-slick stretch of clay and here come that dumb damn tree.
Crossed that little Toyota's slanted little eyes I did. Got out wading
around in the mud and rain, roaring with the joy of it all.

The sane part of my brain peeked out. "Now why'n hell did you do a thing like that, Bax?" "Hotdammit, man, 'cause there wasn't nothin' left to do!"

Well, if I was going to make a living as a writer, I better be finding me a publisher. Went to Vidor and hit up Merle Luker for printing me in the *Vidorian*. First thing he had done when he took over that paper years ago was run me off. Now he said, "What makes you think you can write for Vidor?"

"Well, Merle, I got all the Vidor qualifications. My wife is barefooted and pregnant, and so is the kitty, I'm fired and out of work, and I came home drunk in the rain running through the woods last night and hit a tree and wrecked my pickup."

He hired me. Now I got seven papers. If I had seventy I could make a living at it.

But I missed radio, and that surprised me. I thought I had done all there is to do in radio and it really was time to be going on. When I first keyed the mike in 1945 radio was rigid and formal. The announcer sat in his little booth, waiting for his cue. What he was going to say was formatted in other people's minds. Then Arthur Godfrey fathered the human sound, and for a few bright decades radio was live and real and even the smallest town had some little Godfrey, who, bad as he was, had the sound and flavor of that town. Then the Top 40 format spread from California and radio put its chains back on. Today the "jock" sits tight in his little booth, waiting for his cue. They are all named "Ron" or "Ken"; they interchange plug-in with any control board in America. I wouldn't do it, and I went offstage thinking I may have lasted too long.

Now in the sudden silence I sat on the bottom step, looking out over the creek, thinking how great it is to dream up a kick-it-all, mid-life career change, and how scary it is to do it.

Diane sat beside me, swollen with the bud of life inside her, and her own fears. And courage.

The lazy hum of bees among the summer flowers sounded like stress lines in the air. Old Wolf sat puzzled, shoving his head up under our hands, looking for our eyes.

"Diane," I said, "maybe I could go into politics. Judge Baxter, Law West of Village Creek . . . no? Well, how 'bout if I opened up a faith-healing and fortune-telling booth in that old watermelon stand out on Eastex Freeway? Ok, suppose I go on TV?"

"What would you do on TV?"

"I could be that cute weather fellow that comes on right after the news," and I scooped up a handful of Pearl's kittens, "—that's the news, now, here's the fourcats. . . ."

All this tap dancing on the coffin lid. All this midnight elbow on the table, sipping good whiskey, and expounding on "mid-life career change" with your former associates who have come out from town to see if you're ok. Them wearing sensible shoes and socks and the all-season wrapper of payroll checks and group Blue Cross, and hearing me tell the story I was beginning to tell very well. Me and Dan Green, legends in our time.

"Actually, Dan, I precipitated the firing. Just didn't have the guts to quit a sixty-a-year job and go find out if I could write for the national market. . . ." A quick, boozy flash of the national market. Writers in the poultry section, plucked, but heads and feet still on, hanging in a pale row on strings. Maybe swaying a little. . . . "You know I've been a stringer for *Flying* magazine about eight years, Ziff-Davis is going into hardbacks and their first offering will be a book I'm putting together. I'm really hungry to get out and see if I can go national, and radio was soaking up all my time. Man ought to see how high he can claw his mark on the tree. . . ." Quick flash of me wading up out of the baygall, fangs, all covered with grizzly black hair. Letting out a roar and raring up on my hind legs and slashing a big, bark-flying mark on a cypress tree. And Wolf and Groveler and all the squirrels falling down and rolling all around laughing their asses off. . . . "Diane says we can afford to lay out about a year. Actually, Dan, I've bought myself a summer off."

Actually, Dan, I'm scared.

The other few in sandals, open necks and light gold chain could hear the replay of how radio had given up its heritage and become a sound in the wall. And, yes, I had blown it all away for personal principle. And right now I was coming out of the triple flip, no net, the other trapeze in sight and the timing still good, but not a finger on the bar yet.

Probably a little bit of the truth in all of that. And by the way, the program audience ratings went up with the new guy doing my show.

I stayed dropped out, picked up a little free-lance stuff and some of the secret panic began to die down inside. We made a whole lot less, and found out we need a whole lot less. The Morning Man ritual hung on. The aviation book was still for love but it flowed best starting before daybreak, watching over the typewriter as the light changed on the creek. I could push past the first bloom, but the stuff after the first four or five hours was just typing, not writing, although I couldn't tell the difference until reading it over next day. All newborns are beautiful to their mothers.

The social high-point of the days became the couple of miles through the woods with the dogs to contact the outside world at the mailbox. The commonplace took on wondrous profound meanings.

I Been Studying Armadillos

We were trotting back from the mailbox when Wolf passed me with an armadillo in his mouth.

It was a small armadillo, about the size of a lady's evening bag, with little pink toes curled up and a long hairy tail. I said, "Wolf! Put that armadillo down." And the armadillo said, "Yeah, Wolf, put that armadillo down." He had a high, thin, little voice, like Truman Capote. Wolf said, "Murph, mumps, marble." I said, "Wolf, how many times I got to tell you, don't talk with your mouth full?" "Yeah," said the armadillo, "your mouth full. Oh, my God, that's me."

Wolf put the armadillo down in the short grass beside the sand road. The armadillo closed his eye and gave a final shuddering sigh. He was leaking a little too. I said, "Wolf, now look at what you have done. His mainspring is broken. Guess I'll have to finish him off." I raised the shovel point.

"Now hold on there!" His eye had snapped open; he was looking at me with his little pearly eye. I put the shovel down and apologized. Explained that I just didn't want to see him suffer, die a lingering death out here in the woods. The armadillo assured us there was nothing the matter with his mainspring. "Good as new. See this?" And he made little running motions with his hands and feet, lying there on his side like that. I didn't have the heart to tell him but it was sort of ratchety. You know, like a dropped clock, his mainspring was plenty wound up tight all right, but not all of his little gears were tracking anymore.

Wolf meant no harm. He's just like all the other big dogs up here in these woods, can't miss a chance to go strutting by with his head held high showing off whatever he can catch.

Hell, anybody can catch an armadillo. They are slow and dumb-looking and on my road we stop the car and yield the right-o-way to armadillos. You might think they are too slow and stupid to be scared, but I have been meditating on armadillos and have come up with what might be fresh new thinking which I would now like to offer to the scientific community or any college students who may be reading this paper and want to dazzle the professor.

The armadillo is a very ancient mechanism and according to fossil findings he was topped off and finished in the evolutionary scale of things about a million years ago. That is to say the armadillo had already reached a state of perfection when your folks were still living in the trees with nothing to do but hunt, fish and make babies. They hadn't even gotten around to inventing work yet.

Now the ancient armadillo shared this earth a million years ago with a lot of really elaborate, huge and fancy creatures. Where did they all go? Why is the armadillo still shuffling along?

Well, I have only one fragment here in my theory, but think about this: When the armadillo is ambling across my road and all of a sudden he sees me come around the bend in my car, he does not jump up, scream and run for the bushes. Why should he? A hundred thousand years ago he shared that same road with saber-toothed tigers and long-tusked, hairy mastodons big as a house. Why should he jump up and run just because he sees a little queer French diesel car bearing down on him? He's seen far worse than that. Seen us all come and go. He might know something we don't know. I been studying armadillos.

While I went through all these theatrics of elation and despair, Diane was listening for the phone to ring. At the end of March the call came, the cell culture had not developed, we would have to do it over. Her neat little set of odds had just doubled—against the baby. She said, "I want to go to church this Sunday." Going to church? That horse parade of clothes? We never had, although she had said that after the baby is growing up she wanted him to know. "To belong, to see that people do that." Now she just said, "I want to go to church . . . before we risk our baby's life again tomorrow."

After the second time she began severe cramping. They put us in a little white room. "Call us if there is any bright bleeding." For a few hours we became one of those hospital couples who sit in silence and watch the hands of the clock jerk by, waiting for life or death.

She sent me down the hall after a while, to find the cold drink machine. I was sprinting down corridors, twenty-seven floors of elevators, but I could find the tension running out of my legs in this hospital maze chase. And I suddenly realized why, in the ole-time movies, they always sent the husband out to boil water. It gave the dumb son of a bitch something careful to do, and got him out of the room. Nobody needs all that hot water.

Two weeks after we were home safe, we were sitting on the couch, throwing our heads away on the *Tonight Show*. Diane had no troubles since we left the hospital, the report had come through that the fetus was normal. We could almost feel the mischief in the office girl's voice as she looked at our files, knew the sex of our child and saw the notation not to tell us. Suddenly Diane gasped, and sat bolt upright, clutching herself. "Life! I felt life!" I remember looking at my watch; it was exactly 11:47 P.M.

She had suspected the small flutterings under her heart all day, but the kid had just made a definite statement and there was no mistaking it. Now she held herself and blushed in the excitement. She grew inward into herself and her child. She looked up at me and her eyes were brimming over, then she lowered her head.

Wherever you travel, little person of the twenty-first century, you have caused your first faint tremorings here on earth on the ancient banks of Village Creek.

Tilley's Fire

"Gordon, come quick. My house is on fire!" It was Tilley on the phone, hoarse, his voice faint. He was getting over a throat operation. Can you imagine anything worse than having your house burning and can't yell, "Fire"?

Soon as we saw it we knew it was too late. Pure red flames were gushing out of the upstairs windows. Tilley's house was dying. Norma Jo was standing out there, lighted in her grief. Diane went to her. I ran to help Tilley, dragging stuff out of downstairs. The house was starting to tremble and roar, Gates, Ward, McFarland all heard it now, came running.

Tilley staggered out, streaming smoke, both arms full. I dashed in, stood in the comforts of Norma Jo's life; what to save first? The ceiling was starting to tremble, things were exploding, marking the swift closing minutes. I grabbed their big color TV and somehow got it out the door. Back in again, I ran along the hot walls scooping off the pictures of the people whose voices and love have filled this room. Even saved the picture of Ole Tater, Tilley's best deer dog.

Now there were fewer running shapes through the smoke. I quit too, when the last chair I got was already burning.

Diane, big with baby, had gone down the road in the truck to meet the Silsbee Volunteer Fire Department. It's twenty-five minutes from town, and no way you can describe over the phone how to find this place.

The house was a roarer and a burner, and here came those two little old trucks. What could they do now? The flames were higher than the great magnolia tree by Tilley's back door, and it was dying too. All I could think of was, What if this was our place? What could we do if this was all our treasures going up? I guess I would go out on the sandbar and sing and dance and caper by the light of it.

In a few minutes all there was going to be left of Tilley's would be a mound of coals glowing on a blackened slab. Tilley held Norma Jo, their breathing was hoarse and deep, sobbing.

Now the firemen, who really ain't nothing but Silsbee business-men, were putting up ladders, stringing out one pitiful little hose and climbing up to a burning window, right into the jaws of fire. And suddenly it was all over. About four minutes, actually, and there were no more flames.

The place was boiling with a mass of gray stinking steam. Steve Caraway, the car dealer's son, was coming down the ladder looking boiled. "This is a fog nozzle, Bax; you catch a nice confined fire like that, the fog flashes to steam, no more oxygen, no more fire. Smoth-ered out. We been to a school, man."

The top half looked like blackened crucifixes, the bottom half was saved. God, it was beautiful. And then the parade of pickups began. They carried stuff until Gates's house was filled up, then through the woods to ours. The little children rode on top of the loads. They carried stuff in: "little stuff for little hands." Like a procession of ants, they moved mountains. Norma Jo's nice clothes hung from our downstairs plumbing in sooty rows.

That night we huddled together at our house; the awfulness set-tled down on them. Tilley was hanging down his head. "I'll never build again. Too old. Finished." We tried to comfort them. To reach them. Our house looked too clean and nice all of a sudden.

Norma Jo had been staring out the windows of our Glass Room. It's beautiful in there at night with the outside floodlights making a fantasy world of living up in the leafy trees. Norma Jo began to make little sketches on a scrap of paper, looking out our upstairs glass walls. "Look, Tilley, we could do the whole front of our living room like this, have a view of the creek . . ." The destruction had run its course. Rebuilding had begun in a woman's mind.

Her face beautiful, coming up out of its grief, she began to softly kid Tilley.

"I ever tell you about ole hard-luck Tilley? He come from a little East Texas town that was so poor it didn't even have a name. They just called it '—across the river from Louisiana.' Times were hard, but Tilley worked so hard around the place that his folks decided to give him a BB gun for Christmas. They gave him a Daisy Red Rider and one of those little cardboard tubes that holds two hundred and fifty BBs. They warned him to not waste a shot, because that was all he would ever get.

"That night, alone in his room with his new BB gun, Tilley did the same thing that has happened to all of us. He tipped over the tube of BBs and they spilled out all over the floor. Only there were big cracks in the floor of that old house, and every one of them rolled through a crack and dropped out of sight.

"Tilley thought about trying to crawl under the house and find them in the dark, then decided he knew where they were, and he'd go under there and get them first light of day.

"The chickens ate every one of them."

After that story Tilley got to laughing too, and leaned over and began to plan with Norma Jo how the new upstairs would look.

John Kirby put the Tilleys up at his place up the creek from us. Tilley had once gone down there after a freeze and found all the pipes busted. He saved Kirby's place from water, Kirby was saving him from fire.

The next Saturday all the men who work with Tilley out at the Goodrich plant came out to the creek to help tear off the upstairs burn. I've never seen such big men, working so smooth together. By noon the burn was down and hauled off. Now the bottom half looked clean with hope. Their women all came too, bringing cakes and pies and pots full of a big Eastex collard greens and pork dinner. We made a spread out under the trees and all ate together.

Then the hammers and saws began to sing. They started decking and raising frames. There was a swing to it, a rhythm and a joy that flows through it. Their speed and grace were deceptive. The men on the ground were cutting what the men above would need next. The language was good-humored, but almost a terse, shortcut code. They razzed each other without mercy. To the man swinging a hammer, toenailing studs and missing a lick or so: "You sure leaving big mule marks, boy."

To the young guy with a newly developing beer paunch: "How many months you along, Bubba?"

"Any good craftsman builds a shed over his tools," said Bubba, hitching his crotch.

I was doing wiring. "Hi, easy money, we sure miss you on the radio mornings."

" 'Preciate that. I miss me too."

"Where'd you learn to be a 'lectrician?"

"Reading the Sears catalog."

He watched me making up terminals with bare, bright, new copper wire gleaming. "I wouldn't touch that stuff."

"Carpenters always say that. You guys in the trade sure stick together don't you?"

"So do bankers."

By Sunday evening they had that place decked, framed and partly sheeted. I had no idea that new construction could go so fast. Said so. "Yeah, Bax, we have to watch it sometimes. One time we planked in a rabbit."

That next week I came down and ran circuits so I could stay ahead of them. I enjoyed working alone in the still evenings, and working with wire. One day son Jim came along to help me pull cable. "Dad, look at how this house grows. What these men do is so pure. And people can live in it. They must know a lot of satisfaction at the end of a day. Ain't it funny how the paper shufflers and money changers look down on workingmen? It ought to be the other way around."

I told him it might very well be.

Tilley and Norma Jo laid out a big barbecue venison spread on the planks out under the trees when they raised the rooftree and moved back in.

Jenny Born

All we had come into town for Thursday was a roll of wire and some groceries. What we got was Jenny. It was Friday, August 26, 1977.

We had stopped at the Ramada to have dinner and sit at our favorite table by the window where the light is golden at sunset. Jack Cook saw us come in and smiled from across his organ keyboard in the corner and swung softly into "Greensleeves," which is Diane's song. Then he played "Wildwood Flower" for me, real slow. An evening like this is the classiest thing we do.

Diane was shifting, uncomfortable. "I think I'm leaking." She had started, but we didn't know it. I guess we thought the water breaking would be a dramatic gush, a spilling of the dam. Our chick had only pipped a very small hole.

We went on to Gerland's to buy groceries. In the poultry department Diane took my arm suddenly and said, "Let's go." We met James Byrd and his wife at the door; James is a gentle and religious man, he built our kitchen cabinets. I stopped to vist, Diane kept shifting around, trying to whisper something into my good ear. I still didn't know we were having a baby. She wasn't sure, but what she was saying was, "I don't want to hurt anybody's feelings, but will you please shut up and let's go."

It took us a half hour to drive back to Village Creek, and she came out of the bathroom, all heavy and worried. "I just don't know what's going on." We had seen Dr. Dennis Black, her OB doctor that day too. "Any day now, Diane, and you're fine."

"Why don't you call Black at home, we better find out something?"

She said, "I don't want to bother him at home, and what if this is nothing? We'd look foolish." I reminded her that's what we were paying for, medical advice. "Call him." Black said, "Meet me at Baptist Women's and Children's Hospital. Start now."

Diane activated her Plan Baby Day. There was a list of who to call, labeled, precooked meals were in the freezer, Tilley would take care of the dogs and cats, gowns had been selected. She swung her old million-mile airline hostess tote bag up. "Let's go." These are the times when Diane is at her flat, steady-eyed best. And I was all awash in the emotion of it. I had a fresh-made beautiful drink in my hand; we were standing in the bedroom. I wanted a little scenario. "Here, let's drink a toast to the kid, then let's kneel right here and pray." I was elated. And may have been writing good copy.

Diane eyed the drink in my hand and said, "Please don't throw your head away. Not now. I need you, let's go. Now."

Goddam, that made me furious. One drink, which I needed badly, is not "throwing my head away," and five seconds' worth of praying isn't going to wreck anybody's timetable. Hot words, anger flashing. The glass of whiskey and ice hit the wall with a loud swack! Ice and shards lay between us. It was one of the good set she had given us for Christmas. The heavy thick bottom cut a crescent in the wall. It's still there. Mark of the beast. How can one of our most tender instants turn so swiftly into a little everlasting memento of shame for me and hatred for her? How do we keep doing such to each other, when my whole arms ache to just hold her a moment, make it go away?

I swung her heavy bag onto my shoulder and guided her down the stairs. We drove to the hospital in silence, full of love and prayers and dull anger.

It was midnight. Black said, "My game plan is to induce labor. She's got a safe twenty-four hours with the fluid out, then infection sets in." At 2:00 A.M. labor began. The little white room was crowded with four or five of us at any time. I counted a total of six wires and tubes that connected Diane to the fetal monitor and all the other apparatus. "I feel trapped, tied down, all of you over me. There is no air in this room."

Husband-coached childbirth is every bit as good as they claim it is. My being there was bonding me to our baby. When I could get her attention the long-practiced patter of "—now it's coming, shallow breathing, shallow, find your fix point, relax, you're making fists, relax all over. Good, go-od, only thirty seconds more. There. It's passing. Now rest. Rest, you got two minutes. . . ."

The only misnomer, the flaw, is calling it "husband-coached childbirth." This implies that the husband is in command of something. That the wife will just lie there and obey. There needs to be a review of the limits of some women to the idea of a "husband-coached" anything. Especially to some son of a bitch who started the first day of the baby's life by throwing a glass of whiskey past your head.

When it worked, it worked good. I could read the fetal monitor and see how she shortened and dampened the peaks of the contractions where we got into the trancelike state of Lamaze. She was thirteen hours in labor, and she was heroic. None of us knew that this was not going to be a normal delivery.

It was noon, the next day, Diane was in the very crown of her life, she was having a baby, but we were running out to the limits. How much of anything can a person stand? I knew I needed to be more forceful with her, but how could I when she crumpled. "I'm a failure. I can't do it. Go on, knock me out, drag it out. Do anything!"

I went out in the parking lot and sat way off in a corner and cried. A black woman, I never learned her name, she took over. She had learned Lamaze from watching, and she gave Diane relief. Dr. Black said, "She's crowning, but the baby is posterior, face up. Diane, I am going to sedate you from the waist down. Try to push. Only you can do it."

Diane drew up her knees and she pushed. She pushed one minute on, one minute off, for an hour and twenty minutes. The fetal monitor went off the 100 percent scale, a measure of pain, or force, that was beyond the machine. But when we asked Diane not to shout again she would say, "I'm sorry." I have never seen such blaring force in a human body, or such raw bravery. Nothing moved.

"High forceps," said Black. We all suited up and went into delivery. Cliff Dunlop's wife Kathy had arranged to be her anesthesiologist. Black put those big tire irons into place, he gripped, pulled, rotated. Me and Kathy held Diane's shoulders to keep her from sliding down the table. The block was working, she felt no pain, and watched in the mirror, and between times raised her face to nuzzle against mine. Everything you ever heard about a husband being with his wife at the time of birth is true.

Black said, "I'm not going to subject that baby to any more trauma. We'll go in the other way."

In the delivery room Diane had been triumphant, renewed. I put my head next to hers and drew strength and love from her. This would be the big finish. Now they were preparing to move her into surgery.

"If my hips had been two inches wider we'd be home by now."

"If your hips had been two inches wider you would never have gotten there in the first place."

"Are you disappointed?"

"I'm grateful. If we had lived in my 'circle the wagons' time you would have been one of those women who died screaming out on the prairie."

As they wheeled Diane through those swinging double doors, she blew me a kiss, as though she were passing through a garden gate.

In the little anteroom I sank into my private hell of father guilt. Cliff showed up from somewhere to daddy-sit with me. I babbled, he listened. Listening may be the friendliest thing a person can do.

After about a hundred years those doors popped open and here came Doc Bridges, pediatrician, wheeling one of those transparent-top cake cases that new babies ride proudly down the hall in. He said what only we had not known all along: "It's a girl."

Doc, you looked like you had just gone three rounds with Ali, in your rumpled greens and the mask down around your neck and the sweat still shining on your brow. There was a beautiful look in your eyes that I hope you never lose though your phones may ring at midnight and you bring a thousand new babies into this world.

"They are both ok; Diane will be in surgery about another hour. She'll be sore as hell, but ok, and there is nothing wrong with this big girl."

Jenny, if you read this fifty years later, I want you to know that no man ever fell more in love with you at first sight. You came into this world all roses and cupid bows and that astonishing shock of golden red hair. I just stood there, knowing this was one of those moments that would remain clear forever.

You went off to the nursery and I went off to wait for your mom. She came drifting back into the real world just about the time they brought you in to her.

Diane sucked in her breath and reached out her arms. She cradled you to her breasts. "Ours. I just can't believe this is all real." And she held you. Fulfilled at last. She held her head back and high, biting her lip, then Diane bowed forward, clasping you to her breast, closing out the world. "At last. Thank you, God."

Then, making little sounds to you, your mother began an inch-by-inch peeking and touching of all of you. I believe if they had left you two alone she would have started purring and cleaning you like a mamma cat.

Finally I got a hold of you. Fed up with all this being outside and being hefted around, you puckered up, rared back and expressed yourself. A trait I pray you may never lose.

I really don't know why I did what happened next, it just seemed the natural man thing to do. I did it, and it's worked with you ever since, when nothing else would. I raised one leg, stomped three times on the floor, and burst out a-singing an awful old hillbilly tune called "The Wabash Cannon Ball." You looked up at me kind of funny for a minute, then you sighed and relaxed and we stomped and sang awhile. The hospital people all thought that was kind of funny. It worked all during your infancy; we called it "Daddy's trick." It still works now that you are older. I can hold you and calm your little fears. Only now it's more like crooning.

Jenny, you filled a place in my arms I never knew I had before.

I moved into a hospital cot beside Diane. Black warned us: "She's open at the bottom, open at the top. It was a normal procedure, but she's almost sure to get an infection."

I made a run to the creek. There is a little magnolia tree fighting for a foothold on the edge of the sand bridge. I had never noticed it before. I stopped and cleared the junk weeds from around it. The magnolia was about the same length as Jenny. Jenny's tree. It will shade the passing footsteps of the young woman. They will blossom in about the same years. I will tell her this is her tree. Oh, the terrible risks of loving living things.

I swam in the creek and all the critters came down to be patted on the head. In the stillness of the cabin I could see a future Diane and Jenny sitting on the floor cutting paper dolls as she and her mother had done before. I opened the mail, there was a letter from Ari Cohen, that old soldier of the war of the revolution who had been our friend and our guide in Israel. There was an official document inside. Ari had planted a tree for her among the six million to be planted in Israel's living memorial forest to the Holocaust. "Here is the number of her tree, I pray God for peace, and that someday she might come here and stand beside her tree here on this hillside and look down upon our beloved Jerusalem. . . ."

That was how it was, Jenny, the day we made room for you on earth.

Jenny's Home

After ten of the longest lost days of our lives the doctors agreed that although Diane was neither strong nor well yet, the curingest thing to do would be to put that new baby in her arms and send us on home.

The long, long recovery was simply because Diane is allergic to penicillin and she must lie and get well slowly like people used to back in the old days.

The grimmest day in that hospital was on the second day. Diane had only held her baby one time when they found she had an infection. The moved her out of the nursery and into the surgery wing isolation. How jealously they guard that nursery full of newborns from any infection that may be floating in the air. Separated from her baby, Diane wept most bitter tears.

Diane whispered, "She doesn't know who she is. She doesn't know she has all this love waiting . . . she just lays there in the glare and the row of cribs . . . a nonperson. . . . Please go look again, come and tell me every word of what she looks like, what kind of person she is. . . . Please, go look and come tell me again."

And I stood outside the window and watched. I had become the old phantom of the hospital, ten days the drifting wraith of the corridors, the chair sleeper. And the ladies of the nursery, rocking, holding, patting babies, came out and told me, "Your only trouble will be going home with Jenny—will be that we spoiled her plumb rotten with love."

And then at last the doctors agreed that Diane and the kid could just as well be isolated at home, that I could care for them. They placed Jenny into her mother's arms at the hospital door. There were affectionate farewells to those who cared for us with that special love that most hospital people have, and then we were alone. Just us, a family, driving slowly home to the woods in disbelief of such happiness.

Before we went into the cabin I borrowed from one of the most beautiful passages in Haley's book, *Roots*. Like the tribal father in ancient Africa, I waded out into the clear shallow waters of Village Creek, and with all our critters sitting as solemn witnesses, I whispered, "Your name is Jenny Tittle Baxter." Then I held her up to God. "Behold, the only thing greater than you."

Then we crossed the sandbar to bring her into the cabin for the first time and I told her at the foot of the steps, "You are ours, until someday, God willing, I walk you back down these same broad steps in your wedding dress and give you away."

Diane's mother gave us some time alone, then she came and taught me how to change a diaper and bathe a tiny bottom. I had never done this. I missed all that the first time around. "Too busy. Woman's work." The folly of a young father. Now I held the little red head and fed her and rocked her in the little rocker that had been her great-grandmother's. And the women put their heads together and passed along from mother to daughter generations of learned wisdom about new babies.

Jenny and I rocked and crooned, with no feeling of any yesterdays or tomorrows. Then Diane's mother, a woman about my age, said, "Gordon, I take back all the rotten things I ever thought about you." We laughed, and there was love in the house. That special miracle of a newborn. Jenny's home.

The Hell with Housework

The hell with housework. I have never put in such hours and had so little to show for it. I wash down a stack of dirty dishes, and while I have my back bent over the sink drying, somebody puts a new dirty stack right behind me. I got three stacks of laundry. The dirty clothes to go in, the clean stuff to put in the dryer, the dry stuff waiting to get folded. I have learned that no matter how fast or how slow I gallop around these stacks of clothes, they will always remain the same size. And there is no sensible way to fold a fitted sheet.

All day I carry sacks up and down the stairs. I carry sacks of groceries up the stairs, I carry sacks of garbage down the stairs. Now I am a fairly sane and reasonable old man, but will somebody please explain to my why the garbage sacks are bigger than the grocery sacks when we done ate up the groceries that were in the grocery sacks?

And after I have made a lightning sweep through this house and got it all picked up and sparkling bright, what causes these pockets of ghetto litter to spring up right behind me? Who's doing this? Not Diane. She's in there lying in the bed about to laugh out a thousand dollars' worth of stitches.

I got everybody fed and in bed and we had a power failure and the kid woke up with the colic. Everything I have started defrosting or yelling all at one time. I cradled the kid and thought I had both ends tended to when she did all the things she has learned how to do in just fourteen days on earth. She threw up all her formula, and fired a suppository clean across the room and the cat got it. Then the air-conditioner drain line plugged up and water started seeping out from under the closet door. I made a one-handed grab for the paper towels, and instead of tearing off a sheet the whole roll popped out and unraveled into the sink. I looked at it carefully because I could not tear off a sheet even holding it with both hands. It was the only defective roll of paper towels I have ever seen. No dotted lines to tear off a single sheet. I decided that God was fooling with me.

Diane got up and ordered me to bed. Just as I sunk completely under bliss the phone rang. It was some guy calling from a bar, wanting me to settle a bet about whether Bob Wills was still alive, and did he actually write "San Antonio Rose"? Diane said what I did to the phone was childish. I told her that man should never be summoned by bells.

Diane said she would take the night shift if I would catch the morning feeding. Jenny sent for me at 4:30 A.M.

That part is ok, really. That's when we have our private picnic and play pigpen. I spread out a quilt with all her stuff on it beside the sunrise window of the Glass Room. We just fool around. Sing a little, sip a little, and watch the light change as the sun comes up over Village Creek. It's the only unsupervised time we have together, Diane is getting girl sleep, me and the kid waller around, look into each other's eyes and talk about the mystery of it. You would be surprised how much an old person and a brand-new person have to tell each other.

About midmorning Diane wanders in, looking rested and cheerful, and finds us both on the floor, asleep in the litter.

"Look at both of you. What happened to your shirts?" I explain that we ran out of dry stuff hours ago, and anyhow, skin is better. We may be a little stuck together, but it's just us.

Back when I first went to sea, I was down on all fours cleaning toilets on the ship and the steward came in and watched awhile and then said that if I did a good job of cleaning toilets now, it was a sure sign that I would be a success in later life. I thought about that, as I was down on all fours, cleaning the toilet.

Sometimes the housework really gives me the hoo-hahs but listen, ladies, let me apologize now for the misspent life of thinking how tough we men have it. If I were a housewife and some man came strolling in after his eight hours, union rules and coffee time and said to me, "I'm hungry, where's supper? And while you're up, fix me a drink." And then patted me on the fanny and said he sure was horny, do you know what I would tell him to go do to himself? In fact, I'll bet that phrase was invented by a housewife.

Now if you will pardon me, I got to go. The garbage bags seem to be up and running wildly around the room.

The Bending In

It was the night of September 30. Still about broke and out of steady work, we had just got the news that my agent Connie Clausen had signed the contract in New York for the book on flying. And Diane had just come from her six weeks' checkup after the birth of Jenny, and she had been officially declared a girl again. It was a time for rejoicing, a time for the gathering of the clan, for wine, red meat and the telling of good stories.

We hired the famous 300 Room at the Ramada, the one where LBJ entertained his cronies, and I called in the Baxter Brigade. That's a little band of writers, artists, thinkers, talkers, beloved to each other. The outside world has heard of none of us yet, but if we ever get to be as good as our dreams you won't be able to afford the price of a ticket to come see us.

The night was warm and rich. Diane and I went home to each other's arms. The next thing I can recall was my neighbor Norma Jo leading the ambulance crew into my bedroom and Diane was kneeling at the bed, crying, "Oh, Gordon, I love you so. Please don't die! Gordon . . ."

They said I was having some kind of an awful convulsion. I remember none of that. I felt nothing. I could see them sometimes as though from the other side. I remember them carrying me down the front steps of the cabin on a stretcher and remember wondering why? I could walk, couldn't I?

I remember short bits of the ride down Eastex Freeway and I seemed to know we were headed for the hospital in Beaumont. Mostly I was thinking calmly of how loud that siren is, mounted right above me on the thin metal roof. And thinking next time I see that ambulance coming with all those lights flashing I will say a prayer for whoever is in it.

I remember Bernardo getting into a hassle with the cops in the emergency room. I was still going into convulsions and we needed him. The cops kept throwing him out, he kept coming back. And we had just left the party it seemed. Hi, Bernardo, what's going on?

They told me they were looking for the obvious worst things first, brain tumor or spinal disorder. But it was none of that. And I really didn't care. I felt a strange sense of peace when I was awake.

I kept drifting back and forth from the far side of Jordan. Sometimes I could see how it was going to look to leave them all. Sometimes I got unremembered glimpses of the other side. My brother came and he had been gone a long time. And waking at any hour in those lost days and nights I would look over in the corner and there would be one of my sons or one of the close friends, looking like wood carvings of themselves.

The tests all came back, good news and bad. The bad, some malformed tiny blood vessels in the back of my brain had flickered my lights. The good news: same thing had happened once when I was ten, once again during the military service. Events so small I had almost forgotten them. "If whatever you got was going to get you, Bax, it would have got you long ago."

Then the docs came and stood round my bed with faces as long as Bob Wills's fiddle. "Name your three favorite things." I did. "Now choose one." And that's how come I gave up whiskey and airplanes.

Well, the good Lord let me run wild and free for fifty-three years. Ain't much I didn't do, or at least have a good try at. Now comes the time of the bending in.

The Stearman

These were difficult times, and I wasn't sure how to think about the rush of events. There was a new baby lying in there. Curled up in unbelievable golden beauty and utterly dependent on us for a long, long time to come. She was soft, and woke up smiling. And we were soft to each other, we three.

The regular beat of my radio show lingered, I coasted, the thought that this might be an ending had not caught up with me yet. My fling was over. Grounded, but all of us were careful with the playhouse idea that this was only temporary, maybe a year. I needed a drink, but drinking was done with too.

Circling, I saw all this as a diminishing of my powers. For the first time, there were things I couldn't do anymore. The first sure sign of the aging process, that door I had been guarding forever. These were the first irreversible things. Too soon, too soon. Edges of panic. There had never been anything I couldn't talk my way out of except for someday the box end of a coffin. Is God bringing the bill to my table? No. It's the same for all of us. Well, you couldn't ask for anything fairer than that. But the end of radio, the end of flying . . . I heard that as them starting to stack the chairs in the back of the room. It doesn't really last forever, does it? I had never been here before. Suddenly the expression "killing time" seemed obscene.

Quitting the booze was the easiest. We both did, and Diane and I decided to put that never-missed twenty or thirty a month into a going-to-college savings account for Jenny. Picture the kid, now a handsome red-haired woman, mounting a stairway of unopened whiskey cases to walk across the stage and receive her diploma.

Any remorse about radio was just theatrics. There were offers. Without shoving, or even blackmailing, Diane said, "We can afford a year of writing, and you should, but your true genius is in radio. You were a forum; the town is poorer without you."

I explained to her why it was easier for me to tell a story on the radio than in the lonely awkwardness of writing. "You see my tongue flaps freely and the other end of it is moored only a few inches from my brain. In writing, the thought has to travel all the way down my arm, and that's about a yard, and my arm is stiff, it has a bone in it.

I really want to leave a good book on the shelves. Writing lives on. Even the very best of the radio shows had blown off the towers and were gone. They belong now to the birds.

"What does your daddy do?"

"Tell them I'm an author."

"But you were thirty years on the radio; people grew up with you."

"Tell them I played the piano in a whorehouse."

I had the tight little doors to the publishers open in New York. I wasn't even having to drop stuff over the transom and into the wastebasket anymore. But I wasn't listening to my old radio station either, or that rooster who was crowing off the top of my dunghill.

I went out and walked the sandbar in the cool night. Down to the willow grove at the far end, my sand-floored cathedral. Wolf and Groveler were back in the thicket, playing cowboys and Indians.

Pearl and Gimpy were little quick darting shadows in the shadows behind me. Keats was in front arching, playing fall over the cat.

The creek really was flat and fragrant. In the starlight I could barely trace ripples of current moving. I stood awhile, looking at that. Compared to the events of coming here, seeking peace, some whole earth slogan like "a quality of life," Village Creek had felt more like Niagara Falls. I pictured my barrel popping out over the sheen of the lip of Horseshoe Bend, end over ending for the rocks and spray below, me inside, jacked out in a four-way brace and being philosophical.

I looked up at the star. "God, You really are up there, aren't You? I mean You wouldn't kid us, and let us invent You just because we've always needed You?"

I stepped out from under the willow overhang and looked to find faint Polaris. The polar star was there, steady as ever. In my mind I tried to imagine the whole universe, and us riding it, wheeling about that star point. And that beyond that, there is neither a beginning nor an end. He's up there.

All the critters had been sitting, enjoying. Now they were turning, looking back toward the cabin. The cabin lighted at night; again I thought of how its delicate, half-hidden tracings looked like a fine packet steamer, passing on the river.

We had carried every one of those boards up here on an eight-foot trailer, we had cleaned and scaled each one and carried it up and nailed it. I know every board in that place by its Christian name. Where were all those people now?

There was movement against the light, the dogs were up and trotting there, tails over their backs, wagging. It was Diane, in her full-length dress, moving slowly, barefooted over the sand, the baby on her hip. Slowly she came, bringing our tomorrows.

"Are you all right?" Her voice was soft.

"It's just the flying."

"I know. And I am sorry. But look at all you had. That's more than most men ever will know."

Well, she was right about that, but Diane never made little of the loss of flying. She had been a part of it herself, of the being exclu-

sive. She would say, "I was air crew with Braniff. A flight atten-
dant." She never spoke the vulgarism of "stew," or "stewardess."
She belonged to the club. "Remember the night over Knoxville in
the twenty-seven when we flamed out two and lost pressure at
thirty-one thousand . . .?" or, "Yeah, we had St. Elmo's Fire one
time. It was back in Convairs on the Denver-Memphis trip. The
wings were outlined in blue flame and there was a circle of fire
around both props. . . ."

She knew that part of my attraction to her in those days was that
she was offering up her precious body to airplanes. "When you're
standing out on the ramp facing the wind with your hair blowing
and the uniform pressed up against your body like that, the mounds
of your breasts remind me of the twin cowlings on a Convair. Go
on, turn around and look. Can't you see the same lines?"

Diane knew about such things. She even knew about Stearmans.
I told her that making love to her was almost as good as flying one.
And she had listened to all my Stearman stories. About the time,
coming home in a cold twilight, when I had released the seat belt
and stood up in the cockpit to see if I could reach up and touch the
center section of the top wing. In the First World War the British
SE-5 fighter plane had a Lewis machine gun mounted there. Ace
was changing ammo drums.

Diane has never flown in a Stearman, but she has flown on one.
Standing up on the center section of the top wing, going by at a
hundred feet and a hundred knots. She did that after we were married, just before she got pregnant with Jenny. That might have been
the night we made the baby, I don't know. I had finished emceeing
the Lake Charles Air Show and Wayne Pierce had done his wing act
and now the crowd was going home and he was going to park his
Stearman on a nearby field.

"Diane, you want to ride the wing?"

"Why not?"

I asked her later why she did it. "Because nobody might ever ask
me again."

Was she scared? "No, it was beautiful. I had a little trouble
breathing at first, standing right behind the prop like that, but I

wasn't scared. Wayne is good. My role was passive." I wish you could have seen the strawberry glow in her cheeks and the lights in her eyes after they landed and Wayne helped her down off the top wing of *Ole Smokey*.

Airplanes are so alive with beauty and truth. I once let the Stearman get as slow as it could, upside down, in the top of a loop to see which would happen first: would the engine starve and quit, or would the airplane stall and spin? Really. The answer is yes. It did it all. Another time I tried to fly the Stearman upside down. There I was, four thousand feet, flat on my back, hanging from the straps, when the seat came loose.

The seat, and seat belt, travel on a long pair of tubes attached to the framework of the airplane. Many little holes in the tubes allow for short pilots, long pilots, riding low in the cockpit or sitting up high. All that happened was the catch pins came out of the holes and the seat traveled its full extension and hit the stops.

I only fell out of the cockpit about four or five inches. It might as well have been the rest of the way. The mind can gather all the information it needs about falling out of an airplane that quickly. The other four thousand feet would have only been repetitious. I clearly remember this as one of those moments of being more alive than I have ever been.

The Stearman's birthday is 23 June 1944. It will not haul freight and carries but one passenger; it has done only one thing all of its life, what it was built to do, teach pilots. I have known the Stearman, Biblically, for over twenty-one years. On its birthday I usually go out to George Mitchell's hangar where it lives, teaching ag pilots yet, and buy it a case of cold beer.

The wings of the Stearman are cloth, tautly stretched into shallow scallopings that catch sun shadows. The ribs beneath the fabric are of the most delicate tackings of tiny bits of spruce and gusseted corners. The upper and lower wings are supported by tall struts between them which leave the shadow of an N crawling over the yellow fabric when banked against the sun. Thin bracing wires of flat steel cross in between the wings. When the yellow-winged Stearman is twisting against the sky like a blown leaf, the moan and scream of its wires can sometimes be heard over the roar of its naked engine. At such times the forces will bend and bow the wings enough to tauten one set of wires like the strings of a violin being played, and the others slacken enough for cello chord harmonies. And when a pilot has done all he can do with Stearman, and is gliding back down to clover, the engine mutters to itself and the wires go "wheee-eee," like a child in a swing high against the sky.

They called me from the shop out at M & M Air Service after I was grounded and told me I ought to come visit the old "two holer." New fabric, new paint, and they had put a 450 P & W engine on her, replacing the balky old 300 Lycoming. "Boy, you ought to come see her." I never went. Norbert Slepyan, my book editor in New York, had shown me the artwork for the book jacket; it was my face, with the old Stearman in the background. The artist had every detail perfect. She was in a climbing attitude, her wings under-lighted, almost translucent with lift and the mystery of flight.

I held the artwork up for Diane to see. "That's who I always wanted to be."

"It's really beautiful."

"Maybe I ought to start building a case and try to get reinstated with the FAA. I was only out for a day, and I can remember nearly everything that happened in the hospital."

"You were out five days," she said gently.

I quit going to the airport. People began to ask if I wanted to sell my little airplane. Friends said I should; "Get it over with." Still I hang on, not yet ready to give up the idea of flying.

Elmer Lee and Elaine Ashcraft came out to the woods to see if I wanted to sell the Mooney. My wings. Clipped now. I still couldn't turn loose. I told them I would sell half of it, the half that eats. They laughed and we became airplane partners. They are a gentle young couple, slender built, both redheads, they look like brother and sister. Both are pilots; Elmer Lee is a certified flight instructor. They both feel spiritual about the old Mooney; it's not a "useful tool" as the trend word speaks of today's aircraft. They took the keys like they were part of the Holy Grail.

I can fly with Elmer Lee anytime, fly left seat, because he is an instructor. They were full of rosy visions of the four of us going, urged us to. But I didn't need any words for them to know why I stayed away from the airport now. One evening I went out just as Elmer Lee was landing. Watched our sharp P-51-looking little airplane flash in the sunset, stood against the airport fence as he taxied by, sitting up there, strobe lights winking, that old Lycoming muttering its strong song. That used to be my airplane. Gahdamn! The gall rose up in my throat. The airplane was becoming theirs. They were free to fly, nobody had to come tuck the blanket around their old legs when they got in and took the familiar controls. I walked away full of tears. Seeing another man flying my airplane, like watching someone dance too close to my wife. I could tell the Ashcrafts all that and they would nod. "You know we would do anything we could, Bax."

The Lord giveth, the Lord taketh away. Bax, you are really sickening. Wait. Don't go stand against the setting sun yet. The violins are not ready.

There was someone else I could dance close to now anyway. There was Jenny. We had a new person in the house. I had never thought of a baby as a person. As a being I could make friends with. Diane cut me into the loop of her and Jenny.

"She had colic, y'know. Just screams and rigid sometimes. Gordon will take her out in the Glass Room and dance with her in the dark."

"You mean Gordon does that?"

"I wish you could see them together. . . ."

We would dance in the dark, with the underside of trees lighted from the outside lights and old Sister Creek flowing by out there. I could dance her to sleep anytime. And all the time the voices inside me were saying, "This is real. This may be as good as it ever gets. Hang onto every minute of this. You'll never see her a woman of thirty like the distant Molly is now. God let you play the hand one more time. Let you go round one more time. Don't miss a minute of it."

Diane would stand in the doorway, watching me and the kid.

Jenny was easy to dance with, just like a real girl with her arms around you and her head resting on your chest. Better'n a real girl. With Jenny you don't have to worry about where her feet are.

I could feel her breathing change. I knew when she was asleep, and then after that when she was really asleep and I could put her into Diane's arms for beddy-by. I was surprised when Diane suggested it was time to go have her baptized.

"What faith?"

"Catholic, of course."

Baptism

Jenny did not cross Jordan quietly. She went into the mighty river of Christianity at the top of her voice. Jesus, Moses, Abraham, all of them, could hear her coming for miles and miles. The angel Gabriel laid aside his mighty trumpet to admire all that lung power. You should have heard Jenny being baptized.

At three and a half months she was not much bigger than a good-sized Opelousas catfish, and she had gotten here on earth absolutely helpless. But the Good Lord, in his infinite wisdom, had provided her with what she needed: her voice.

Like a carborundum circle saw blade, Jenny's voice will easily cut through walls, glass, ceramic tile, shatter crystal on distant shelves. She can raise her voice and flatten the cat against the wall. When she is really in a rotten humor and in full cry, it shows up on the local TV area radar weather forecast as a small, isolated thunderstorm located in Hardin County.

Jenny also knows when to open the gates of mercy. Just at the time she has Diane's hair matted in green beans, her blouse turned halfway around backward, and Diane looking vacantly off into nothing, what the Marines used to call "the ten-thousand-yard stare," then Jenny will let the sun come out.

She breaks out in the twinkles. A three-cornered cat grin, those clear blue eyes looking directly into your soul, a little starfish-dimpled hand reaching up for your face. You would not suspect that a person who has been here only ninety days could learn to direct her affairs so well, so quickly.

During the times of the storms I have taken Jenny to walk the long sandbar with me. I raise my voice to match hers, there in the starry night; echoing off the other creek bank I bellow to her the great songs. We do "The Roving Gambler," "Rye Whiskey," "Do Lord," and all the dirty-word limericks I know, starting with "There was a young lady from France . . ."

Gradually I feel the closeness of me and God and Jenny soaking right through my soul. At least something is soaking right through me. And she goes to sleep. Think of some future psychiatrist trying to unravel the woman Jenny's penchant for walking lonely woods roads beneath the starry skies and singing old songs of ribaldry and religion at the top of her voice.

But she knows God. They were formally introduced at these rites of baptism. Or what we call "The Baptism of Attila the Hun."

Betty Em and Bernardo were there, the godparents; so were most of the other kids. And other families too, eight of them. Father Nick Perusina, who knows me from lots of other old movies and is still my friend anyway, said this gang baptism was the way they used to do it in the old days. He wanted us all up around the altar. "Like you are all one family. . . ."

Diane had Jenny all gussied up like a Clabber Girl calendar picture. Some of the stuff that was going on would break your heart. The baptism cap was a little laced-trimmed thing made to be folded up and carried later at her wedding, as "something old."

There was a girl playing folk guitar. Jenny was ok long as she could hear guitar music. But when it got to the serious part, and they dipped her rosy little fanny in that cold water, man, she cut loose.

She purpled. She stiffened up. She roared. The other little peaceful, brand-new Christians raised up their heads and stared. Who is this kid water skiing on the River Jordan?

I could see that the rites were still going on. I could see the padre's lips moving. Diane was in a four-handed fight to put the beautiful little christening dress on her. Jenny christened Diane. She gave the kid to me, and Jenny stuccoed my marrying, burying and going-to-Jerusalem suit. Tossed up lunch. Made me an admiral with all that fancy decoration on my shoulder. I handed the kid back to Diane. She handed me a wet diaper. Out in the crowd, Jenny's older siblings were trying not to crack up. I rolled up the wet diaper and tossed it at them. Frank Gerrietts fielded the toss. Frank, the artist. Said he was going to save it and give it back to her on her wedding day.

Outside for the picture taking, the kids were still laughing.

"Pops, why didn't you stomp the floor three times and do your 'Wabash Cannon Ball' thing?"

"What, in church?"

"Why not? You've done everything else."

That night I had a bad case of the Novembers. November is when I always quit, get fired, run off with the circus. The main thing is if we can make it through November.

The Novembers

Thin clouds covered the glow of a full moon. Village Creek ribboned its trek wetly through the wilderness below. It was Yangtze yellow yesterday after all the rains. Now she was deep green again and breathing serene, lying halfway up on the bosom of the sandbar. The forest lay absolutely still, wearing her winter gaunt. Sounds carried farther, vines stood out, things that had seemed far away seemed like such a little ways with the screen of leaves down. I had missed the day the beech leaves all turn to bronze and evening light makes a golden tunnel where the sand road passes under them. The storm had beaten it all into a mulch. I take the baby buggy through there on the afternoon mile to the mailbox. Jenny likes the rattle and the moving, she peers up in wide blue eyes to the forest passing overhead, then quickly goes to sleep, her lips moving. "—angels are talking to her." She is all golden curls and roses. A tiny perfect leaf of yellow and gold drifts down and touches her tucked-in blanket so lightly that it seems to hover. I left it there. These, I was thinking, are times to remember.

Yesterday when the storm came through, blammity, blamming in the night, I woke up. Listened. I looked beside me at the mother and tiny daughter, curled in upon one another as they had been most of the time before they breathed separately just ninety days ago. They had been up with their own struggles from midnight till two. Earache, bellyache, tried everything. Dead tired, had given in to her instincts, brought the infant to her arms, her own bed. I had slept through all that. Now they slept through the storm. I studied their faces in the half-light. No picture, no painter, could ever catch that, I thought.

Lightning split a tall cypress in the baygall. The house jumped, etched in pale blue. The dogs slammed themselves up agains the door. Walleyed.

I listened to the storm beating up the woods. "For once I am glad I'm not a pilot anymore."

Next day I went in to produce three TV spots. That was about my main source of income those days and I worried sometimes that the income ain't up to the outgo. But that is what we had agreed on, to make time for the book writing. We could stand it awhile longer. I thought what a funny thing it is about TV. I had been in radio thrity-one years, a newspaper writer twenty years, but only thirty seconds on the TV and I was a recognized celebrity in the supermarket. Every kid, every black, did the double take: "—ain't I seen you on the TV?" I liked it. And the little old ladies said, "Miss you on the radio." And the store managers and doctor said, "Sure enjoy your columns." I was in danger of making another one of my oversimplified judgments about the audience.

Producing the three thirty-second spots took half a day. It went well, but I got home in the dark. The baby was still hurting. Screaming. Diane had that keen look of desperation in the corners of her eyes. She had had it. All day. Her arms were like lead. "—and I haven't got a thing done . . ."

I hit a few licks of housework, told her to go take a hot bath and I fixed her coffee. I picked up the screaming kid, put her up on my shoulder, shut myself to her rigid screaming, went out on the dark porch and settled into Grandma's old wicker-bottomed white oak rocker and started to rock. I thought of hiding out in Houston.

Running off to Mexico. Clenched the pipe in my teeth, rocking, singing a tuneless tune, decided I could do this for three days if I got to.

Outside, the thin clouds covered the glow of a full moon. Village Creek ribboned wetly through the forest. The cabin was the only glow of lights for miles, gleaming out on the water. In the distance an owl hooted. Slowly peace came under the roof. All I could hear was the little skwonk-skwonk of Grandma's old rocker, and Jenny's deep, steady breathing, snuggled up by my ear.